D1452744

The Art of
ANTICIPATION

Values and Methods in Forecasting

The Art of ANTICIPATION

Values and Methods in Forecasting

edited by
Solomon Encel, Pauline K. Marstrand, William Page
SCIENCE POLICY RESEARCH UNIT, UNIVERSITY OF SUSSEX

PICA PRESS

NEW YORK

Published in the United States of America in 1976 by PICA PRESS
Distributed by Universe Books
381 Park Avenue South, New York, N.Y. 10016

© 1975 Science Policy Research Unit, University of Sussex,
England.

Library of Congress Catalog Card Number: 75-34506
ISBN 0-87663-719-5

Printed in the United States of America

Contents

Preface   vii
Contributors   ix

Part I: Setting the scene

1. History and the Future   3
2. Forecasting and Planning   9
3. Values and Objectives   14
4. The Art of Anticipation   18

Part II: Problems and principles of appraisal

5. Assumptions and Dilemmas   23
6. Some Logical Points   41
7. Eight Critical Issues   52

Part III: The state of the art: an appraisal of current methods

8. The Assessment of Forecasting Techniques   63
9. Computer Models   92
10. Cost-Benefit Analysis and Technology Assessment   116
11. Survey Research and Psychological Variables   141
12. Numerical Moralities and Social Indicators   174

Part IV: An international perspective for values in forecasting

13. Scientific and Traditional Technologies in Developing
    Countries   223
14. Reducing World-Wide Inequalities   250

Bibliography   265
Indexes   280

Preface

To anticipate the future is one of man's oldest desires. For millennia the bases of forecasting were divine revelations, oracles, crystal gazing and dreams. The desire, indeed the need, to forecast is now as strong as ever. But while there is no record of anybody asking Joseph to explain the theory on which he interpreted Pharaoh's dream so that a degree of planning could be introduced into Egypt's agricultural economy, modern forecasters are in a less enviable position. They engage in their tasks *qua* scientists and they cannot escape the intellectual obligation to examine their forecasting activities in the light of the assumptions and procedures which give them their identity as scientists. Forecasting is a hazardous enterprise, presenting a large number of tough intellectual problems which range over the entire field of epistemology in the natural and the social sciences and, to the extent that assumptions differ in these two major branches of the pursuit of knowledge, cover the problems of their co-operation.

These problems cannot easily be resolved, nor can they be avoided. Between the Scylla of total involvement in problems which centuries of philosophy have not yet solved, at the expense of getting on with the central task, and the Charybdis of apparently ignoring them at the expense of introducing tacit and naive assumptions, a middle course is indicated which consists in making explicit the logic of procedure – even where it is tenuous – in the expectation that periodic stocktaking as more concrete work proceeds will reveal where positions need to be changed, where some dilemmas can be resolved and where new ones arise.

Such reflective exercise is in sharp contrast to the breathless quality which pervades some forecasting studies – not only Toffler's

Future Shock. The sense of urgency is understandable at a time when pollution, for example, touches upon the personal experience of millions of people in the world's technologically most advanced countries, and we share it. But however strong and important the social impetus for forecasting research, it is only the impetus and not a substitute for clarity of thought and assumptions.

In what follows we raise some of the issues on which all concerned with the future must sooner or later take a stand. They have, of course, been raised before (*Daedalus,* 1967; Young, 1968; de Hoghton *et al,* 1971). That they need to be raised again is an indication of their fundamental difficulty.

The contributors to this book are all members of, or associated with, the forecasting programme of the Science Policy Research Unit (SPRU) at the University of Sussex. This programme receives its central support from the Social Science Research Council, with additional support to the main activities coming from the Leverhulme Foundation. Contributory studies have been carried out on a shorter-term basis for several other sponsors. The present volume follows the programme's earlier book, *Thinking About the Future: A Critique of 'The Limits to Growth'* (published in the USA as *Models of Doom*).

Each chapter, though originally written by one person, was subsequently discussed and altered by all of us, so that most of them are now a composite effort. Because we feel that it is the teamwork and the debate to which we expose each other's work which makes our approach what it is, we have decided not to attribute any of the chapters to an author, not even the two or three which are in fact the work mainly of one person. Instead you will find a list of authors with their original discipline and relevant research interest.

Contributors

J. A. CLARK, B.SC., D.PHIL. (Research Fellow)
Physicist/systems analyst/modeller. Working on dependencies in agriculture sector.

H. S. D. COLE, B.SC., A.R.C.S., D.PHIL. (Research Fellow)
Ex-Physicist. Urban planning research. Concerned with the application of forecasting and planning methods. At present studying world models.

R. C. CURNOW, A.R.C.S., B.SC. (Senior Research Fellow)
Mathematician/systems analyst. Research on forecasting techniques, systems behaviour, theory of modelling.

S. ENCEL, M.A., PH.D. (Visiting Professor from University of New South Wales)
Sociologist concerned with innovation, science policy, relations between social and technical change.

C. FREEMAN, B.SC. (Director of SPRU and R. M. Phillips Professor of Science Policy)
Economist. Working on R & D measurement and diffusion of technology.

J. P. GARDINER, B.SC., M.A. (Associate Fellow)
Biologist/Physicist. Interests in philosophy of technology, especially in agriculture, energy and electronics.

A. HERRERA, M.S., DR.SC. (Visiting Fellow from Department of Natural Resources, Fundacion Bariloche, Argentina)
Geologist. Leader of Latin American world model project.

SPRU work on generation of technology by developing countries.

MARIE JAHODA, DR. PHIL. (Professor Emeritus Social Psychology, Chairman of the SPRU forecasting group)

PAULINE K. MARSTRAND, B.SC., M.SC., M.I.BIOL. (Senior Research Fellow).
Biologist. Interested in environmental and health aspects of changes in technology. At present working on Agriculture and Nutrition sector.

R. M. MACLEOD, A.B., PH.D., FRHIST S. (Senior Research Fellow)
Historian of Science. Concerned with history of science and its relevance to current problems. Reader in History and Social Studies of Science, University of Sussex.

R. McCUTCHEON, B.SC., M.SC. (Postgraduate student)
Engineer. Work in construction aspects of 'shelter' section.

J. M. McLEAN, B.SC. (Postgraduate student)
Logician/systems analyst. Working on concepts and computational techniques relating to behaviour of large systems. Stability of ecosystems in relation to food production.

I. D. MILES, B.SC. (Research Fellow)
Social Psychologist. Work on assessment of quality of life, interplay between society, science and technology.

C. H. G. OLDHAM, B.SC., M.A., PH.D. (Deputy Director of SPRU)
Geophysicist. Responsible for unit programme on developing countries.

R. W. PAGE, B.A. (Research Fellow)
Social Psychologist. Work on issues of technology assessment, (non-modelling) forecasting techniques and in materials sector.

P. J. SENKER, M.A. (Senior Research Fellow)
Economist. Work on manufacturing sector and effects of technical change on skills.

Part I

Setting the Scene

1. History and the Future 3

2. Forecasting and Planning 9

3. Values and Objectives 14

4. The Art of Anticipation 18

Chapter 1

History and the Future

Modern history, writes E. H. Carr, begins when history becomes concerned with the future as well as with the past. 'Modern man peers eagerly back into the twilight out of which he has come, in the hope that its faint beams will illuminate the obscurity into which he is going' (Carr, 1951). Flechtheim had a similar thought when he coined the word 'futurology' in 1943, at a time when speculation about the future looked uncommonly risky. The future, he contended, could be made available to us by examining its growth, its rootedness in past and present, its potential being. It was too easy, in an age of crisis, to assume that the future would be radically different from the past, and especially that it would be worse (Flechtheim, 1966). T. S. Eliot was concerned about a similar problem when he looked back at the twenty wasted years of *entre deux guerres*. In *Burnt Norton*, he contemplated, the 'still point of the turning world . . . where past and future are gathered'. In *East Coker*, he began with the pessimistic line 'In my beginning is my end', but concluded more hopefully: 'In my end is my beginning'.

The study of the future can only be conducted in relation to history, and one of the recurrent problems of forecasting is to utilize historical explanations without projecting them naively into the future. Popper has demonstrated the fallacy of Comte's attempt to do just this; so also, more concisely, has de Jouvenel. Nevertheless, historical interpretations provide an indispensable theoretical basis for the prediction of large-scale social changes, and the progressive testing of predictions within the framework of an historical interpretation is a valuable scientific activity (Gibson, 1960). Without exceptionally powerful evidence pointing to a radical break between past and future, forecasting is possible only through the projection into future time of social phenomena which can be shown to exist somewhere in the present.

Thus, the study of society along a time dimension is the essence of forecasting. For this insight, we are largely indebted to H. G. Wells (MacKenzie, 1973). The sub-title of his book *Anticipations*, published in 1901, sets out much of the agenda for forecasting in the 20th century: 'the reaction of mechanical and scientific progress upon human life and thought'. In a subsequent lecture, *The Discovery of the Future*, delivered at the Royal Institution in 1902, he called for the study of 'inductive history' or 'human ecology'. Inductive history would be concerned with working out the biological, intellectual and economic consequences of the social forces unleashed by technology, and by charting the possibilities of the future it could be used to provoke man into making sensible use of those possibilities. The future, he argued, could be foreseen and a study of it would help to liberate us from the dead hand of the past. 'It is our ignorance of the future and our persuasion that ignorance is incurable which alone has given the past its enormous predominance in our thoughts.'

Wells' faith in the application of knowledge to human affairs (inspired by the millenarian views of the 17th century Puritans) and his belief in a scientific élite or 'open conspiracy' which would set the world to rights (largely inspired by his reverence for T. H. Huxley) were responsible both for the enormous popularity of his writings before 1939, and for its subsequent rapid decline. E. H. Carr rightly asserts that we cannot understand historical writing except in terms of the historian (Carr, 1961). Any author's view of the future should be related to the period in which he wrote. The pessimism of Malthus is rooted in the political and economic straits in which Britain found itself in his lifetime. The varied writings of Wells reflect both optimistic and pessimistic tendencies in British thought at the turn of the 20th century. Spengler's apocalyptic picture of Occidental decline was a reaction to the decadence of the Habsburg and Wilhelminian empires.

In the 1920s there was a striking efflorescence of futurist writing, to which historians like Charles Beard made some notable contributions. One of the most interesting products of this period was the series called *Today and Tomorrow*, embracing 104 titles published in London between 1924 and 1936. Although some of these were merely whimsical, like Robert Graves' *Lars Porsena, or the Future of Swearing*, a number were both serious and influential, like J. B. S. Haldane's *Daedalus*, which was a source for the biological fantasies of Aldous Huxley's *Brave New World*. One of the contributors claimed that the series had 'made us think of our institutions merely as expedients for the achievement of social ends. It has made us consider what, if any, are the social ends we *should* set before us' (Hall, 1928).

This emphasis on historical relativism is an essential counterweight to the 'scientism' which lurks behind a number of contemporary attempts to find a systematic framework for the study of the future. The determining role attributed to technology – a topic which figures at several points in this book – is a product of a particular historical situation, whatever its objective validity as an historical inference. Current ventures in forecasting have a number of features which differentiate them from their predecessors. The *instruments* of anticipation are different – mathematical models, systems analysis, multi-disciplinary research teams. Expectations are different. In the 1930s, Bernal, Mumford, Beard and others believed that science was the key to social progress if it were correctly applied. In the 1970s, science itself has become ideologically problematic, and technology appears to be disruptive rather than deterministic. Daniel Bell's picture of the post-industrial society, although derived from earlier notions about the social role of science and technology, is touched by this pessimism; society in the year 2000, he observes, will be more fragile and open to polarization along many different lines (Bell, 1967). Forecasting is less concerned with straight-line predictions and more with alternative futures.

The idea of the future as potential history dates effectively from the 18th century French *philosophes*. The current boom in forecasting has its counterpart in historiography, for which new roles are opening up. This may be seen, for instance, in the growth of 'cliometrics', which is a form of forecasting in reverse ('retrodiction'). Cliometrics attempts to use quantitative methods, largely derived from econometrics, to test established propositions about the relations between social processes, for instance, the contribution of the railways to economic growth in the 19th century. The prospective use of cliometrics has already been exploited, for example in an attempt to assess the impact of the U.S. space programme on American society. Historical evidence, however, can be used without a cliometric filter, in the re-interpretation of 'conjectural history', in tracing the historical origins of current assumptions about the future, and in correcting various forms of reductionism to which forecasting is prone in its attempts to build workable models of the future.

Conjectural history has a special relationship with utopian fantasies about the future. Utopian writing, which stretches back to the very beginnings of literature, is the original *genre* from which other forms of forecasting and prediction have developed. It follows several well-worn paths. Generally speaking, utopias are non-realistic. One of Thomas More's recent editors insists that the word should be translated as 'Noplacia' (Turner, 1965), although More himself implied that it could be derived from Eutopia ('Goplacia'). Utopian romances tend to portray authoritarian societies, isolated in time and insulated from contact with disruptive forces, where social harmony is enforced and well-being is mandatory.

Turner suggests that the origin of utopian fiction is to be found in the Sumerian epic of Gilgamesh, with its portrayal of a place beyond the grave where there is no death, no sickness, no old age, no lamentation. Development since then has taken place through the addition of new themes. By the time More invented the word Utopia, the *genre* included a mixture of 'paradisiac, political, and travelogical themes'. More himself added topical realism, and Bacon, in the *New Atlantis*, added science. Turner also locates the origin of 'dystopias' in 1600, with the work of one Joseph Hall, which was light-heartedly satirical. Since Hall, there have been few light-hearted dystopias. In particular, science and technology play a sinister or at best ambiguous role in the work of writers like Swift, Samuel Butler, Aldous Huxley, Zamyatin, Orwell and Čapek. Wells was one of the last utopian writers to treat science with reverence. Clarke observes that the message of modern dystopian writing is that the only enemy of man is man himself. The traditional utopian fantasy looked forward to a time when man would transcend the limitations placed upon him by nature; fictional dystopias are concerned with the enormous powers of destruction placed at man's disposal once he has transcended natural limitations (Clarke, 1971a).

Utopian and dystopian fantasies will continue to be written so long as men find them a useful device for drawing attention to abiding moral issues. The new company of prophets and predictors, in their concern with the dangers that confront mankind, are animated by 'the two most powerful drives that have decided the shape of ideal states ever since Plato's *Republic* . . . the desire for social harmony and the demand for general well-being'. In this way, apart from their intrinsic interest, utopian works continue to exercise a powerful influence on systematic conjecture (or forecasting) about the future (Moore, 1966). Indeed, an over-emphasis on the 'scientific' character of forecasting can obscure its dependence on utopian moral assumptions. Winthrop has observed that 'scientific' forecasting attempts to escape from utopian holism by studying segments of society about which detailed information is available. This attempt generates its own difficulties because of the unco-ordinated and piecemeal character of predictions made in this way, and efforts to overcome these difficulties often involve a concealed resort to utopianism (Winthrop, 1971). Forecasters and writers of fiction face the same epistemological problem – i.e. how can we know the future? (Friday, 1972) – and forecasters are often prone to accept the insights offered by free-floating imagination.

Science fiction is another category of imaginative writing which has exercised, and continues to exercise, a strong influence on forecasting. In the simplest terms, it may be said that utopian writing is predominantly political and moral in its inspiration, with science and technology introduced in an attempt to increase the degree of reality; science fiction is predominantly concerned with science and technology, and treats society as the dependent variable. The distinction may be epitomized by comparing Wells with Jules Verne. Verne's romances combined systematic analysis of scientific progress with naive optimism about the social consequences of technological change; Wells was not simply an optimist, and his use of science is frequently incidental to a moral and political argument. Technological forecasting, whatever its serious purpose, may be traced back to science fiction (and is liable to similar errors); social forecasting is closer to utopian writing. Compared with Verne, science fiction writers are much less optimistic (indeed, their success is often related to their ability to give us the creeps), but their work continues to reflect the character just described. These distinctions are shifting ones, and in the work of particular writers they may disappear. For example, one well-known contemporary author, J. G. Ballard, has stressed the need for science fiction to deal with 'inner space' rather than 'outer space'. The distinction is nevertheless important, and its implications may be seen throughout the literature of forecasting.

Chapter 2
Forecasting and Planning

Since 1914, writing about the future has split into separate areas of practice. 'The drive for world improvement, which once found expression in so many utopias and ideal states of the future, switched from fiction to the exact statements and precise schemes of expert economists, engineers and town planners who described ways of anticipating and preparing for future changes' (Clarke, 1971a). The impact of the 1914–18 war, and of the great depression which followed it, were powerful stimuli to the growth of futurist thinking, reflected alike in utopian writing, science fiction, and systematic conjecture, as well as a variety of sub-genres. Technological forecasting was officially encouraged in the United States, its best-known exponent being the sociologist W. F. Ogburn, much of whose work was done for President Hoover's Committee on Social Trends, and published in a series of reports in the late 1920s and early 1930s. The famous report of the U.S. National Resources Committee, under the direction of Ogburn, was also concerned with technological unemployment, obsolescence of capital equipment, and science policy (National Resources Committee, 1937). Erich Jantsch, in his well-known survey of technological forecasting (which he defines as the 'probabilistic assessment of future technology'), traces the development of the technique from this kind of generalized concern to its application in the fields of commercial planning, military strategy, and industrial management (Jantsch, 1967). Many of the techniques used for social forecasting have been derived from technological forecasting, including growth functions, envelope curves, analysis by precursive events, Delphi studies, cross-impact matrices, and morphological studies (de Hoghton *et al*, 1971).

The attempt to develop forecasting as a 'scientific' activity is related to the growth of long-term planning by governments and other large-scale organizations. The idea that governments could plan for the future is itself an outgrowth of the 19th century optimism (as expressed, for instance, by the English historian H. T. Buckle) which assumed a steady improvement in the condition of man by the progressive application of science and technology. In the capitalist-industrial states of the Western world, the concept of planning has had three particular aspects in this century which relate to the inadequacy of *laissez-faire* as a basis for economic and social justice. Two of these, city planning and economic planning, both date from the end of the 19th century. The English businessman Ebenezer Howard conceived the idea of garden cities, and set off the modern town planning movement which has tried to design pleasing urban environments. Economic planning was envisaged by the English Fabians as a necessary antidote to the unsatisfactory features of a capitalist economy, and its technical basis was laid by the application of mathematical methods to economic analysis. Social planning, to provide an adequate level of public services like education, health, pensions, communications, and housing, is partly an outcome of the great depression of the 1930s, and partly of demographic changes.

All three forms of planning have shared some basic assumptions. The first is that the world tomorrow will be much like the world today or yesterday, and that its goals and values will not be very dissimilar from those with which we are familiar. Secondly, that the capacity of the earth to sustain the demands our plans make on it can be taken for granted. Thirdly, that a continuous programme of economic expansion is the core of all plans for the future. Fourthly, that science and technology can be effectively harnessed for these purposes.

Planning and forecasting are also related to much more radical demands for social reconstruction, generated not so much by utopian visions as by the actual experience of industrial society and powerfully stimulated by the impact of war, depression and revolution in the 20th century. The concept of planning on a national scale first took effective shape during the 1914–18 war, when the embattled countries of Western Europe found that modern warfare demanded far-reaching control over resources and manpower which could not be provided by *laissez-faire* capitalism. The directors of the German war machine, Rathsnau and Moellendorf, projected the continuation of 'Planwirtschaft' into peacetime as the permanent answer to the problems of a modern industrial economy (Bowen, 1947). The influence of these ideas is manifested in the work of the German sociologist Karl Mannheim, much of whose writing was devoted to the theme of 'reconstruction' and the necessity of combining the planning mechanism with democratic control (Mannheim, 1951). The idea of planning was in fact taken up in the Soviet Union, where the first national plan – the GOELRO scheme for electrification – was inaugurated immediately upon the end of the civil war in 1920. As Carr has written, this was merely the first of a number of plans for increasing industrial and agricultural productivity through a deliberate and centrally directed reorganization of the national economy. Since then, the idea of planning has become one of the principal aspects of Soviet influence on the rest of the world (Carr, 1946). The essential notion of the GOELRO plan – the use of technological change to effect social change – remains deeply embedded in the ideology of Soviet communism, now increasingly expressed in terms of the 'scientific-technological revolution' which is to transform society. 'For socialist society the scientific and technological revolution is a natural continuation of the planned implementation of social transformations. Socialism places the scientific and technological revolution at the service of social progress and uses it for further perfection of the social structure and social relations' (Gvishiani, 1974).

In the command economies of the Soviet Union, Eastern Europe, and China the nature of planning is highly centralized and dominated by ideological objectives. In the capitalist-industrial countries planning is both more fragmented and less ideological. One result is that the various branches of planning activity are dominated by the conventional wisdom of specialized disciplines or professions such as economics, architecture, engineering, medicine and education. In a rapidly changing world this can lead to serious errors, and especially to a failure to prepare for new problems instead of extrapolating the solutions to those with which we are already familiar. It is not only generals who are always preparing to fight the last war; most of us are in much the same situation. A provocative examination of this tendency is to be found in the BBC Reith Lectures for 1970 by Donald Schon. The structure of government, he remarks, is ' a series of memorials to old problems', and society in general is tending to become a cluster of 'threatened institutions caught in the grip of an imperfectly understood instability'. Schon enunciates a facetious 'law' which asserts that no currently accepted idea is appropriate to the circumstances of its time; hence, because finance is only made available for studying acceptable ideas, work on real problems does not obtain support. Our organizational map, he suggests, is 'perpetually mismatched to the problems that we think are worth solving'. In an unstable world, new forms of research are essential if we are to keep abreast of change; traditional methods, which depend on establishing in detail what has already occurred, yield information which is obsolete by the time it is collected. Forecasting is preferable even if it is based on inadequate data or no data (Schon, 1971).

This kind of thinking about the future embodies what might be called a 'craft' approach, i.e. a mixture of specialized knowledge with the practical wisdom of long experience. A common alternative to the craft approach is the attempt to find 'technological' solutions, in the hope that complex socio-technical problems can be resolved by a technological 'fix' or 'breakthrough'. At its best, technology can achieve a great deal, especially if applied on an experimental basis which provides for improvements in the light of experience, but its recurrent failures are due to an absence of proper appreciation for the second-order effects of technological change, and a lack of insight into the complexity of the relationships between technology and society.

Forecasting may be seen as an attempt to make planning more informed, more rational, or more 'scientific'. Mario Bunge suggests that forecasting entails the addition of research to planning, rather than relying on experts. There is no special technique available to experts which can save us from research. The scientific approach requires us to build a conceptual model of the problem with which we are concerned and to improve it progressively by testing its applicability to the data (Bunge, 1973).

The most systematic attempts yet made to relate forecasting and planning are associated with the various groups linked with the French Commissariat du Plan. The 'Plan et Prospectives' group, for instance, has defined its task as identifying *'faits porteurs d'avenir'* which, though difficult to quantify, are likely to be significant in shifting the direction of change. These include population growth, demand for goods and services, income distribution, consumption levels, and the use of space and time. Ideally, they acknowledge, this requires a systematic theory of social change. Since no such theory is available, a less systematic approach based on these *'faits porteurs d'avenir'* is the available alternative. By developing such studies, it should be possible to plot major social trends (*'tendances lourdes'*) and to import a longer-term perspective to the planning process (Cazes, *et al*, 1972). This approach has much in common with the arguments developed in the present book.

Chapter 3
Values and Objectives

Forecasting is not, and cannot be, a purely objective exercise. The future does not exist; forecasters try to invent it. In doing so, our presuppositions about what *ought* to happen are intertwined with assumptions about what *will* and what *can* happen. Forecasting is an attempt to gain what Baier calls 'meliorative knowledge'; hence it involves assumptions about the causal roles of events, things, and human endeavours in generating the future. Such knowledge depends on value judgments, which are not merely expressions of the emotions or exhortations to better behaviour, but are susceptible to logical examination (Baier, 1969). Winthrop, in an examination of the contribution made by the social sciences to the study of the future, describes the notion of 'value-free' speculation about the future as complacent self-deception, and insists that forecasters must choose the values which their research will serve (Winthrop, 1968).

Edward Gibbon described history as a record of the crimes, follies, and fortunes of mankind. Evidently he did not have much faith in the possibility of achieving a society in which decisions would be taken on the basis of available information, and his view is, in a way, an expression of the ultimate in determinism. If we believe that people make technology and that people can choose whether and how to use it, then some methods of evaluating different ways of achieving society's goals are necessary, and indeed some way of analysing the assumptions underlying the goals themselves. Only by postulating goals and understanding why we select them rather than others, can we assess the ways in which technological change might interact with society – whether it be large-scale, such as a radical change in the transport system, or small, such as a new motor technology for a particular form of transport. Of necessity, this assessment involves some forecasting. We want to know not just how the change will or will not fulfill our postulated goals now, but also how it will affect them in the future, for one, two or even three generations. To do this requires some exercise of the imagination, and we have to move out of the quantifiable and verifiable into the unknown.

Contemporary concern for the quality of life and work, and the fear that misuse of technology is causing irreparable and insidious damage to the natural world, are a continuation of the criticism expressed by earlier social critics and reformers. Fourier, Marx and Russell castigated the use of knowledge in ways which increasingly separated the majority of people from responsibility for social decisions. Fourier, in 1822, criticized the 'learned men who for thirty years have neglected the science of associative mechanisms'. It is the 'science of associative mechanisms' which we are trying to develop in the attempt to assess the ongoing effects of technological change. In doing so, we are anxious to avoid the strong bias towards historicism and determinism which characterizes much forecasting in both capitalist and socialist economies, and to underline the positive social aims towards which technological progress should be directed. 'Only in this way can we design technologies to serve human beings rather than extrapolate technical changes and think of ways to adapt human beings to these requirements' (Freeman, 1970).

Popper (1945) and others have pointed out the tendency towards despotism in all utopias. The dreamer is so anxious to impose the good society on mankind that he commands it to be done. This danger can only be avoided if the widest possible sections of the community are enabled to take part in decision processes. Part of our concern, then, is to demonstrate the inter-actions between a variety of technologies and social processes, and to compare their probable effects on society and on the natural environment.

The kind of social goals that could be examined by a fore-casting group could include:

(1) Social change should be directed towards the reduction of inequalities. By this we refer not only to material living

standards, but also to non-material values such as education, leisure, and the availability of participation in public decision-making.

(2) In particular, social policies should be designed on an international basis to raise living standards in the 'under-developed' countries and to narrow international disparities.

(3) The choice of technologies to meet social demands should be directed towards those which are likely to generate the least damage to physical environments and social relation-ships, and which do not create excessive social or environmental vulnerability in the event of internal or external disturbances.

N.B. We recognize that social transformations are not possible without disruption. Too much disruption is generated, however, because of lack of intelligent fore-thought about the effects of new technologies.

(4) Social and technological changes should increase rather than decrease the social options available to communities, so that the exigencies of making a living are less significant by comparison with opportunities for personal involvement, development of a diversity of life styles, and the cultivation of rewarding social relationships.

We believe it is particularly important to stress the long-term importance of reducing inequalities between nations. Population growth, economic expansion, and technological change are the great moving forces of our era; when they act together, their usual effect is to enlarge and deepen existing inequalities across the world. Left to themselves, these forces are liable to aggravate existing inequalities, and thereby to increase tension, conflict, and the threat of international violence.

'World equality' would be a grossly over-simplified and sloganised representation of what we are advocating. There are many types of inequality which we believe it is undesirable to eradicate, and still others which we believe it is impossible to remove. For example, we accept the evidence from molecular biology that every individual is unique in terms of genetic endowment. There is a rich diversity among the different cultures of the world and it would be a great loss if this diversity were sacrificed in the move towards a more egalitarian situation. Such things as food, art, music, style of clothing and housing all contribute to the diversity in life styles around the world. Furthermore, climatic and other geographic variations make an enormous difference to life styles and these cannot be changed. As Part IV makes clear, we would hope that scientific research and technical innovation might contribute to the enhancement of this diversity rather than its elimination. Variety is the spice of life, and many inter-personal and inter-cultural differences will and should persist indefinitely. We accept the point of Bernard Shaw's dictum: do not do unto others as you would be done by, because their tastes may be different. We do not want to see every remote tribal culture forced to assimilate.

But cutting across all this desirable diversity there are other sorts of inequality. We believe that the degrees of difference in levels of nutrition, housing, health, and income that now exist, say between India and the United States, will become increasingly unacceptable as we move towards and into the 21st century. They are unacceptable to us now. For this reason we have formulated as a major value-based objective 'the reduction of world-wide inequalities'.

This choice of emphasis may appear to some as eccentric or misplaced, to others as undesirable or outrageously radical, to still others as hopelessly naive or utopian in the bad sense of the word. We do not hope to convince them all, but to persuade at least some such readers that there are very strong arguments for looking at the world's future in this perspective, which is examined further in Part IV.

Chapter 4

The Art of Anticipation

The title of this book warrants some comment. Forecasting, it need hardly be said, is an uncertain exercise, plagued with fallacies, uncertainties, and ignorance. It cannot aspire to be called a science, and it must avoid the dangers of pseudoscience. Insofar as forecasting is successful, it requires an imaginative synthesis between what is known and what is unknown, between what is (relatively) certain and what is indefinite. This is properly described as an art (or a craft). Art, declares Herbert Read (1967), is not an ornament to society (contrary to the philistine view of H. G. Wells) but a mode of knowledge, as valuable to man as philosophy or science. 'Indeed, it is only when we have clearly recognized art as a mode of knowledge parallel to but distinct from other modes by which man arrives at an understanding of his environment that we can begin to appreciate its significance.'

Our distinguished coeval, Bertrand de Jouvenel, appropriately titled his work *The Art of Conjecture*. We have tried to go a little further in our analysis of the problem and the methods available to deal with it. The relation between prediction, forecasting, and anticipation is explored in several parts of the present book. As we are sceptical about prediction, and have not endeavoured to make specific forecasts, anticipation may be regarded as our major theme. Our work has six distinguishable aspects, which collectively make up what may be called the 'Sussex approach' to forecasting:

(1) An emphasis on the need for choice of social and technological alternatives (hence the name of our project).

(2) The definition and exploration of moral and ethical criteria

to be applied to the choice of alternatives in a changing world.

(3)   An emphasis on three massive forces for change (described elsewhere as 'escalator processes') – population growth, economic expansion, and technological change.

(4)   Analysis of sectors rather than forecasting of a generalized future. This also entails a study of interactions between sectors (e.g. food supply, energy, materials and transport), and detailed small-scale analyses or 'micro-studies'.

(5)   The concept of 'socio-technical systems', i.e. a clustering of physical technology, social organization, and social institutions in response to the satisfaction of human needs. This clustering makes it possible to provide systematic analysis of sectors and their inter-relations, and to build 'projective models' for forecasting purposes.

(6)   The use of dynamic modelling techniques to explore, test and quantify relationships suggested by logical reasoning and data collection.

The structure of the book is a result of this approach to the problems of anticipation. Part II deals with a number of common dilemmas, errors, and logical difficulties entailed in attempts to make forecasts or predictions. This general account leads into Part III, which is the most substantial section of the book and represents a detailed critical appraisal of current methods used in forecasting, in technology assessment, and in the identification of the *faits porteurs d'avenir* already referred to. Part III may be seen as the continuation and completion of the critical analysis of forecasting methods undertaken in a previous volume, *Models of Doom* (Cole *et al*, 1974).

This book should not be regarded as dominated by the perspectives of the affluent, urban, industrial, Western countries. For this reason, if for no other, we do not pretend to be able to predict some kind of global future. Nevertheless, we believe it is most important to provide an international perspective. Part IV draws attention to the special problems of raising living standards in the developing countries, and to the technological and social choices which will be required to invent a tolerable future for the majority of the world's population.

Part II

Problems and Principles of Appraisal

5. Assumptions and Dilemmas 23

6. Some Logical Points 41

7. Eight Critical Issues 52

Chapter 5

Assumptions and Dilemmas

Predicting future history?

Notwithstanding the categorical assertion in some published forecasts about what this planet will be like in 30, 50 or 100 years, no serious forecaster, when pressed to the point, will maintain that the shape of things to come can be delineated in the here and now with any degree of precision. This cautionary attitude is in part the result of looking at previous forecasts already confronted by historical fact with the easy wisdom of hindsight. Most of these were proved wrong; occasionally there is one nearly correct, but for the wrong reason. To take some examples: the notorious groundnut scheme which the British government initiated after the war was based on a forecast of an imminent severe shortage of fats. That the scheme failed for technical reasons is almost beside the point, for the predicted shortage never developed. Other historical forecasts, for example some in demography, were right for the wrong reasons. A U.S. forecast based on birth and death rates agreed exactly with the subsequent census. But the result was not due to the predicted increase in births and decrease in mortality; it came about through large-scale immigration at the time (Page, 1973). A lucky hit. Other examples are quoted by Michael Young (1968) who says that 'it is (far more happily than unhappily for mankind) part of the definition of the future that it is unknown'.

Why should this be the case? There are some who believe that such uncertainty will gradually diminish as methods become more sophisticated and more reliable data about the current situation become available. They have the full force of the deterministic world view behind them. But given the assumptions that our knowledge of the world as it is at any moment will always be imperfect and that any scientific representation must always be a simplification of such imperfect knowledge, the aim of precise predictions recedes beyond man's intellectual powers. Even such an arch-determinist as Freud (in much, though not all, of his thinking) regarded prediction as virtually impossible because the relative strength of current characteristics defies efforts at exact definition of their development, and settled for post-diction (Freud, 1920). In the natural sciences, probabilistic thinking is replacing simple determinism because of the operation of random factors. But in forecasting social events the natural science solution is not easily applicable because whatever the likelihood that pollution, for example, will continue to increase, a decision to introduce counter-pollution measures is possible. In other words, the probability of any predicted future is subject to major modifications by deliberate action and decision-making within the time span for which the prediction is supposed to hold. These actions may well be the consequence of the prediction having been made, thus leading to a self-defeating prophecy. Whether man's deliberate decisions are in themselves determined raises the philosophical issue of freedom which we do not wish to discuss here because we have nothing new to add to the age-old arguments. Anybody who has ever been involved in any major or minor decision will confirm that such determinism is certainly hidden from human experience. The question for us is not to decide the philosophical issue, but rather to select an image of man that corresponds to the manner in which decisions affecting the future of mankind are actually made, that is man as an actor rather than as a passive robot driven by inexorable forces to fulfil his fate (Chein, 1972). This is, of course, not the only possible image. Whole civilizations are presented as based on the Nirvana principle of contemplation and renunciation of choice and purposeful actions. They would hardly have survived, however, unless this ideal had been restricted to a spiritual élite, while lower castes risked reincarnation into a lower form of life if they engaged in contemplation.

The general mood of our times often appears to support a fatalistic view of man's future, certainly among many intellectuals (Heilbroner, 1974). If one dared to attach a date to the change in the climate of thought in the Western world, the concentration camps and Hiroshima and Nagasaki might mark the water-shed between the period when the idea of progress and decency based on effort and purpose was central in the climate of thought and the current period in which fatalism replaces it. The atomic bomb provided a rational base for the fear of the future; the growth of technology helped to make the individual feel power-less in stemming the tide; the camps demonstrated the power of evil in the 'civilized' world.

Data on the mood of the population in general are sparse; where they are available they seem to indicate that the present is compared unfavourably with the past (Part III and Harris, 1974). Important though it would be to understand the general climate of current thought better, it could not form the basis of forecasting exercises. Nor can technological determinism fill that role. Yet the assumption that the future can be predicted from the extrapolation of technological trends, that 'progress' means the replacement of one technology by another, and that man's adaptive actions can be ignored, seems to dominate a large amount of forecasting work. On the basis of our assumptions this is at best futile and at worst dangerous.

If predicting the historical future is therefore not the central task of forecasting studies, what is?

Alternatives for the future

The emphasis on man as an acting, purposeful, goal-directed being and not a robot occurs in many forecasting exercises as an afterthought. Apart from the danger of crying 'Wolf' too often, apart from the psychological inappropriateness of a power-less plea to those who feel powerless to change the world, this is intellectually unsatisfactory just because action comes as an afterthought rather than as an integral part of the forecasting exercise.

Now it is easier to complain about this than to improve on it. The major difficulty stems from the fact that while the physical properties of the world are quantifiable, goals, intentions, pur-poses and their expression in policies are, as a rule, not. Where efforts at measurement exist, as for example, in the field of attitudes and aspirations, the units of measurement are not easily compatible with the units used for GNP or pollution or material resources. Where efforts have been made to convert human values into monetary terms, as in cost-benefit analysis, for example, the arbitrariness of the conversion is open to serious criticism. Methodological ingenuity has on occasions produced a satisfactory solution to the measurement of intangibles, as Sinclair (1971) demonstrated in his investigations of the value attached to the risk of life and limb in industrial accident prevention costs. But this is the exception rather than the rule. Pending further progress in convincingly converting values into monetary terms, one way out of the dilemma lies in combining qualitative and quantitative data in models of the future. Admittedly, the qualitative part will not lend itself to computerization, at least not yet. This is a disadvantage but one with which one has to live. It is certainly not an excuse for ignoring aspects of social structure and function which are essential influences on the shape of things to come.

As Bertalanffy (1956) has pointed out, when he said that structures are slow processes of long duration while functions are fast processes of short duration, the distinction between them is less radical than is often assumed. The point is important when discussing forecasting, for it would be a serious mistake to regard social structures as unalterable givens, even if one avoids the even greater mistake of ignoring social structure completely as if the future could take off from a social vacuum. Feudalism, capitalism or communism, international or national organizations, whether industrial or military, are aspects of the social structure which must be considered in more sophisticated efforts to spell out alternative futures.

Among the functional aspects, there are at least three types of qualitative factor which should be taken into consideration; first policy decisions; second, goals and purposes; and third, those factors which are often subsumed under the still vague label of 'quality of life'. While all three interact, of course, in feedback loops, there is a clear distinction between the first two and the third: what happens as a result of (1) and (2) affects (3) over a time-lag; in other words, (1) and (2) are analogous to independent variables in experimental design, and (3) to a dependent variable.

Of course one can argue that the third factor, quality of life, could be regarded as the independent variable which pressures public goals and enforces policies, after a time-lag. But since we cannot start with a *tabula rasa* but must begin thinking about the future in the here and now, it is more practical to ignore the past time-lag. There is also a time-relation between policy decisions and goals. Ideally, the formulation of goals should precede policy decisions. In the real world matters are different. Policy decisions are as a rule much more urgent than the adoption of long-term goals. And even where long-term goals have been adopted, the lack of visibility of interactions in the complex modern world often makes it impossible to see how an immediate policy decision bears on the long-term goal. Here lies the social justification for research on the future, because free from the formidable pressure of daily decision-making, research can simulate the ideal world, start with long-term goals and examine the policy decisions which need to be made in the continuous process of approximating the goal.

All too little is known about the manner in which decisions are made which commit the future. Whether the decision-maker is a national government, an international agency, a multinational firm, or a political movement, decisions inevitably involve an anticipation about future developments, even when they are made in order to deal with immediately pressing circumstances. Implicitly or explicitly, however, each decision bears on some more long-term goal.

But what are the goals and who chooses them? Of course, national governments, political parties, private firms, and individuals differ widely in this respect. It would be politically intolerable and practically futile for a research group to pretend that it can dictate the goals. The way out is to present alternative possibilities which indicate what is implied at the various points and to leave the choice between them to the political process where it properly belongs. But it would be foolish to pretend that forecasters themselves are outside the political process. They are not and cannot be. For even when they deliberately adopt a neutral position *vis-à-vis* major goals, such neutrality is in itself an expression of values. A minimal safeguard against bias stemming from value commitments in research is that they be made explicit, so that others can check whether and to what extent such commitments have inadvertently influenced method and argument. An additional and more powerful safeguard is the introduction into the body of research of alternative goals in terms of basic values. As the last chapter of this book will make explicit, the value on which all contributors to this book are agreed is the reduction of inequality within and between nations. The commitment to the tracing of alternatives will be implemented by thinking through possible futures in which this value is either implemented or ignored.

These are the reasons why we want to adopt the tracing of possible alternatives for the future as the central task for forecasting studies. The implications of this reformulation are considerable. Above all it means advocating a normative approach, i.e. the specification of various goals. It also means that forecasting groups should view their work not as prophecy but as contributions to an essentially political debate about the future of the world.

What goals?

It could be argued that not only all forecasters but all mankind are united in one goal: survival of life on this planet. True. In astronomical time perspective this may be unachievable. But we are talking in human time perspectives, that is to say about the next few generations. In forecasting, where controversies are so much more numerous than agreements, it is important to underline the consensus on survival. The point at issue is not this, however, but the identification of policies necessary for the survival of future generations. Forrester and Meadows, for example, regard 'overshoot and collapse' as almost inevitable unless economic growth is very soon brought to a halt. If they were right the prospect would indeed be grim and draconian measures justified even though it is hard to see by what powers they could be implemented in the short time available. Perhaps these powers would emerge, as they did when Fred Hoyle's black cloud approached the planet. But are the forecasters of ultimate crisis right? This is a technical question which we have recently tackled in an examination of their assumptions, techniques and data, and we concluded that they were not (Cole *et al*, 1973). Here, it must suffice to refer to one of their predicted modes of 'overshoot and collapse', namely that produced by pollution, to illustrate why we find fault with the notion that all economic growth must cease, even though we agree that in some places on the globe pollution requires the immediate attention of policy makers. Catastrophe through pollution is predicted with the help of the following assumptions: pollution is assumed to be an inevitable consequence of industrial investment and it is aggregated for the globe, ignoring the differences between, say, Africa and the metropolitan concentrations in the United States. Since very few data are available on pollution as a totality, and none based on systematic repeated measures, guesses had to supplant data for estimating the increase of pollution. Pollution was assumed to grow exponentially. Lord Ashby who was chairman of the Royal Commission on Environmental Pollution in the U.K. gave, in a lecture to the Royal Society in 1973, a number of fascinating and detailed case studies which demonstrated the lack of plausibility of these assumptions. Only one can be sited here:

Carbon monoxide is stable in the air and it is broken down photo-chemically (except perhaps at the top of the troposphere, and this is uncertain). At this rate it should be accumulating sufficiently to raise the background concentration by something like 0.04 parts per million per year, and by now the background concentration should have reached about one part per million. But so far as we can discover, the background concentration has not changed for 25 years or longer. It remains, with some local variations, of the order of 0.1 part per million. This is a vitally important piece of evidence, for if the background level of carbon monoxide were accumulating in the way the level of carbon dioxide undoubtedly is accumulating, something drastic would have to be done. But there are scavengers which keep under control the global reservoir of carbon monoxide. The most likely scavengers are micro-organisms in the soil, which convert the carbon monoxide to methane. So we are deeply in debt to these micro-organisms, which save pollution from carbon monoxide from becoming an international problem of the first magnitude. The evidence at the scientific end of the chain of decision-making does not, in my view, justify top priority being given to this issue at the administrative end. I believe we, and the Americans, have over-reacted.

In other cases, legislative action has been highly effective in reducing pollution where it is a more serious threat.

Moreover, the goal of survival may plausibly be interpreted as justifying a higher priority for the prevention of war than of pollution. Survival is insufficient as a goal in itself since it implies indirectly many other subsidiary and associated goals and since it cannot be divorced from the quality of life for the survivors. What goals then should be specified toward which various forecasting exercises can be geared? Depending on the focus and scope of such endeavours, the choice is large. In the light of what has been said before there is only one requirement for the formulation of goals: it must be stated so as to include alternatives for choice. Suppose a forecasting exercise is concerned with the future of the motor car: by our standards it would not be enough to consider the replacement of internal combustion engines by electrically driven cars; other possible goals, such as replacement of cars by public transport or the technological improvement of cars would have to be considered to permit informed choice.

Even the relatively small goal of dealing with the excesses of the motor car, heralded at the beginning of this century as the answer to the pollution of cities by horse droppings, already contains all the problems of goal setting in the modern world. There is good reason to believe that car ownership, notwithstanding its generally recognized nuisance value for public amenities, offers to millions of wage earners a sense of personal freedom, of being one's own master, at least on the way to work, which enriches the quality of life. In the 20th century it is no longer possible to establish limited goals as if they had no repercussions for the rest of the world. The long-term goals must always be examined from the point of view of *cui bono*. The increasing interdependence of the modern world has only highlighted the vast inequalities which exist within and between nations, inequalities which seem to be linked to deep frustrations and political dangers. This is why we have chosen to make a decrease in existing inequalities the dominant value guiding our forecasting exercises but also to introduce as alternative outcomes of policy an increase of inequalities or the maintenance of current disparities in standards of living.

The scope of forecasting

Forecasting exercises can vary in scope along at least three dimensions: topic (from, e.g., motor car to economic growth, quality of life or natural resources); geographical limits (from, e.g., a city to a region or the planet); and time perspective (e.g. next year, next 30 years, next 100 years). To make one's choice along these dimensions involves in every case a set of dilemmas to which there are no easy solutions.

If one regards any topic, whether specific like the motor car or general like natural resources, as a socio-technical system, that is as a system involving people, their environment, institutions, material and technology, then the specific topic must be regarded as a wide-open system, subject to interaction with surrounding systems which are neglected only at the risk of making the specific exercise less realistic. If one selects a global phenomenon the system can be regarded as closed, but there are two major difficulties: first, data are usually simply not available on, say, all natural resources and guess-work will therefore have to be substituted for a firm data base; secondly, the utility of forecasting research depends on linking it to decision points at which note can be taken of its results and policies appropriately adjusted. In a world in which all major decisions affecting the future of mankind are in the hands of national governments or at best associations of national governments, there simply does not exist an international machinery to take note of, say, the oil crisis in the world. Forecasts may then at worst be nothing but an admittedly fascinating game which academics can play for their own satisfaction; at best they can be an input into international decision-making to the extent that this takes place. But most important, the aggregation of problems which have such different aspects as, say, economic growth in the developed and the developing world cannot be regarded as a reasonable input to decision-making anywhere.

Much the same arguments apply to choice on the geographical dimension. Even though the problems of the world have become so inter-related that decisions in one block of countries have repercussions in another, the urgency and nature of many problems vary enormously from one part to the other. If world models are considered important, they must be built up from the analysis of smaller units. This raises the question of the most appropriate units to choose from those which jointly make up social life on this planet. It has become customary to think in terms of two basic units: the developed and the developing world. Whether this is good enough is a moot question. It could be argued that the Latin-American block, for example, fits neither group; its problems are certainly very different from those of the new African states. Where units smaller than the world are chosen for forecasting exercises, they must, of course, be treated as open systems.

The time perspective of forecasts must vary with the topic; forecasting road deaths will undoubtedly be done for a shorter period than, say, the future of natural resources. The safest forecasts are generally those with the shorter time span. But the nature of many of the urgent problems does not permit such narrow vision. The British Ministry of Transport, for example, tries to think ahead for thirty years in making decisions on the construction of motorways. The *World Dynamics* models aim to predict for the next century. And the year 2000 has not yet lost its glamour and millenarian connotations for forecasts, even though its inexorable approach will sooner or later diminish its attractiveness.

Given that the nature of the problem must have influence on the choice, perhaps the specification of terminal dates is not quite as important as it may appear at first sight, particularly when one is concerned with alternative futures. For while the scenario for twenty, thirty or fifty years ahead is an important aspect in establishing targets in the light of goals, even more important is the prospective tracing of processes which approach the alternative goals. Time, said St. Augustine, is a three-fold present: the present as we experience it, the past as a present memory, and the future as a present expectation. (*Pace* Daniel Bell, who used this beautiful statement in his introduction to the 1967 *Daedalus* issue on the Year 2000.) The future which we can now envisage should dictate the actions taken now. But as they proceed to produce consequences some will emerge which have not been anticipated. The intended and unintended processes which will result from purposeful actions will, in turn, shape our visions of the future which, as Augustine implied, will never be here but always ahead of us. Forecasting must then be conceived as a continuous process in which broad goals may remain stable for decades but in which policy recommendations must be revised as praxis and process unfold. To give an example, Britain has had in the 1950s and 1960s an influx of coloured immigrants who came for economic reasons of their own and in the economic interest of the host country. When Roy Jenkins was Home Secretary he formulated a goal for Britain, namely that she should develop into a multi-racial society. In the interest of this goal a control of the immigration process was instituted to avoid the upheaval for natives and immigrants of a sudden and massive influx. When Amin suddenly expelled some 30,000 Asians from Uganda, Britain's goal was not changed but the policy rightly was. And the forecasts of how the transformation will occur and which actions will help or hinder the approximation to the goal must be modified in the light of this new fact of life in this country.

Propaganda or research

In what has been said before, much emphasis has been placed on the need to relate forecasting to policy formation and implementation; not only because the motivation of researchers engaged in this field is, as a rule, embedded in a sense of social responsibility for the future, but as an inherent intellectual requirement of the approach to forecasting which has been sketched here. If one believes that the central task is the tracing of alternative ways to alternative goals and that the choice between the various paths can be influenced by purposeful action, that we are not totally at the mercy of uncontrollable forces, then a preoccupation with policies is inevitable.

Under every form of political regime, even a totalitarian one, policies are carried through more easily if they have a resonance in the population; indeed, sometimes – and more often in democracies than under dictatorships – policies are conceived and implemented only under the pressure of public demand. Public demand for future-oriented policies, or at least a favourable attunement in the population to such policies, is, in turn, not likely to occur spontaneously. Most people are understandably so preoccupied with their own lives in the here and now that they do not give a concerted effort to thinking about future generations. Propaganda, on the other hand, can produce an atmosphere in which policies for the future become acceptable. In his previously quoted lecture Lord Ashby draws attention to the genuine dilemma these considerations raise for the scientists concerned with policies emerging from work on the future:

> Generating concern among millions is a job at the other end of the chain from the scientist's job. . . . To create popular concern about the future of the environment is an art which, like dramatic art, requires the gift of make-believe. . . . this is something alien to the scientist. . . . And yet – this is the dilemma – it is the headlines which generate interest; the small print has no appeal to the public.

He takes *The Limits to Growth* as an example which he criticizes in its data and assumptions, but he concludes with the dilemma still wide open:

> . . . suppose the tentative and quite undramatic truth had been told: would the work have aroused public interest? Would the press have taken it up? Would even Whitehall have felt obliged to set up a unit to study it? I suspect that the answer to all these questions is no.

At the very end of the lecture he says:

> So the ethical problem remains: is it moral, for the sake of a good end, to refrain from telling the whole truth?

The resolution of this dilemma is a very complicated matter, but since scientific research is a collective rather than a one-man enterprise, there is a corrective mechanism in the criticism of others who can demonstrate where propaganda and research get mixed up in a non-permissible fashion. It must be recognized, however, that this is no solution for the original dilemma posed by Ashby. We must admit that when we tell the whole complicated truth about our projections for the future, with all the if's and but's needed to qualify basic assumptions, the most likely result is that it will not influence the climate of opinion very much, and may not make future-oriented policies which require some immediate sacrifice more acceptable even when strongly indicated; it may even encourage complacency. All we can do is to recognize that we have no solution and decide to stick as a research team by the scientific approach, whatever other mistakes we inadvertently make. There are two rather diverse comforts in living with this unsolved problem. One is to say Thank God for Ralph Nader who, without the prestige of science, is an effective and unashamed propagandist for a good cause. The other is the fact that for the last 5000 years or so scientists and philosophers have lived with the unsolved problem of determinism versus free will, and yet have done good work in the process.

Methods for forecasting

By general consent forecasting profits from being undertaken by interdisciplinary teams. The justification for this practice is obvious: the physical, social and psychological attributes of human existence on this planet continuously interact as they are shaping the future. Whether the topic is water resources or the nuclear family – habits, feelings, attitudes, values and aspirations are involved as much as natural resources, technology, biological aspects and economic conditions.

The difficulties often experienced in the co-operation of natural and social scientists are sometimes attributed to the different state of development in the two broad fields, the social sciences being generally regarded as three or four hundred years behind in their development. While this is undoubtedly true it is not the entire explanation. One consequence of the late development of the social sciences is that they have taken their older brother as a model to emulate, and they have learned a lot by doing so. In particular, the pressure for greater precision, the introduction of empirical methods, the search for the elegant abstraction of mathematical models and, lately, their translation into computer simulations have considerably advanced knowledge of man and society. But there is a debit side to this learning process. Much current work on the social science side or in interdisciplinary efforts is based on the tacit assumption that there should come into existence a unified science in which the old distinctions disappear, that there is no fundamental difference between the

two spheres and that the natural sciences have made the conceptual and methodological breakthroughs which permit this
to happen.

While the prediction of scientific thought is notoriously the
most unmanageable area for forecasting and while we would
not dare to venture a guess as to whether this assumption will
be justified at some time in the distant future, we believe that
within the limited time span of our working lives, it is dangerous
to accept this assumption *in toto*. Particularly dangerous because
it is largely valid; but not altogether, and the small difference
is of major importance. Throwing the baby out with the bath
water is as inconvenient as letting it drown in it. The crucial
difference, small only in relative terms, lies in the nature of the
phenomena with which the natural and the social sciences deal.
At least in the modern age the assumption that inanimate objects
have purposes and intentions is generally regarded as inappropriate. On the other hand, the assumption that man does not
influence the course of events through purposes and intentions
is equally inappropriate. It is, of course, possible to study man
in a mechanistic fashion. But nobody could communicate such
a study without purpose and intention. Scientists cannot claim
for themselves attributes which their science denies to the rest
of mankind. This is why concern with conflict, purpose and
intention, concepts so alien to the natural scientist's way of
procedure, must be included in forecasting exercises by the
social scientists in an interdisciplinary team.

These inevitable differences in the nature of basic concepts
become a problem in forecasting where quantitative methods are
employed. With Delphi methods and the development of
scenarios, co-operation is as a rule much easier; while they have
their good use, in isolation from other techniques they imply
the danger, even more than all forecasting, of remaining fanciful
rather than convincing. At the other extreme are extrapolation
on the one hand and the development of systems analysis on the
other, which lend themselves to computerisation with all its
enormous advantages, but usually at the expense of excluding
human factors. These points highlight the sad fact that notwithstanding many years of efforts in interdisciplinary work, the
concept is still unclear. Kahn, for example, seems to interpret
interdisciplinary research as the elimination of all separate

disciplines; hence he produces large lists of important factors, without apparently profiting from the great amount of thought that single disciplines have devoted to some of them. As has been indicated above, our own interpretation is decidedly different.

This is not the place to discuss in detail the variety of available techniques and their possible combinations. These matters will be dealt with in Part III of this book. In any case, even though appropriate techniques are crucially important for the quality of research and, as the subsequent discussion will show, are never perfect but present various mixtures of assets and liabilities, they cannot be applied mechanically to new problems. It is in the nature of research that the progressive improvement of the formulation of a problem leads to adaptation and modification of existing methods, or the invention of new ones. Here it should be emphasized that even before work on techniques begins it is necessary to clarify the method of thought which is to be applied to forecasting, that is the basic framework within which one decides to think about the problems of the future. It is in this sense that Kahn, for example, proposes 'surprise-free' projections as a yardstick for evaluating the unfolding future, when he says:

> The most salient of the projections we can make is one that is 'surprise-free', nevertheless it would be very surprising if in any thirty-three year period the world did not produce many political and technological surprises. For the skeptical reader this 'surprise-free' projection may be useful chiefly as a norm for comparison and disagreement.

Another method of thought about the future is that of Forrester and Meadows who have chosen to think primarily in terms of physical attributes of the world.

We have taken a somewhat different approach. Attempts to relate social and technological change require a suitable intellectual framework, which may be found in the concept of a 'socio-technical system'. This may be defined as a complex model of the connection between human needs, demands, and imperatives on the one hand, and on the other, the inter-related networks of institutions, social roles, physical techniques and instruments which arise in response to these needs, demands and imperatives. A socio-technical system is not a comprehensive description of the structure of organized society, but an analytical and heuristic device for examining the processes of social change, especially the interaction between social institutions, social behaviour, technological change and the natural environment. In this context we readily accept one of Kahn's objectives for future-oriented policy research, namely to 'create propaedeutic and heuristic methodologies and paradigms'; regrettably his own work does not implement this. Food, energy, transport, the use of materials, the provision of shelter, health, and communications are examples of sectors which should lend themselves to this kind of model building.

Forecasting – cui bono?

Forecasting, particularly normative forecasting, is directed toward influencing social policy. Social policy, in turn, is more and more explicitly concerned with improving the quality of life. This is why forecasters must come to terms with this elusive phrase, which goes beyond the advocacy of social institutions and regulations which are only means to an end. The phrase implies that the life experiences of individuals are the ultimate yardstick for the quality of a society to the extent that they are shaped for better or worse by the nature of the society in which they live. A subsequent chapter describes in some detail how various researchers have defined and measured aspects of quality of life. This is not the place to anticipate the advantages and disadvantages of various methods and measures discussed there. Here, the problem is to identify one or the other assumption and dilemma which underlie all such efforts.

In the long-standing debate about the attributes of a good society the emphasis has not always been on people. Plato's *Republic* suggests a system of orderly institutions, aesthetically pleasing in their smooth hierarchical structure, but – at least explicitly – unconcerned with the way of life of ordinary people. Modern thinkers are more often concerned with the consequences of institutions on individuals. The greatest happiness for the greatest number as much as 'from everybody according to his ability, to everybody according to his needs' are two of the most powerful examples of this changed emphasis.

However admirable the morality inherent in such ideals, when one attempts to apply them as indicators of quality of life, their apparent clarity disappears; they raise unanswered, perhaps even unanswerable questions. The utilitarian dogma presupposes that we know how to define happiness, and that, whatever definition emerges, the organization of a society has a clear bearing on it. Freud, in *Civilisation and its Discontents* (1930), gives a powerful negative answer to both these problems. Though many strive for happiness, he argues, the human condition is inevitably tragic; suffering and unhappiness even in the best conceivable society will stem from three unalterable conditions of our existence: the decay of the human body, illness and death; the occurrence of natural catastrophes; and what people can do to each other in their personal relations. While there is certainly in the last of these three conditions also the source for happiness as understood by many, through its own dynamics and as influenced by the other two, it remains a fleeting experience that cannot remain stable for very long; what is more, it is certainly outside the power we are willing to grant policy makers. The search for happiness is better left to individuals in their efforts to make sense out of their lives; it cannot be tackled by policy makers and, therefore, *a fortiori*, should not be tackled by forecasting.

Marx's definition of socialism is unfortunately no better guide. To use it for policy formulation presupposes that what people need can be specified. Perhaps such specification is possible in terms of minimal material standards of living, and some forecasting efforts have indeed taken, for example, the calorie intake of food necessary for keeping alive as a yardstick for forecasting food requirements. Useful though this may be for some purposes, it does not approach Marx's ideal. For it is in the nature of human beings that their needs have broader scope, that basic needs fulfilled give rise to new ones, that aspirations met will guarantee only one thing: new aspirations will arise, not only in each individual case, but from one generation to the next. All forecasting rests on the solid basis of events, needs and aspirations in the here and now. In fifty or a hundred years from now material and other needs of human beings may have changed beyond recognition.

The forecasters' problem in dealing with quality of life factors is further complicated by the stark fact that we live in a world of scarcity and will do so for the foreseeable future. Meeting the needs of some may inevitably imply not meeting the needs of others. Or, as Heilbroner (1974) implies, meeting the material needs of the world may be possible only by sacrificing all other needs – for freedom of movement and thought, for decency of man to man and all humanitarian ideals, for culture, art, and play. These needs are real too; to sacrifice them is a counsel of despair. Yet these non-material needs are, occasionally, referred to by some forecasters as a cheap way out of the problems of material scarcity. The implicit argument is that if non-material needs were to replace material ones, the scarcity argument would lose its force. There can be no doubt that the extreme materialism of the industrialized world is self-defeating; shifts in values must occur. But the argument about spiritual values substituting for material ones has no power for the developing world. There is good evidence to show that non-material values do not flourish on an empty stomach.

How, in view of such considerations, can forecasting come to terms with the idea of quality of life as the ultimate yardstick? There is no easy answer. The best one can do is to reduce deliberately the level of aspiration in the forecasting enterprise itself. Since we do not know how to make everybody happy, to meet their needs and aspirations, nor what these needs and aspirations may be for some future generation, all one can do is to aim more modestly for an elimination of social conditions which are experienced as constraints, preventing people from shaping their own lives. A society in which people have food, housing, work and security from physical violence does not guarantee happiness nor fulfilment of all higher needs, but it gives people a better chance to find their own purposes for their existence than a society in which these constraints are high.

Chapter 6

Some Logical Points

Throughout this book, frequent references are made to 'systems' and 'models'. The logical status of these terms, and their relationship to one another, is often taken for granted. Attempts to study the future should take as little as possible for granted, and in this chapter we have therefore included a brief discussion of these basic concepts.

A typical definition of a system is one which describes it as 'a complex of elements or components . . . [in a partially ordered] . . . network, such that each component is related to at least some others in a more or less stable way within any particular period of time' (Buckley, 1967). In simpler terms, a system can be identified as a unit with a defined structure and components. The concept of system owes its generality to the wide interpretation of what constitutes 'structure' and 'components'. Generally speaking, however, there are two types or families of systems: (a) empirical systems, most frequently used by technologists; and (b) theoretical systems, most frequently used by scientists.

This distinction is not always clear-cut, and indeed scientists and technologists often use both, but with a preference for one or the other. Regardless of how systems are characterized, there is one central practical problem: almost without exception, the most important and the most interesting systems (e.g. health, energy, production) are all very big and very complex. This immediately leads to the very natural conjunction of models and systems. Seemingly, this tends to be a constant conjunction between the two. But this is not at all surprising as the fundamental role of models is to provide a simplified and under-standable *representation* of systems – especially the very big and the very complex.

A ship is an empirical marine transport system. The naval architect with his plans and drawings decides on the *structure* of the system (or ship). Similarly the estimating engineer with his bill of materials and specifications sheets orders the *components* of the system (or ship). From the very earliest Chinese or Greek boatbuilders to the most modern Japanese shipyard, there have always been models representing the particular design of ship being built. None of these boat models for a marine transport system were in any sense toys. Rather, these were empirical models for empirical systems which were constantly referred to, formerly by the carpenter and more recently by design engineers with their testing tanks.

Classical physics is a theoretical *world* system. The *components* are point masses and the *structure* is Newton's laws of motion. As with empirical systems, this theoretical system has theoretical models of the way point masses collide and the way point masses orbit in gravitational fields. The older 'billiard ball' models, and the newer 'air table and puck' models, give clear and distinct representations of the essential features of the Newtonian theoretical system.

In both previous examples, the respective empirical and theoretical models could logically have been discarded in favour of their parent empirical and theoretical systems. Nevertheless, the models were not dropped, and if anything, it is to be noted that models have had increasingly stronger roles to play in the modern world. Many governments have large econometric models, nuclear scientists have families of nuclear models, aeronautical models are developed for each new generation of planes, prototype models are used extensively by production industries, circulatory and respiratory models produce standards for judging biochemical results in modern medicine. What then, makes models so strong and valuable?

Perhaps their greatest virtue is that they are relatively both transparent and useful, in the sense that the bigger parent system is made more understandable and manipulable at certain sensitive points. As it turns out, this transparency and utility of models tends to be a self-fulfilling characteristic. Those representations which are not transparent and useful should not be called models; they are often viewed just as alternative formulations of the system under consideration.

Granting this characterization of models, the question of transparent and use 'to whom?' naturally arises. It is the people that work with models who ultimately decide their detailed characteristics. Since there are large numbers of specialized working groups, it is not surprising that there are numerous types of models. There will probably always be some sort of confusion or imprecision when the word 'model' is used in various discussions, but the chart on page 44 may help by outlining some of the senses of 'model' (adapted from Bunge, 1967, with additions).

Breadth of models

In the construction of models for forecasting, there is in principle no constraint on the breadth of the model. Frequently, the breadth is decided by the practical constraints on feasibility. Nevertheless, the guiding dictum should be that models must be sufficiently wide to enable the implementation of effective policies. Forecasting models, which are narrow and unspecific, are only blunt policy implements.

Stacking of models

Realistic enquiries into systems necessitate the recognition of the fact that a number of models are layered one on top of the other. Ignoring different layers can produce very skewed results. One example occurs with some of the Middle East oil producing nations, where per capita GNP is very high in a 'top layer' national model. The underlying industry model is dominated by the oil and gas resource sector. Beneath this is an employment model, distorted by almost feudal family connections and by a large work force of non-nationals. At the bottom level, there is a population model with a huge gap between male and female labour participation rates. Boring down through a stack of models shows that an overlying high per capita GNP is almost totally

Ideal Model involved in a theory
— Iconic (e.g. the lock-and-key model of engineers)
— Symbolic (e.g. the democratic society in political science)

Theoretical

Interpretation of an abstract theory
— Conceptual (e.g. an arithmetical interpretation of group theory)
— Factual (e.g. physical interpretation of Euclidean geometry)
— Mixed (e.g. general automata theory)

System

Empirical — Material Analogues (e.g. a hydraulic model of a country's economy)

Mechanical (e.g. prototypes, aeronautical 'scale models')

Black Box (e.g. input/output models, stimulus-response models)

Representational (e.g. animated displays of railway or electricity systems)

Note: In forecasting, 'Computer Modelling' by itself appears to be a combination of Mixed and Material Analogue types of models. As inputs, sub-routines, and sub-systems, many of the other types of models appear; thus computer models are 'super-models' on the backs of many smaller and more specific models (see Part III).

irrelevant to the numerous non-national female domestics in that country.

Accepting the above points reinforces the view that, for large systems, there must be width as well as depth in the forecasting models. This may be hardly surprising, but it can be easily under-estimated. For a country such as Britain, forecasts of primary energy requirements generally have errors of ± 1 per cent per annum. After ten years, the forecast can be wrong by ± 10 per cent, a figure which in itself does not seem too bad, and might at first glance be acceptable. Unfortunately, ± 10 per cent does not mean that the structure and components of the primary energy field change individually by ± 10 per cent. Rather, it may mean building or not building a new refinery or nuclear station, or it may mean sinking or not sinking several new coal mines – all of which are ten-year projects. Without good width and depth in forecasting models, important choices, alternatives and decisions are hidden from view.

Model input/output compatibilities

The output of one model is the input of the next, and in big systems the links have to be homogeneous, or else contradictions will arise. Conversion factors and standard units are frequently introduced, but not without difficulties. Models of electricity generating systems use kilowatt hours (kWh) or kilogramme coal equivalents (kgc.eq.). For forecasting there are several problems. When compared to coal- or oil-fired stations, the coal equivalents of hydro-electric or nuclear stations are (in practice) under-estimates of the power outputs and over-estimates of the power inputs. In fact conversion factors have been changed as 'standard' coal stations have become more efficient through time.

In addition, the whole notion of conversion figures completely masks the *system* differences in changing primary energy into electricity by the contrasting conversion processes of coal, oil, gas, hydro and nuclear stations. Hydro and nuclear conversion processes are highly capital intensive, and thus their costs are very sensitive to changes in interest charges for capital. Coal, oil and gas stations are highly resource-cost sensitive and any change in the price of fuel is immediately and strongly reflected in production costs.

The upshot for forecasters is that, contrary to the normal forecasting approach of using input/output models (i.e. 'black boxes'), something approaching representational models has to be used whenever possible. Representational models can increase the level of reality in the analysis. Compare 'black box' energy models for a horse and a tractor; both have inputs in terms of so many kcal/day input and so many h.p./day output, but clearly the horse and tractor are not the same, even though they can be given comparable standard units and conversion factors.

Cost-benefit studies of traffic accidents in Britain currently calculate each personal accident at £1600. Totals for accidents can be numerically set against the costs of new safety measures. But any representational model has to include the actual deaths and serious injuries and not just the standard units of costs, i.e. money. The figure of £1600 is a black box which hides any representation of the very real situation – death and injury.

Superficially, this seems to run counter to the large push in forecasting increasingly to quantify and attach numerics to factors. More deeply, it is the demand that the utility of computing with numbers should not be allowed to hide what the numbers represent.

Confirmation—refutation

Data versus systems

As events unfold, even so-called neutral forecasts are not strictly speaking being tested in the way an astronomer tests a hypothesized orbit against the observed orbit of a new comet. Forecasts are not directly tested; rather the concurrent policies are what are being tested.

Given this restricted appreciation of testing policies, then indirectly forecasts can be said to be right, or wrong or nearly so, within certain limits of error. Taken together, forecasts and policies can be self-confirmed or self-refuted. If an electricity board forecasts a large increase in demand which does not seem to be developing, marginal cost pricing and special low rates for large customers have frequently been introduced, so that the forecast is self-confirmed. If an iron and steel refinery forecasts increasing iron ore resource costs because of expanding demand for shrinking supply, then the forecasts can be self-refuted by adding an up-grading plant which permits the use of a larger supply of a lower grade ore. Within the system being forecast there is generally a balance of self-confirming and self-refuting elements. Basically this is simply that positive or negative extremes are offset or counteracted by the natural conservative character of most productive systems.

Even when the basic self-confirming/self-refuting aspects of a system have been detailed, can forecasts be said to be 'right' or 'wrong'? The simple answer is no, since no piece of data or data series can be said directly to confirm a forecast. It is perhaps surprising that this state of affairs is in no way unscientific. The problem is that any specific set of predictions involves so many 'special cases', 'boundary conditions', 'idealizations' and 'initializations' for a whole series of models, that the final forecast is at best a caricature of reality. The forecasting of a system is exactly parallel with forecasting of naval bombardments in the military sciences, and with forecasting the weather in the meteorological sciences. In all three cases the forecast is only a caricature of the very big and complex systems which are being predicted. If a naval fire control officer or a meteorological officer produces a forecast which is 'on target' even then it may not be a strictly confirming instance (and similarly, a strictly refuting instance). A shell can still arrive at a target even though its weight was too light, because this was offset by a slightly more explosive charge being used. This is a case of compensatory changes in 'initial conditions'. The forecast of high temperature for a particular day may be reached only because of an anomalous disturbance at the boundary of two weather cells, i.e. a sudden gap in the clouds on an otherwise cloudy day. In the same way, forecasted increases in European energy consumption made during the late 1940s and early 50s for the 1960–70 period were generally 'on target' for predicting an exponential increase. What these forecasts did not predict was the huge flood of Middle Eastern oil coming into Europe such that the dominant role of coal over oil was completely reversed.

If forecasts cannot be directly checked because it is never quite clear whether the data indicate strictly confirming or refuting instances, then how are forecasts to be checked? They have to be checked *systematically*. Naval fire control officers and weathermen have their forecasts checked systematically. Their forecasts do not rise or fall because one shell misses or it rains when it should be sunny. Rather, their forecasts are scientifically checked (often with the aid of probability analyses) to see if the overall evolving pattern matches reality. Similarly, forecasts for an agricultural system can be checked systematically. At the micro level (a home garden) or a macro level (a continental granary) the failure of one crop or one poor year in ten does not strictly refute or confirm a forecast of an increase in agricultural output. The original forecast would have been based on 'boundary conditions' (e.g. the number of frost-free days), 'initializations' (e.g. planting dates and seed types), 'idealizations' (e.g. no labour disputes or tornadoes), and on a number of 'special cases' (e.g. frequency of the use of seed dressings, herbicides and fertilizers). To check an agricultural forecast, provided it has sufficient width and depth, it has to have its predicted pattern, i.e. its systematic characteristics, compared *in toto* with the evolving natural pattern of agricultural production. When there is a good match between forecast and the agricultural output, then a 'good' forecast has been produced, or alternatively, if there is a poor match, then a 'bad' forecast has been produced. Very highly aggregated forecasts which do not permit systematic checking of the pertinent details are neither good nor bad, but rather are obscurantist. Undetailed forecasts are in practice useless for systematic examination or the development of rational policies, and are useful only in one very dubious way – that is the support of emotional appeals. A population forecast which predicts that 'someday the world will be 100 feet deep in people if there is no birth control' is only useful as an emotional scare, and wholly useless scientifically and rationally as there are no details of the relevant population socio-technical system. 'Boom or doom' forecasts support extreme cases only. Moderate forecasts with some width and depth of detail, which can be systematically checked, hold the middle ground where the world is neither as good nor as bad as it might be, and are a basis for trustworthy reading.

Species/individual problem

Forecasting shares with biology a species/individual problem. A very real and frequent difficulty in biology is to check whether a particular individual is a member of an evolving species. Often in these identity checks there is recourse to ideal models which set certain standards and if the overall difference (again systematically checked) is too great for an individual it is said to be a member of a new species. In forecasting, predictions are also made for evolving species. When a new socio-technical individual appears it has to be decided whether or not this is a variant or a new species. Television is a new species when compared to its parent, radio. Colour television can be said to be a variant individual of the older black and white television system. But the decision is not that simple in other situations. There is telegraphy, radio telegraphy (RTTY), telex, and PCM broadband operation (Pulse Code Modulation) all of which can be said to form an evolving socio-technical system for *coding* information. Are they each variant individuals and/or new species? In biology there can be a string of types, each of which is a variant with respect to its immediate neighbours and a new species with respect to more distant neighbours. In between there are many sub-species, as often happens with dog, cat and cattle populations. This can lead to two very real practical problems in forecasting. The first is that if one cannot decide if a new type of individual (e.g. the video-phone) is a variant or a new species, then it cannot be checked against the prediction of a forecast (i.e. are video-phones to be counted along with ordinary phones). The second is that a new species of socio-technical system can initially be nearly indistinguishable from the existing members of a socio-technical system (e.g. the early versus late versions of the Boeing 707 in which the most recent members have twice the payload, twice the range and cater to quite a different air transport sector). In spite of these difficulties, it is important for forecasters to try to identify variant individuals and wholly new species as they are often key features in what makes the future not quite like the present or the past.

Classification of data

The classification of data for use in forecasting produces both assets and liabilities. On the asset side, data provide a 'real' basis for the model; as a liability, they introduce 'noise' (random factors) and arbitrary judgments about relevance and significance. Energy statistics are a good example of this two-edged situation.

Most energy forecasts assume that the meaning of 'energy' is well understood. In reality, the use of the term frequently contains implicit definitions which go beyond the language of the physics textbook. In practice, energy bridges the operational terms, 'power' and 'fuel'.

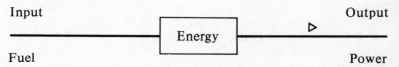

Input   Output

Energy

Fuel   Power

where fuel can be wood, coal, oil, gas, geothermal, nuclear, and power can be heat, mechanical, electrical and chemical.

Energy, as an umbrella concept, is a tremendous systematizer in forecasting because it ties together, through a common denominator, such different sectors as population, transport and agriculture. Energy forecasters can draw up energy balance sheets which show the distribution of energy across all sectors. For all the unity and coherence brought about through systemization, energy is still just the bridge between fuels and power. At this bridging point there are a multiplicity of non-identical conversion processes. In human populations these are metabolic energy conversions. In transport, they are steam, internal combustion, and turbine energy conversions. At the same time, technology has equally increased its role in the acquisition of fuels and the consumption of power. Conveniently, energy classifications unify the fuel, conversion, and power complexes and their respective supply and consumption networks. In spite of this convenient systematization, energy classifications are quite opaque to the very different underlying technologies and particularly their working life-times in terms of plant and equipment.

All classifications bring certain features to the fore at the expense of burying complementary features in the background. Sectoral forecasting lessens the danger of unacknowledged assumptions which are readily concealed by over-aggregation and by reliance on apparently quantifiable data series.

Chapter 7

Eight Critical Issues

In this chapter we briefly summarize some of the issues which can arise in making forecasts. The way in which these issues arise and are handled will vary from forecast to forecast; as Part III shows, they are definite sources of 'error' and defect in some cases, while in others they may be handled wisely, or a means of side-stepping them may be devised. It is important to note that perfect solutions are rarely available for these problems; compromises have to be made.

Many of the issues raised here are taken up in Part III of this book, where they are also illustrated by reference to specific forecasting exercises. Consequently the purpose of this chapter is not to provide a detailed, comprehensive and illustrated analysis of all the possible dangers in forecasting, but rather to arm the reader with a set of issues to look out for in Part III.

The 'over-selling' of forecasts

It is dangerous to assume that forecasts are equivalent to predictions of the future. The word 'prediction' implies a degree of certainty which, in practice, can rarely be justified. One can sympathize with those decision-makers in government, industry and elsewhere who seek a precise, accurate picture of the future environment into which their plans must fit. Demands for knowledge of future population size, GNP per capita, and the like, frequently represent such needs. However, not even in these cases are predictions possible which are both definitive and non-trivial.

A number of different types of forecast can be identified. Firstly, there are attempts at identifying the 'most likely' future, either explicitly assuming that certain preconditions will exist or even taking these as part of the 'most likely' forecast itself. Secondly, there are attempts at devising or exploring alternative futures which may, in practice, cover a wide or narrow range. Lastly, there are forecasts, such as those contained in much utopian literature, which orientate more towards stimulating thought than to providing a plausible description of the evolution of the future from present trends. This list can be translated into considerably more refined terms, but in its present form it helps put the term 'prediction' into perspective. In other words, clients who expect predictions, or forecasters who offer them, merit strong scepticism with regard to the assumptions and constraints under which the forecast was made.

Determinism

Technological determinism, as used here, can be defined forcefully, if inelegantly, as the belief that the social and political context of a technology has no moderating influence upon its impact; that, for instance, introducing a high-yield crop to an area will have the same social impact, be that area in India, South America or Europe. It would be unfair to argue that many, if any, forecasters would defend such a view if baldly stated as a principle of their belief. However, in practice it is necessary to guard against the naive use of this assumption. For instance, the unquestioned assumption that, because a technology arose and had such-and-such a course of development in place or culture x, the same technology will also arise, and have the same course of development in place or culture y.

Determinism applies not only to technology and technological change; it is equally easy uncritically to assume that the impact of a specific item of, say, economic, legislative or labour relations policy, will be the same in other places as it was in the first place. This belief does not reflect only (or even necessarily) the assumption of cultural homogeneity between places; it overlooks the possibility that man can intervene to forestall the future and the problems he foresees; it ignores the influence of outstanding individuals, be they thinkers or actors; and it fails to recognize the significance of social action as against the apparently ineluctable character of social processes.

The reader should note that it is not necessarily inevitably mistaken to make some of the assumptions mentioned above, but it has been emphasized that they should not be made unquestioningly and uncritically. Indeed, there are cases where such assumptions can greatly assist the forecaster – but he should be aware of their existence and probable limitations. In turn, the forecaster is morally obliged to make these same limitations explicit to his public.

In addition to the above varieties, forecasting can be biased by other types of determinism. At the core of the Nazi movement, up to and through the Second World War, there was a social determinism, to the effect that they were the master race, and the forecast for the coming Nazi millennium was that they would displace all other races. At great final cost of life and resources, this social determinism was proved false. Secondly, biological determinism imparts to forecasting the view that man has reached the apex of the ecological system – yet the age of man may pass the same way as did the age of dinosaurs. In short, man is neither ascendant over, nor independent of, the ecological system; he is only one part of the natural world, and can be subject to the same forces. A well-known illustration of this variety is seeing the human population explosion as having only a lemming-like solution.

Continuity

The assumption of continuity is often associated with that of determinism, although there is no necessary link. There are many circumstances in which an apparently clear-cut trend is produced in respect of a particular phenomenon by the processes underlying it. However, the assumption of continuity in such a trend requires examination, since the underlying processes may, for instance, exhibit instability of various kinds in the short or long term, or ceilings may become apparent and critical threshold values may be reached. It is of great help to be able to make simplifying assumptions, such as that certain processes on the boundaries of the areas of interest will continue much as they are now (or have been in the past). The mistake is to believe in the absolute truth of the assumption.

a) Trends

There are many circumstances in which an apparent continuity stems from the stability of a particular mechanism underlying it, and in general we call these trends. If forecasting were a pure science, then these trends would be backed by laws; but forecasting is an applied science, if not a craft, for which the trends are based on empirical generalizations or rules. As there are no laws available, empirical trends are handy tools for forecasters (hence the long survival of moderately accurate trend extrapolation techniques). Without continuity there can be no extrapolation. Over the long term, the degree of continuity alters and thus severely limits the accuracy of trend extrapolations.

b) Distinguishing the short- from the long-term

Short-term trends often differ from long-term trends: the danger is that of confusing the two. What turns out to have been a short-term trend may have been initially interpreted as a shift in the long-term trend; the opposite can occur equally easily. An example of the former misinterpretation led to the widespread belief in the 1930s that the population of many Western nations was about to decline rapidly; an example of the latter might be the scare about high levels of mercury pollution in tuna fish, at first believed to reflect recent industrial activity, but later shown to have been present for many decades. This problem applies not only to trends in a narrow statistical sense, but equally to political moves, expectations of breakthroughs in pure science, and so on. The moral is that caution should be exercised when interpreting and particularly when extrapolating recent trends. The difference between the two is that a short-term trend is only a perturbation in the basic continuity of the existing system, whereas a new long-term trend reflects a more severe and permanent discontinuity.

c) Historicism

The identification of trends which have existed for a very long period can lead to the application of historicism to forecasting; locating historical trends in social phenomena should not be mistaken for the establishment of fundamental and permanent laws of such behaviour.

Working more at the level of cultures and civilization than of, say, specific communities or industries, certain historians (Spengler, Toynbee, Sorokin, etc.) have suggested paths of development which are followed by civilizations. More recently, Kahn and Wiener, Daniel Bell, Talcott Parsons and others have applied similar 'laws' to anticipate the future directions of society. At a more humble level, many corporate planners appear to have models (sometimes implicit, sometimes nebulous) of how companies develop, with some kind of 'law of company development' not too far away. Many of these historical developments are seen as following fixed evolutionary pathways.

Goldthorpe (1971) has demonstrated the Western and technocratic biases of historicist futurology, in which 'Western' political systems and industrial organizations are viewed as the ultimate stage of growth for developing countries in the foreseeable future, with East and West eventually converging in post-industrial societies, dominated by scientific and technical élites. The problem for forecasting is that this sort of historicism has patterns of development dominated by particular features. For instance, post-war developments in the West have seemingly been dominated by the emergence of the 'Plastics Age'. Contained within this historicism is often the determinist implication that Third World countries will follow similar evolutionary patterns through to their own 'Plastics Age'. But equally apt (or inapt) descriptions could be 'the Age of Stainless Steel', or 'the Aluminium Age'. This highlighting of one particular feature is representative of an over-simplistic aspect to historicism.

A more balanced approach sees history as providing the prognosis rather than the more simplistic and definitive casting of the future implicit above. A good parallel exists between the forecaster and the medical practitioner. In the same way as the doctor has to take into account the past medical history of his patient, the forecaster has to take into account the past development of his socio-technical system. Historicism, as historical prognosis, provides the forecaster with some (not all) of the roots of the future. History can constrain the future, but it does not necessarily control it.

Simplification

As a methodological principle, simplicity is highly desirable in forecasting. The pragmatic problem is how to simplify processes, events, etc., so as to come to grips with them analytically, without omitting so many of the elements as to lose touch with the real world. In demographic forecasting, the under-simplification of retaining all people's names is as equally undesirable as ignoring the sex of the members of the population. The balance between under- and over-simplification is difficult, and in the main is influenced by the system's description, the level of aggregation, the availability of data and theory, and the type of model being built – amongst other things.

One common variation of simplification can be described as crude reductionism. In one case this applies to theories and, in another, to data. In the case of theories, it is the transfer of an explanation for forecasting purposes from one field to another; for instance, from sociology to psychology, and even to behavioural biology. As applied to data, it implies the provision of certain definite 'standard yardsticks', such as reducing coal, oil, gas and nuclear fuels all to coal-equivalents, or reducing economic activity and welfare to GNP. Reductionism undoubtedly provides some simplification, which is a prerequisite for analysis and forecasting, but it must be noted that this introduces a new weave together with a new pattern into the forecasting fabric. It is thus a fallacy to believe that simplification provides a totally satisfactory approach to analysing major problems of the future, given the extremely complex nature of such problems. Simplification permits capture of only a few aspects of the big and important problems. In the end, approximations and simplifications must be integrated into a more comprehensive (albeit less detailed) picture of the future.

In all-embracing accounts, holistic approaches are frequently introduced as forecasting simplifications. Holism attempts to take into account the fact that the sum of the parts does not always equal the whole. For instance, the concept of a city as a social system is greater than the sum of its constituent parts (people, housing, transport, industry, entertainment centres, etc.). By itself, holistic forecasting is incomplete in that the underlying subtlety and detail of the sectoral mechanisms is ignored, with a resultant unrealistic, science fiction type of forecasting. In sophisticated forecasts there is a mutual interaction between the complementary aspects of holistic and sectoral approaches. The value of holism lies in providing a system of checks and balances for the more detailed sectoral forecasts.

Quantification

There is a certain appeal in numbers and quantification which can exaggerate their true validity and justification. Numerical precision tends to give the impression that some quality is accurately described, whereas non-quantified characteristics may tend to be viewed as much less important; this is a recurrent theme of Part III. The dangers can be put into two categories: those arising when quantification is conceptually tenable, and those arising when it is not.

In the first category are the problems of data collection and processing, which are discussed under the next heading. The second category stems from the fact that, over time, it can be more than simply numerical values which change; the underlying structures can also change. For instance, imagine an attempt of a century ago to forecast the future energy supply position: as it has turned out, many of the sources of energy have changed since then; peat, windmills and the like are now of minor importance, while electricity from coal, gas, oil or nuclear fuels would then have received no attention.

The problems of quantification and inadequate data are not problems unique to forecasting. As with other disciplines, experience, trial and error, and intellectual initiative are the main means by which these problems are controlled.

Inadequate data

As with others of these issues, Part III of this book will elucidate and illustrate the problems of data. The main problems are that data may not exist or, if they do, they may be inaccurate or not actually refer to what they purport to. It is often the case that the data available to forecasters were collected for other users, whose needs may differ. Thus the forecaster must do his best with data which were collected for a different purpose, or which have been analysed and presented in a different form.

Frequently direct measurements are difficult, impossible or simply not available; hence the use of surrogate indicators. (For example, reported crime rates for criminal activity, or, in ecology, the use of an indicator species in measuring the health of the environment.)

The warning is against believing that data problems do not influence the resulting forecasts. For instance, the doomsday forecasts of *The Limits to Growth* have been shown to be highly sensitive to some changes in the interpretation of certain data. For presenting conclusions, forecasters should point out the background and the margins of error for the data employed, and attempt to assess their implications through, for instance, sensitivity testing.

Relating forecasts to decision-making

The objective of the kind of forecasting discussed in this book is to help shape present-day policy decisions and actions. Firstly, present-day actions will influence the future in the short term and perhaps in the long term; some of the consequences of this influence may be regarded as undesirable (important options may be closed off, etc.) or, alternatively, they may be desirable (e.g. when thresholds are reached, permitting new stages of development). Secondly, to the extent that goals, objectives, aspirations and the like can be set for the future, present-day actions should be directed towards meeting them. Given these policy and planning considerations, the forecast can be designed in terms of the desired accuracy of the forecast, the degree of explanation and level of detail being sought and accessibility for any other parties to whom the study may be relevant.

Once again, there is need for a balance: it must be drawn between the forecaster working closely with the users of his reports (so that they are relevant to the users' needs and compatible with his room for manoeuvre and implementation) and, on the other hand, the need for the forecaster to be sufficiently divorced from his clients so that he can maintain his independence of critical and constructive thought.

Isolationism

By isolationism (sometimes synonymous with élitism), we mean the danger of the forecaster losing touch with the real world around him. Forecasting in the sense discussed here, is linked to decision-making in a more or less direct manner. Through this, it can have an impact on the real world; it should therefore start off with roots in the real world. This does not exclude idealism, or mean that the forecaster should always attempt to remove his own aspirations, personality and so on (i.e. values) from his work.

What this does mean is that he should not believe that he is necessarily providing an accurate reflection of the views and aspirations of the different parties who may be affected by his forecasts. At one level, this implies a need for co-ordination between forecasters in different social and economic sectors (e.g. the different suppliers of energy); at another, it means that forecasts may be used to propagate the views of cliques and élites, and as a means of forestalling debate about a wide range of alternative futures. Those whom the forecast concerns should be prepared critically to assess the interests and priorities of those involved in its construction.

There is an obligation on the forecasters themselves to be open to both internal and external criticism. Internally, minority views, when present, should be included in final forecasting reports; externally, comments from peer groups and the public at large should be sought.

PART III

The State of the Art: An Appraisal of Current Methods

8. The Assessment of Forecasting Techniques ... 63

9. Computer Models 92

10. Cost-Benefit Analysis and Technology Assessment 116

11. Survey Research and Psychological Variables ... 141

12. Numerical Moralities and Social Indicators ... 174

Chapter 8

The Assessment of Forecasting Techniques

Around 1872, according to the historian G. T. Chesney, there was a German invasion of Britain. The British armies and fleet, it will be remembered, were at that time scattered across the world – quelling an Indian mutiny, protecting Canada from an expansionist United States, guarding Ireland against an attack by Louis Napoleon, and so on. Consequently, the home defences were minimal when, one March morning, German boats set out across the North Sea. What Royal Navy there was left in British waters soon went under to the German mines and torpedoes – weapons developed in secrecy. British land forces suffered not only from their lack of numbers, but from their inadequate training and discipline combined with an out-dated philosophy of warfare. The great stand at the Battle of Dorking failed; the Germans conquered. (See I. F. Clarke, 1970.)

It does not matter that this story is totally untrue. When Chesney (an 'historian of the future') published it in *Blackwood's Magazine* in 1871, it was a plausible account of a hypothetical sequence of future events, intended to stir the military establishment into rectifying the many defects he portrayed. The result of publishing *The Battle of Dorking* was, in Clarke's words, a 'political sensation'. Prime Minister Gladstone attacked it strongly, both on its plausibility and the wisdom of open publication of such alarmist views (especially given the fact of an international audience). A wide-ranging debate had been set in action, and some changes did indeed occur.

This, in essence, is what forecasting techniques are all about.

Chesney presents (by implication) alternative futures: the one outlined above, and (at the start of his article) an indication of how pleasant English life would have been if the attempted invasion had been made impossible. There is a strong data base, in that he exploited his excellent knowledge of how military matters work (he was a Lt. Colonel). There is ample use made of imagination, visible in both what he communicated and how he did it. He also explores many of the interactions of several items in his system – events in India, technology, social attitudes, etc., all play a part in his scenario. Finally, he brings out the crucial decisions, and, implicitly if not otherwise, shows how things could be done differently.

The one characteristic of Chesney's scenario which may be thought undesirable in an ideal model for other forecasts is the strong campaigning or lobbying element. He was no passive analyst, but a man with a political case to argue. This offends the idea that forecasts, and the methods used to derive them, are part of an objective and value-free search for what is often called the truth or, alternatively, described as information for use by decision-makers. However, had Chesney played down this lobbying role – had he put in the shades of grey – his message would probably not have overcome the deafness of the desired audience. In such cases it is not easy to define the morality of being objective against being heard. Equally important was the fact of a public debate: Chesney was not a confidential consultant to the government and could (as indeed he was) be openly challenged. Normative forecasting, when done under certain conditions which include openness, can be quite respectable.

The purpose of this chapter is to pursue some of these issues. It should be emphasized that it is neither a textbook nor a full critique of forecasting techniques; these already abound, and any more would be redundant (see, e.g., Jantsch, 1967; de Hoghton *et al*, 1971; Maestre and Pavitt, 1972). It is more a review of the assumptions on which the various techniques are based and so reflects some of the important considerations in selecting and applying a specific technique. Forecasting assumptions and evaluation criteria are the focus, but we conclude with specific comments on scenarios, Delphi, cross-impact matrices, extrapolation and morphology.

The characteristics of the techniques

One point of the introduction to this chapter was to emphasize that forecasting techniques are not always intended to produce 'forecasts' in the sense generally understood by that word. The word 'forecast', as already noted, is far from being clear and unambiguous. Occasionally it has the connotations of an absolute, unconditional prediction. Forecasts made during the first half of this century, to the effect that no man would ever be able to leave this planet, were often of this nature; the laws of nature could never be beaten by man (see A. C. Clarke, 1962). The 'most likely' future may be meant, with all the problems of how to judge a likelihood; many population forecasts are implicitly or explicitly in this category and, as the situation changes over time, they can reasonably be updated (see O.P.C.S., 1971–3). Delphi forecasts may also be in this category, but they give a range of forecasts as well as a single 'most likely' estimate. Then there are those which are not always used in either of these ways, but to provide a 'guideline' into the future; we shall argue that extrapolating is such a technique, as surely scenarios are too. Model building can be used to generate alternative futures which, to some extent at least, can then be evaluated. And some so-called forecasting techniques make minimal or even zero claims to anticipate the future; morphological mapping never forecasts anything, it only raises ideas.

Techniques abound. Erich Jantsch, in his well-known survey (1967), found it necessary to distinguish roughly one hundred techniques or separate elements of techniques. As well as those mentioned here, these included biological growth analogies, brainstorming, contextual mapping, decision matrices and through Monte Carlo to science fiction.

Several taxonomies have been proposed for introducing some order into such lists; most standard texts offer one. Some attempt to place techniques on a continuum according to, say, their degree of numeracy (e.g. de Hoghton *et al*, 1971), others to distinguish exploratory from normative techniques (Jantsch). Some lists are elaborate; Edwards (1969) gives ten categories of techniques or elements, which we shall discuss shortly.

All these taxonomies encounter the same fundamental

obstacle: all the different techniques draw heavily on one pool of elements, meaning that the differences between them are largely attributable to different combinations or different developments of those elements. Attempts to categorize the techniques themselves are thus prone to producing overlapping groups, and can hinder understanding of what the techniques are really based on. Although overlaps exist between the elements identified below, we hope the list enhances understanding.

To start with what is a general observation rather than true element: most of the techniques are highly structured. In fact, some almost parallel recipes: virtually each step is specified. And, as with great cooking, following the instructions does not always produce good results when there is no 'feel' for the art. One consequence of this structuring can be the dangerous impression that forecasting is easy; that, for instance, it is simple to follow the steps in a Delphi study, and that the results must therefore be trustworthy. (To give references would be unkind.) The desire to believe in the results can be strong amongst 'professionals' as well as amongst 'amateurs'. There is the well-known 'GIGO' motto of computer programmers – 'garbage in, garbage out'. During the *Limits to Growth* debate, one irreverent student suggested 'GIGO-plus' – 'guesses in, gospel out'. Dynamic modelling provides good illustrations of the way in which assiduous attention to detail produces a tendency to accept the first comprehensible and apparently consistent set of results.

There is a related problem also found in dynamic modelling and which may transfer across to these other techniques. Be it for good or bad reasons, it is uncommon to find full details of a study being published. This hinders the reader, user or critic in assessing the value of the work: what data were used and why; how were they 'corrected' (if at all)? Were the reasons for and objectives of the study those claimed – or was there a strong element of trying to prove a point? And so on. Admittedly, excess information can burden most readers, and there is the right to make further enquiries of the original researchers. But most readers will have enough to do to deter them from using this right. Indeed, some cynics claim that mysticism is almost an objective of some work; to clearly present the full story could be detrimental to some studies and groups. Not that forecasting is unique in this respect. We thank our colleague, Martin Bell, for bringing to our attention the following quotation (from a book on the cassava market), which may convey the impact of stark honesty upon credibility. 'The methodology of the report is to apply those techniques of analysis . . . which appear to be best suited to the problem at hand to the data available. Quantitative results are, when possible, validated by best available information. If the results are shown to be untenable, *adjustments are made to the data and/or techniques in order to produce an analysis which approximates a priori expectations.*' (Italics are ours.)

Edwards (1969) provides a list of what he describes as fore-casting methods. We suggest that his list covers not simply methods, but also many of the assumptions which underlie many specific techniques. After briefly presenting his list, we will return to highlight some of these assumptions or, if you prefer, elements on which techniques draw.

Prophecy is the first. While not of obvious appeal to many academics, is it not of interest that astrology appears to be of widespread and increasing interest? Could not the soothsayers, the astrologers, have a major influence in some parts of the world, through influencing conscious or purposive choice at a mass level? Was prophecy a major influence in pre-Christian Judaism? in Islam? in Hitlerian Germany?

Chance. The act of flipping a coin may seem irrelevant to fore-casting, but in a gaming situation (gaming in the mathematical sense; Vajda, 1956) there are many strategies which, regardless of objective, require a random choice. Thus, in the Stock Market, it is commonly held that although 'the Index this morning has fully discounted yesterday', it is also true that 'money can only be made against the market trend'. In such a situation random choice can be shown to be an effective predictor in some situations. If the world situation is regarded as an *n*-person game, with nation-states as players, a similar approach to strategy might determine some of the alternative futures. Indeed, coin-flipping can in many such game-structures be shown to be an optimal strategy.

Intuition. Although the hallmark of true intuition is the total lack of 'explanation', clearly some forecasters do appear to have a good 'track record'. But on closer examination, these track records often are not a multiplicity of independent forecasts but rather forecasts spun off from one main intuited trend. Bearing in mind that most forecasters are, quite naturally, only recognized as being 'good' *post facto,* there must also be a considerable bias in the recognition and acclaim mechanisms.

Analogy. Basically this covers a spectrum of techniques ranging from the trivial to the complexities of modern pattern-recognition (Rutovitz, 1966).

Correlation is used here to describe the mathematical methodologies of measuring association. However, as demonstrated by John Stuart Mill, a greater number of different sorts of observations are required for imputing causality than for simply imputing association. Remembering that Mill's causal canons were written for systems not including elements with the possibility of purposive anticipation (such as humans or nation states), how much more difficult must be the causal interpretation of association data. One pitfall into which correlation methods may lead is shown by Coen, Gomme and Kendall (1969). This analysis related the Stock Exchange Index to previous car production figures and later commodity prices – interesting, but hardly a good basis for forecasting.

Projection. We come at last to the area of much statistical and mathematical artistry and some would say sophistry. Basically, three main levels of projective methodology can be seen; one assumes no change, one continuous change, and the third attempts to identify the underlying mechanisms of the phenomenon being forecast.

Simulation and gaming are essentially variants of each other. Both involve the construction of a model of the system for projection, but in the case of simulation the time evolution of the model is mechanistic (whether fully determined or involving chance elements). In gaming, human beings are allowed to interact with the evolution of the model in a purposive manner.

Invention, as used by Edwards (1969) and interpreted here, would imply a conceptualization of many possible futures for a given social system, and the assignation, conscious or otherwise, of probabilities to each such future. The assignation of the probabilities may be found to have used any, or indeed any combination, of the techniques previously listed.

Elimination. This implies that different possible futures will appear reasonable, depending on what is and is not viewed as reasonable; but, unfortunately, reasonableness varies.

Dialectic. This is a belief that certain fundamental forces will dominate and eventually determine the system, despite the presence of certain temporary contradictions, which may indeed prove to be forces of acceleration. It is interesting that some of the better-known dialectics handle contradictions rather as though some elastically increasing force of restoration accompanied deviation.

These, then, are Edwards' ten items. They provide an introduction to the discussion that follows, in which an attempt is made to identify the main elements drawn upon by the different techniques. We make some general observations on each element, and more detailed comments will be made when examining the individual techniques separately. It will also become apparent that the Edwards' items are not as distinct from one another as may have been thought on reading them.

The first element in the pool from which techniques draw is intuition. Although intuition implies a total lack of explanation, the concept is a messy one because, in practice, it can never be totally devoid of reasoning, analogy and the like. Different forms of intuition can perhaps be distinguished; for instance, that relating to what are important issues, what are their important components, what is feasible, and so on. There is also that form of intuition which merges in with values or the feeling of what is good or bad. Intuition, as manifest in prophecy or Delphi, appears to mean forecasts in which some of the reasoning and data is in fact non-existent, while much of the remainder lies in the privacy of the forecaster's mind (conscious or otherwise). When Delphi is described as exploiting intuitive judgments, this merely means that the respondents (the forecasters) are invited to step outside the usual formal constraints of data, logic and the like. When the Delphic Oracle made its prophecies, we can speculate that it made cunning use of psychological and political insights, exploiting both conspicuous and subtle information in conscious and unconscious ways.

If we accept this broad concept of intuition, we will find most techniques drawing on it to varying extents. When an author suggests nuclear rockets will replace chemical ones as the fastest known means of transport (as in the envelope curve in Jantsch, 1967, p. 161), this is probably not the result of pure, logical analysis alone; or when crowding is taken as a parameter in determining death rates in a world model (Meadows *et al*, 1972), we can suspect intuition has played a role. Again, our mention of morphology at the end of this chapter can be rationalized, but this may not reflect all the reasons behind our attraction to the technique.

Imagination is the second element in this list, despite the problems of definition and of distinguishing it from intuition. Chesney's approach was then novel and imaginative – the story is being recounted by a Volunteer Soldier some fifty years after the events; it is well told and maintains the reader's interest. Had it been badly conceived and written, it is unlikely that the impact would have been significant. Imagination (whatever exactly the term might mean) comes into the selection and/or interpretation of data, into the selection, application and (at times) modification of techniques, and – perhaps most importantly – into finding weak points in a study and strengthening them as far as possible. It could even be said that the role of imagination is self-evident to those people gifted with it – dissenters, beware.

The third element is the concept of continuity: that if population has been growing at 2 per cent per year, it will continue to do so; or, alternatively, if the rate of growth has declined by a constant 10 per cent annually, that this decline will continue. This is another element in extrapolations and, in a sense, in scenarios, in that the latter set out to examine discontinuities as well.

Formal use of association is a fourth element. By association we mean the search for, and subsequent application of, qualitative and quantitative relationships between parameters. Modelling (the theme of chapter 9) and cross-impact matrices are relatively pure and complex developments of this element: relationships are identified and quantified. Extrapolations of different types are operationally simpler forms, with time often being one of the key parameters. Analogy is a variation of this theme, employing the concept of similarities as distinct from direct connections; for instance, there may be parallels between the development of the American railways and the American space programme (Mazlish, 1965), or between biological and other growth patterns (Lorenz, quoted by Jantsch).

Logic and formal reasoning should also be in this pool,

although we sense that they are drawn on less frequently than is commonly supposed. Logical arguments may be thought to underlie envelope curves, for instance. (These are a form of extrapolation, described later.) But is it in fact an axiom of logic to assume past relationships will continue, or simply a plausible assumption? Cross-impact matrices employ the principle that certain future developments will be incompatible with others. Logically, the forecast of a population decline contradicts that of an increase (for the same group at the same time). In contrast, a cross-impact assumption that increased trade between the U.S.A. and the U.S.S.R. will mean reduced arms expenditure cannot be deduced entirely from logical arguments. (And remember that a theme of this chapter is that, poor data and all, it cannot be logically reasoned to prove that a forecast will not materialize.) Logic does, nonetheless, have an obvious role, and especially in 'balancing the books' – a feature of models. Capital expenditure of two units in year y is (given certain conditions) contradictory to having only one unit available for investment.

Assessment criteria

It is often maintained (albeit sometimes implicitly) that the final verdict on the quality of a forecast, in the sense of accuracy, can only be passed when the time has come for it to have materialized. The 1964 Delphi forecast of automated language translation by 1972 can, in restrospect, be seen to have been wrong, whereas we now know the Americans did indeed achieve a manned lunar fly-by by 1970 (RAND, 1964; both dates were medians). This evaluation criterion suffers not only from its dependence upon hindsight, making it too late for most useful applications, but also because the opportunity for the test often never arises: a forecast that there will be serious international conflict, unless the international rich/poor gap declines over the next generation, will not have been tested *if* the gap is in fact reduced; the conditions of the forecast will not have been met. And, as we have argued, some so-called forecasting techniques (and applications) are more orientated towards stimulating thought than towards forecasting itself – as in *The Battle of Dorking*.

This line of argument is important because it shows that, in principle, there is no way of proving the accuracy of a forecast in advance. Erroneous historical analysis, misleading data or contrary evidence can all be claimed, but they cannot provide irrefutable proof that the forecast will turn out to have been wrong; forecasts have been known to be right for the wrong reasons. Having lost this, the most desirable of criteria, we are in a trap: we need criteria to forecast the accuracy of forecasts. We cannot prove that our evaluation criteria are themselves accurate so we must ultimately fall back on what appears reasonable, plausible and, at times, logical – thus using the same elements as go into forecasts themselves. If there is an escape route, it is not apparent. Consequently, values and bias will influence not only forecasts, but also the way they are evaluated.

The basic premise of this chapter is that forecasts based on (or, if you prefer, methodologies which suffer from problems of) dubious data, dubious assumptions or a significantly incomplete set of considerations are unlikely to produce trustworthy conclusions. We put it statistically ('unlikely') because, as hinted above, there is no *a priori* absolute guarantee that any forecast is correct; bad ones can turn out to be accurate and, equally, good ones inaccurate. Therefore our evaluation of the techniques discussed will revolve around such criteria as the scope and reliability of the data used, the implicit (or explicit) nature of the results, the range of considerations included, as well as the assumptions behind the methodology. Such analysis will at least tell us about the pedigree of a forecast, if not about its own individual running chances. We also believe, with many other people, that provoking thought is often as important as accurately forecasting the future. Forestalling may be more important than forecasting, preparing more important than predicting.

The general problems of locating or collecting data are numerous and well known. In summary, the data needed by forecasters (in industry as well as government and elsewhere) have often not been collected; when they have been, doubts can exist as to what exactly they measure and how successfully. Surrogate data are frequently resorted to; for instance, GNP may be used when the need is for a measure of economic activity within steel-consuming industries. There are rarely quick, easy or cheap solutions to these problems, as forecasters well know. Unfortunately, this problem is not always so well appreciated by the readers and users of forecasts. The experience of dynamic models illustrates the point: it can become difficult to appreciate how unreliable some data are once they have been incorporated into a model; the impact of *The Limits to Growth* demonstrates this. Similar problems emerge in cost-benefit studies. A more mundane example, but experienced more often, is the way reports acquire status as they move from handwriting to typing – let alone to being in print. Statistical data can thus be assessed in terms of whether they measure what they purport to measure, and how accurately they do so. Forecasting reports should indicate the reliability of the data used, and, if relevant, the consequences of any errors.

Secondly, there is the scope of the data and other considerations. When Adelman (1972) forecast the price of oil, he concentrated on the costs of production and the competitive element between supplying countries. This suggested a future price of around the $1 per barrel mark. What he did not consider seriously enough was the potential of the situation in the world market and in the oil exporting community to change, and to have the dramatic impact achieved in late 1973. Adelman was not alone in his expectations. This error cannot be attributed solely to consideration of too narrow a range of possible developments; there were convincing reasons for believing that, even if the market changed such that price-raising action were possible, OPEC would not be able fully to exploit it.

A fundamental tenet of many researchers is that important influences are lost by setting boundaries too near the area of immediate interest. This view derives from hindsight experience as well as other sources. Its practical meaning is that the conclusions to be derived from a narrow focus are likely to differ from those stemming from a wide scope. Consider the problem of forecasting the future demand for a metal. At one extreme would be a forecast based on, for example, extrapolating demand over time; close to this point would be employing GNP as an intermediary. More useful information would come from including the potential influence of substitution, recycling, efficiency of use, growth in the end-use sectors, etc. Finally, one could envisage a study encompassing social attitudes to mining, the objectives and policies of Third World producers, the expectations and priorities of industrial R and D managers, the costs and extent of future exploration, competition from alternative products at the end-use stage, and so on. Note, however, that we described the results of these wider studies as 'more useful information', and not as 'more reliable forecasts'. Each element added to a forecast will bring with it some uncertainty; it would be naive to believe that uncertainty about the scope for recycling could be eliminated by considering every conceivable point. What a wide scope does achieve is an enhanced understanding of what is being forecast, with greater ease of tracing consequences, key elements, and sources of discontinuity.

A further area meriting emphasis is the role of peer judgment or the sense of plausibility. Although a distinction can be drawn between these two, the degree to which they are related permits them to be discussed together. They are certainly two of the most influential of evaluation criteria, no doubt for many reasons of social psychology. It is well-known that there are both conspicuous and subtle constraints on the behaviour of a member of a group which induce a degree of conformity in at least some respects. These constraints can apply to professional forecasting behaviour as much as to any other activity. This can reduce the divergence of views within a group, and it increases the need for larger public and professional forums. (Few modelling groups employ members who do not believe in models, for instance.) This means that judgments of colleagues (as an immediate peer group) are obviously of some value – and the more critical, the better – but it also means that the final verdict of such a group should not be taken as the last word. Equally important is the point that not even a unanimous agreement on the reliability of a forecast from every expert in the world proves that the forecast will materialize; all it proves is that there is currently at least one point of agreement.

Lastly, we would follow Amara and Salancik (1972) in arguing that techniques should be capable of generating reproducible results. Application of the same techniques to the same information should, when conducted by a different group from the original, lead to the same forecasts (or at least to comparable forecasts). In the pages that follow, some such comparisons are quoted. Once again, it should be remarked that consensus does not mean accuracy.

Trend extrapolation

There are several techniques which come under this heading (including some regression analysis approaches, envelope curves, etc.), but the underlying principles of association and continuity are always present. Historical quantitative data are collected for a parameter; a mathematical form is found for relating it to a second parameter (commonly time); and by inserting future values of (in this case) time, a future value of the original parameter is derived. This may constitute the final forecast, or may be an input into a further operation. The core assumption is, then, that a simple mathematical relationship claimed to exist between two parameters in the past will hold for the period of the forecast. In essence, this is the beginning and end of the conceptual foundations.

This exposes the reason why extrapolation is not a suitable tool for producing long-term forecasts (although its value under one set of conditions is discussed below). The 'long-term' usually implies that time by when significant structural changes will have occurred (in all likelihood). It therefore makes little sense to employ a technique which rests squarely on the assumption of continuity.

However, it is probably the most commonly used forecasting technique (although it may be only a first step in many exercises). Population forecasts, for instance, often assume that past growth rates will continue or – a variation – that their rates of change will continue (e.g. Office of Population Censuses and Surveys, 1971–73). The U.S. Bureau of Mines (1970), in projecting demands for various minerals and materials, starts by assuming the continuation of past growth rates. *The Year 2000*, Kahn and Wiener's influential book (1967), starts by assuming the continuation of past growth rates of certain economic indices. While the published examples extend beyond this listing, there are countless unpublished examples to be found in industry, government and elsewhere.

Extrapolations of this form can serve one very useful function for forecasters: they provide a baseline into the future, which can then be played with in different ways. Assuming the need for an indication of the future demand levels for minerals or food, say, how is one to start? The future position is bound to change quantitatively, if not qualitatively, with developments in economic activity, substitution, efficiency of use, the introduction of new goods and services and the fading of old ones. The forecaster will be greatly aided by having some picture which (regardless of its other merits) he can use as a basis for exploring the consequences of such developments. The baseline is arbitrary; he could assume 1974 demand levels throughout the next thirty years, say, but it is more conventional (and for perhaps good reasons) to take the growth rates of the last decade or two. (See the U.S. Bureau of Mines, 1970, as a neat illustration of this approach.)

Acknowledgement of the usefulness of extrapolations is as crucial as acknowledgement of their naivety. They are indeed naive, insofar as they are claimed to forecast a likely future while ignoring many of the key determinants of that future. More systematically, the reasons for not believing extrapolations are as given below.

We can argue that the fewer the connections between the item(s) being extrapolated and the world at large, the less the likelihood of perturbations and so the more successful an extrapolation (or indeed, any other forecast) may be. Forecasting events in the Cyprus–Greece–Turkey crisis of July 1974, on a day-to-day basis, was considerably harder than forecasting U.K. aluminium consumption for that period.

We shall consider some specific extrapolations shortly; the best that can be done here is to issue a warning against assuming exact continuity. We can also mention the marvellous illustration of how easy it is to take extrapolation to excess: during the 1920s and 1930s, 'S-curves' were applied to countless different things – including the future size of empires in Asia, lynchings in the southern U.S.A. and the number of countries using postage stamps.

There are, naturally, other qualms to be expressed. An aspect of data not mentioned above involves discrepancies between sources. In most countries, an extrapolation based on birth, death and migration rate statistics can be almost guaranteed to differ from one based on aggregate population size. Should GNP per capita be extrapolated directly, or routed through GNP and population exercises? Materials demand forecasts can be based on per capita consumption against GNP per capita, or they can be derived from consumption per (say) million dollars of GNP against total GNP (time being incorporated in the GNP element). The resulting forecasts can be markedly different (see Brooks and Andrews, 1974).

Our literature search suggests that very little systematic empirical work has been done on this technique. There have been starts – demographers have shown that simple forecasts go wrong (or, at times, are right for the wrong reasons), and that revisions in the light of later data do not necessarily improve performance. But we know of no general studies on (for instance) the increase in error over time, the merits of different mathematical formulations, etc. Perhaps the drawbacks and limitations of the technique are so obvious to those who pose such questions – with experience of such problems – that they see little point in pursuing the matter.

The Year 2000 by Kahn and Wiener (1967) is perhaps the most significant instance of extrapolated world futures. Their Figure 1 (from page 11) gives their 'surprise-free' projections of GNP per capita for ten countries in 2000. Their data consisted of the 1965 GNPs and population sizes of each country, and their past growth rates. The points 'they seem most likely to reach by the year 2000' (p.10) are not actually points, but ellipses suggesting an (unindicated) margin of error. The neat appearance of the ellipses is marred by the use of log-log scales.

Assuming for simplicity that both the 1965 GNP data and the past growth rates are accurate, let us examine the assumption that the future growth rates of the different countries are comparable. Remembering the Bertalanffy maxim, 'structures are processes of long duration, the data parameters are processes of short duration', what is comparability? Do we infer that it is assumed that the economic structures of the various ten major countries are such that the growth rates can wholly represent the evolution of both parameters and structure? The projections are made for a forward period of thirty-five years – is it to be inferred that the assumption of continuity is to hold throughout that time? Did it hold for the previous thirty-five years? And even if it did, does not this further assume that the rate of change of such phenomena will not markedly change in the future?

Delphi

We concluded that extrapolations do have some uses despite their drawbacks; the verdict is less favourable for Delphi. This technique was first expounded by Dalkey and Helmer in 1963, and involves two of the issues raised in the first half of this chapter: the use of intuition, and the social psychological problem in group behaviour.

The first assumption of the Delphi technique is that useful forecasts lie hidden away in the collective unconscious of a group of people knowledgeable in the area of interest. The object of the technique is to extract this forecast with minimal contamination from social pressures – it is, it seems, a frail entity. Bringing a group of experts together, as in a committee, means such contamination: regardless of the merits of their views or arguments, the more extrovert or higher-status committee members will tend to be more influential than the others. Delphi reduces the status problem by keeping the contributions anonymous, and using postal questionnaires avoids the need for a communal gathering. This is how a typical Delphi is conducted. A panel of perhaps several dozen experts is selected, and each member receives a questionnaire listing (say) possible techno-logical developments in the area of the study. This questionnaire may originate with the Delphi organizers, or from editing individual lists previously requested of each panel member. The conventional questionnaire asks when (if ever) each of the specified technologies will materialize; supplementary information may include reasoning, confidence rating and views on the desirability of the technology. The co-ordinators then summarize the responses by such means as quartile dates (the dates by which a quarter, half and three-quarters of respondents expect the development), and perhaps résumées of any arguments written in by the more optimistic or pessimistic respondents. This summary is circulated and the panel members may, if they so desire, revise their past estimates in the light of the consensus and the arguments shown in the summary. There may be two or three such rounds, by which point further rounds would have rapidly diminishing returns.

Does the technique work? Does it, to be more precise, lead to forecasts which can be trusted to materialize on time (unless averting action is deliberately taken)? Little empirical work has been conducted in answer to this, partly because the first Delphi forecasts were only made in 1963 (RAND, 1964); consequently, insufficient time has elapsed to permit such an assessment. Grabb and Pyke (1973) have compared against reality six Delphi forecasts of computer developments. They concluded that these forecasts had, in general, been too conservative; events occurred sooner than expected. This is not a good omen for the trustworthiness of the longer-term forecasts (where it is still too early to pass final judgment). However, the six studies did agree with one another, meaning that the Delphi technique did at least permit reproducible results.

At least three studies have made forecasts of certain medical developments. For some items there was close agreement on the likely dates of actualization. 'Implanted artificial organs made of plastic and/or electronic components' were given medians ranging from 1982 to 1985. In contrast, the medians for the 'chemical synthesis of protein for food' spanned twelve years – 1978 at one extreme, 1990 at the other; the extremes in the case of the 'creation of primitive life form' were 1978 and 'later than 2017'. These conclusions show a wide range of divergence on timing of future events.

Ament (1970) compared some of the 1963 RAND forecasts with the reality since then. Of ten items drawn from the original study, with median dates of 1969 or earlier, eight had occurred (by 1970), two had not; of the twelve for 1970, seven had, three had not, and there were two 'partials'; of the twenty-four 1971-or-later items, three had, thirteen had not, and the remaining eight were 'partial'. We contemplated updating this study, but one reason stopped us: the specialists we contacted, to enquire whether the items had materialized or not, were so frequently unsure of the exact meaning of the items that definite answers were not possible. This meant great dangers in interpreting the results derived from so small a sample. (In fact, around twenty-seven of the forty-seven items selected by Ament have this defect.)

Another approach of equal importance is to assess (again with hindsight) how many significant items have been missed by Delphi studies. An unpublished paper by T. J. Gordon (cited by Amara and Salancik, 1972) mentions twenty-eight events of importance which actually occurred before 1970 but which were not foreseen by the RAND study.

The Ament hindsight work demonstrates one of the problems in Delphi (and of questionnaire design in general): do the respondents all understand the same thing by the question? What is meant by 'reliable weather forecasts', 'feasibility of effective large-scale fertility control by oral contraceptives or other simple and inexpensive methods', or 'widespread use of simple teaching machines'? The more precise items in this list, such as questions on space developments ('U.S.A. manned lunar fly-by', for instance), illustrate a different point: why attempt to forecast items which are subject to planning and human control as was (or is) the U.S. space programme? Surely the interesting question from the forecasting/decision-making point of view is not by *when* is event *x* 50 per cent or 90 per cent likely to have occurred, but by when could the technology (and other associated needs) be available if planning is directed towards such-and-such a goal? The question applies equally to all forecasting; the conditional nature of all forecasts should be perfectly explicit.

To return to the empirical validation of Delphi: many Delphi forecasts have been conducted which may, in due course, be checked against reality. The focus of these studies includes medicine (Bender, 1969), computers (Bjerrum, 1969), social change (de Brigard and Helmer, 1969), the chemical industry (Parker, 1969), railways (British Rail, in progress), etc. So far, then, we cannot employ empirical evidence to justify or to refute the merits of Delphi; or, rather, to identify the factors leading to more or less successful Delphi forecasts.

There are, however, good grounds for scepticism. The two main reasons have already been hinted at: the assumption that intuition provides a sound basis and – related to this – that all the interaction between participants is under the control of the organizers. The argument can be summarized thus: Delphi does not produce forecasts devoid of contamination by social factors.

It should, in fact, be viewed as a form of social survey, whose results reflect the expectations, feelings and (at times) knowledge of official plans among the group members. Thus, there is little, if any, operational control over the influence of such factors as the 'mood' of workers within the area, the published pronouncements of great men, knowledge of official plans, temporary peaks or troughs in optimism coming from recent research successes and disasters, or even such misuses as expressing confidence in the possibility of a development so as to attract funding.

There are several other issues which can increase doubts about this approach. Who selects the panel, with which criteria in mind? Experts have generally become such because of their past ability (or guile) in their field, which can mean that their perceptions of how things used to be will hinder their seeing how things will be: alternatively, it can be argued that their past experience has enhanced their awareness of how things do change. So should there be many or few established experts? Should you include people who, although ignorant of the technicalities and likelihood of a given development, would be influenced by it (as customers or third parties) and so may have views? Such views have been discussed at length (e.g. Amara and Salancik, 1972), but there is still insufficient information to permit a consensus view. For one view as to how technocratic statisticians see Delphi, see Welty (1971).

The practice of asking panel members to rate their confidence in their answers may contradict the spirit of the technique – the ratings will reflect personality as well as the quality of the answers; and, if much more weight is given to those claiming confidence, one of the problems of the committee style is reintroduced. One of the few studies of the effect of personality on forecasts (Weaver, 1969) revealed that some personality types tend to be more easily swayed in a Delphi study than do some other types.

Some of the other difficulties will be known to social survey researchers. That of ensuring consistent panel interpretations of the questions has been illustrated. Questions can also be phrased or arranged so as to bias the answers. The RAND study, in asking questions about future progress in space, arranged them (in our perception) so as to emphasize the American–Russian competition; when will they do x, when will we do x? While perhaps easy to create accidentally, and hard to avoid anyway, such problems exist and require great skill if they are to be successfully identified and conquered.

Other observations can be made and, if the technique is to remain in common use, merit experimental investigation. For instance, it may be dangerous to assume (as is in fact often done) that each answer is given by a respondent without consideration of his other answers; to assume, in other words, that there is no common argument running right through his anwers. This assumption can appear when combining the panel members' responses into, for instance, the quartiles. The questionnaire format can, potentially, hinder those panel members wishing to state subtle views with implications for many of the questions; a committee can often overcome this. An empirical study which showed that Delphi produces plausible results along one dimension was done by Salancik (1973); he found a tendency for median dates to move forward if respondents were told that specific developments (in computer applications) were not only technologically feasible and relatively cheap, but would fulfill a social need.

Delphi does maintain the illusion (perhaps accidentally) that the future can be reliably forecast; this is reflected in both the objective of minimizing contamination of the process by social interactions (as though the forecast is a frail entity), and by the operational emphasis upon single forecasts – the individual panel member is not (in general) asked for alternatives or how new conditions, such as funding levels, would change his forecast.

Since the introduction of Delphi in the mid-1960s, it has been used for collecting check-lists of arguments, and views on the desirability of developments, as well as estimating dates (e.g. de Brigard and Helmer, 1969). Delphi is perhaps a short-cut to generating such information, but it has drawbacks even here. As regards its use in generating check-lists, it does have overtones of asking other people (usually unpaid) to do your work for you. Whether it produces 'better' lists than, say, literature searches or discussions with immediate colleagues or a few outside specialists has yet to be shown. In the context of assessing desirabilities, it is a social survey technique, but one employing a small group drawn from a professional élite. Insofar as this is remembered, it may have uses. However, it could not, under almost any circumstances, be accepted as a substitute on the one hand for a proper, detailed technology assessment/cost-benefit analysis, or, on the other hand, for the wider political processes of decision-making.

To sum up, the merit of a Delphi depends on the expertness (to be proved in the future) of the experts composing the Delphi. One is reminded irresistibly of what a Roman said: *'Quis custodiet ipsos custodes?'* (Juvenal, AD 112, *Satires*, vi, p. 347).

Cross-impact matrices

The cross-impact matrix can be regarded as an analytic tool as well as a forecasting technique. The approach derived from work done by Olaf Helmer and T. J. Gordon for a 'futures game' devised for the Kaiser aluminium company. Gordon pursued the approach with Hayward in the late 1960s.

The principle is simple; it builds upon one crucial element which is often ignored in Delphi-type forecasting studies: the actual and potential relationships between the forecasted events. Using Delphi, it is quite possible that forecast events may be mutually reinforcing or exclusive and thus that a totally unrealistic 'consensus' may be reached.

Single events such as the production of power from the first atomic reactor were made possible by a complex history of antecedent social and technical events. It is hard to imagine an event without a predecessor which made it more or less likely, or one which having occurred, had no influence on the future. This interdependence between events was called by Helmer 'cross-impact', and the technique which sprang from this insight provides a method by which the anticipated probabilities of occurrence of items can be adjusted in view of judgments related to potential interactions of the forecast items.

The use of a matrix is a natural consequence of classifying the interactions between events; if there are ten forecast events, then there are 10^2 (100) possible first-order interactions between them. These can be most easily represented in a 10 x 10 table (or square matrix). The procedure for compiling this matrix is essentially that of Delphi; experts are asked to classify the interactions between events, specifying both the type of interaction and an estimate of its 'strength'. There are three main forms of interaction possible between any two events, A and B. The occurrence of A can either increase or decrease the likelihood of the occurrence of B, or have no effect at all. The first two can be further sub-divided into pairs. The first kind of 'enhancing' relationship is termed 'enabling', the other, 'provoking'. The development of new materials has enabled supersonic jets, whereas aircraft noise has provoked certain legislative measures. The two 'inhibiting' modes are labelled 'denigrating' and 'antagonistic'. While the past merits of ocean passenger liners denigrated the development of aircraft, the need for safety has been antagonistic to cheap fares. It is obvious also that some events can be more enabling, etc. than others. The experts are thus also asked to assign a value, usually from zero to ten, to each interaction – a high value indicating a 'strong' interaction. As should be apparent, each relationship is only a partial determinant – it is their combined influence which determines the final outcome.

The preparation of the cross-impact matrix by obtaining expert consensus is only the first phase of the technique; now follows the computational manipulation of that matrix to produce the revised probability estimates for the occurrence of individual events. This phase relies heavily on simulation; if the experts have assigned a probability of 0.5 to the occurrence of a single event in isolation, and also decided that this occurrence is to some extent dependent on the occurrence of ten antecedent events, then there is *no* analytic method for calculating the revised probability. The approach taken is to simulate the development of the system over time using suitably generated random numbers to determine the course of events according to the given probabilities (this is rather like 'turning a coin'). Numerical reliability is given to the results by taking a very large sample of possible paths into the future and taking the revised probabilities as the *mean* probabilities over this sample.

In the two cases examined by Gordon and Hayward (1968) quite significant changes were brought about by superimposing the effects of cross-impact on original Delphi studies. For example, the probability of deployment of the minuteman missile was estimated to be only 20 per cent in one study. The revised probability given by the cross-impact method, from interactions derived from a consensus of the *same* experts, was 73 per cent. Perhaps the most valuable addition to Delphi studies which cross-impact techniques provide is the certainty that the forecasts are not internally inconsistent.

There are, of course, a number of uncertainties raised by the exact form of the simulation used: for example, the original studies assumed that the probability of events varies in a linear fashion. This is equivalent to assuming that all relationships occur only between pairs of events, whereas in the real world relationships are seldom that simple (the 'eternal triangle' of popular novels is a non-linear relationship). However, the most serious grounds for criticism of the method lie in the dependence of cross-impact matrices on their 'parent' Delphi studies. No amount of simulation and manipulation can turn a poor Delphi forecast into an excellent one. Furthermore, whilst the 'parent' Delphi study has the advantage of being based on 'literary' techniques – in principle, fairly transparent (comprehensible) to the non-expert, the cross-impact approach both tends to conceal the underlying assumptions of the forecast, even more than in Delphi, and at the same time lends the results a spurious air of mathematical reliability and objectivity.

The approach does at least encourage deliberate consideration of interaction between events. This in itself is a good thing, but we would still argue that the value of cross-impact lies not in its forecasting ability, but in the way it helps identify important events and relationships. It is much closer to formal mathematical modelling (chapter 9) than any of the other techniques reviewed here.

To the extent that cross-impact is an analytic tool, it resembles morphology. In morphology, an item (usually a technological device) is dismantled into its conceptual components; alternative 'states' are then found for each component. This will permit the conceptual assembly of new devices through different permutations of the 'states' of each component. The classic example, taken from Zwicky (the approach's originator), is the jet engine. Ideas which emerge from this illustration include units which move through earth, by sucking in rather than blowing out, and which obtain their power from the soil. Clearly, the technique must, at some final stage, be combined with a technological feasibility evaluation. Zwicky is keen to emphasize the need for full problem definition at the outset of any application, a requirement which applies equally to any forecasting exercise.

A morphological approach is likely to miss ideas which depend upon restructuring of concepts. A morphological dismantling of the radio valve, for example, would be unlikely to suggest the transistor. On the other hand, it does have its uses as an aid to analysis and thought. For instance, one can identify some of the elemental features of organizations engaged in minerals – companies, research organizations, etc; state or privately owned; trading internationally or locally; based in rich or poor countries; etc. A systematic listing of all possible permutations produces a more comprehensive list of possibilities than would a less formal approach. Many real-world organizations will fit into some of these categories (e.g. privately-owned, multinational, rich-country based extractive companies); other categories will be more or less blank (e.g. state-owned, multinational, poor-country based technological research institutes). One is then in a position to examine, say, the significance of the blanks.

Scenarios

Chesney's *The Battle of Dorking* has already illustrated the use of scenarios, and shown that they are not intended as 'semi-predictive' pictures of the future, but rather as possible paths into the future. More accurately, they are (in the words of Kahn and Wiener, 1967) 'hypothetical sequences of events constructed for the purpose of focusing attention on causal processes and decision-points. They answer two kinds of question: (1) Precisely how might some hypothetical situation come about, step by step? and (2) What alternatives exist, for each actor, at each step, for preventing, diverting or facilitating the process?'

This formulation of the objectives of scenarios makes sound assessment of the technique hard. We agree that some applications have had great impacts, Kahn's *On Thermonuclear War* and *Thinking About the Unthinkable* being outstanding instances: their influence upon thinking about nuclear strategy has been immense. However, as with *The Limits to Growth*, we must consider drawing a distinction between the merits of a technique *per se*, and the impact achieved by one specific group (or individual) in one specific application. How, in general, is success in 'focusing attention' to be measured and compared with the success of other methods? No sound means exist for identifying the impact of scenarios on real, live decision-makers in making them aware of an increased range of options.

The key issue here is the acceptance of the plausibility of all the evolving futures leading up to the postulated possible long-term future.

Although not quantified extensively – understandably in view of the vast amount of data which would be required for quantifying the whole of a possible pathway – the scenario technique uses the same selectivity in choice of relevant data and assumed mechanisms as do straight trend extrapolation techniques.

Of the scenarios discussed in *The Year 2000*, the following table (taken from p. 249) shows the range of possibilities considered:

CANONICAL VARIATIONS
A. More Integrated:
    Relatively peaceful, relatively prosperous, relatively arms-controlled worlds with a relatively high degree of consultation among nations, and the existence of political co-ordination or even integration among all, or almost all, the 'major' and/or minor powers.
    1. Stability or Status Quo-Oriented
    2. Development or Aid-Oriented
B. More Inward-Looking:
    Worlds that are almost as peaceful and prosperous, but with little arms control or general coordination.
    3. With an eroded Communist movement
    4. With an eroded democratic morale and some Communist dynamism
    5. With a dynamic Europe and/or Japan
C. Greater Disarray:
    Relatively troubled and violent worlds, but in which no large central wars have occurred.
    6. With an eroded Communist movement
    7. With a dynamic Communist movement and some erosion of democratic morale
    8. With a dynamic Europe and/or Japan

Only in the scenario A2 is there foreseen a world in which significant progress is made to a more egalitarian world. Even then, on p.253 there appears the proviso for the scenario: 'There is at the same time a willingness on the part of the under-developed world to work for (and be satisfied with) "reasonable" and moderate short-term gains that carry excellent long-term proposals.'

The definition of the 'short-term gains' for the year 2000 is given on p.254 as most of the under-developed nations being at $500 per capita and all being over $300–500 per capita. This is to be compared with the ten major countries having GNP per capita of about $6000 to $8000.

But even with this framework there has been no consideration of the disparities within nations as opposed to between nations, and *no* consideration of the possibility that such internal disparities may produce forces, either internal or external, which may change the social regime in such a way as to reduce disparity.

It can be argued that responsible scenario-writing should reflect, as far as possible, the likely range of influential developments. Clearly, it is impossible to cover every single possible development in a field, and views will differ on what is and is not important. But it is generally important to capture the extremes – a booming world economy from now to the year 2000, and a major un-alleviated depression, for instance.

The recent shifts in oil prices, following the action of the Organization of Petroleum Exporting Countries (OPEC) in late 1973, shows one difficulty in constructing scenarios. This action has led to considerable (some say, dramatic) changes in the structure of the world economy and the terms of trade. Very few forecasters (scenario-writers included) anticipated this move and, going by the public pronouncements, nobody has been able to give a definitive picture of the full consequences and implications of the change. While illustrating the difficulty of foreseeing possible changes, this example simultaneously reveals the suit-ability of scenarios in exploring some of the paths along which the OPEC action may take the world.

In writing about scenarios, a French researcher (Gerardin, 1973) proposed systematic procedures for finding pathways for evolution at a sequence of time intervals and identifying those thresholds of social tension where social forces will alter or inhibit previous trends. Paraphrasing his comments upon the intuitional use of scenarios, to date these included a tendency to self-persuasion, a bias in future inter-relationships stemming from the use of today's perceptions, and a lack of emphasis upon the fact that today's most important parameters may not be those of tomorrow. Clearly each of these postulated failings involves value judgments upon what are the important parameters, what are the important structures, what are the goals which form those forces.

Such criticisms do tend to knock the sequins off scenarios; they are not a trouble-free way of providing routes to alternative futures. However, to the extent that scenarios do open up new horizons to decision-makers, and provide a broader framework in which to make decisions, they are a good thing. They may also score higher than many other techniques in another way: their ability to communicate ideas on the future without creating such awe (of data, of mathematics, etc.) that the reader's critical faculties are handicapped.

Conclusions

Nobody in his right mind would argue that the future can be predicted – that it is possible to have now a picture of the future, in outline let alone in detail, which can be absolutely guaranteed to come true. The remarkable point is that, de facto, this is the objective for many forecasting techniques and exercises. Often this is implicit; when explicitly stated there are usually qualifications to be found elsewhere in the published reports.

It is easy to sympathize with decision-makers in government and industry who seek a reliable picture of the future situation into which their decisions will fit. The reduction of uncertainty is, after all, generally taken as one of the driving forces behind the behaviour of both organizations and individuals.

We are also very aware of the pitfalls of assessing forecasting techniques against criteria which seek perfection. Just because a technique does not predict the future, we should not condemn it. This does not prevent condemnation of those techniques which, perhaps through no fault of their originators, do imply that they have the Truth. This is why so many negative things have been said above about some of the techniques.

Our main conclusion is that insufficient attention has been paid to the underlying issues. We – together with many other forecasters – would welcome more attention and effort being drawn to attempts at showing the scope and nature of the alternatives which exist. By and large, the wrong questions are usually asked in forecasting exercises. For instance, the question should not be, 'When will the power-to-weight ratio of electrical storage systems reach such-and-such a number?' to be answered by extrapolation of trends, or Delphi or cross-impact matrices. The question should in fact be a set of questions, asking under what circumstances different ratios would become possible – funding levels, R and D needs, consumer needs and so on. The pretence of only one future is untenable in technological, let alone social, matters; if, despite such declarations, the game of 'predicting the future' is to continue, then the users of forecasts (as well as the public) should be more aware of its being such a game.

It is easy to forget that, despite the previous comments, there are situations where predictions are desired, and for good reasons. These are 'conditional' predictions: if x is done, y will follow. It may be possible to alter that y through making different decisions, but this means a further level of complication as distinct from negating the principle. Let us take a practical example. If a Channel Tunnel is built between Britain and France, several things will follow. The present cross-Channel transport facilities will be affected, the rural nature of some areas will go, old jobs will go and new jobs will arise as both direct and indirect consequences, certain trade patterns will change, and so on. Decision-makers will have a completely reasonable desire (if not duty) to forecast many of these impacts. They may start by assuming that they take no action beyond that needed to construct the tunnel system. At this specific point, they are not seeking alternative futures, but only that which will emerge from that set of conditions.

Their forecast will reveal some undesirable changes. Once identified, the second forecasting stage can start; if certain additional decisions are made, what consequences will follow? Will the problem be solved, and will other problems arise? These questions are fundamental to cost-benefit and technology assessment exercises.

To this extent, there is an overwhelming need for improved forecasting techniques. It is hard to see how this need is to be met; the current state of the art in forecasting is inadequate, and there are no obvious routes to improvement. It seems best to continue along two lines. One is the attempt to improve forecasting methodology; the gradual, incremental improvements which should occur with more work on variations of techniques or empirical study of current approaches. There is always the hope of some kind of radical development – even if it is only a hope. The second line is improving and consolidating the means of checking upon the use made of forecasts by decision-makers. For instance, informed public opinion about the Channel Tunnel (and the forecasts on which it is based) is a fundamental means of checking the forecasters and the service they provide.

The other, distinct role of forecasting bears repeating: that of stimulating thought, of opening the minds of all decision-makers (in government, industry and elsewhere) to new horizons. This calls for imagination and good communications; the forecasts must be readable and comprehensible. In this respect scenarios are perhaps the most promising of the techniques reviewed here.

This allows us to conclude with a plea for pluralism in things great and small – in ideas as to where society should head for, as well as in whether to use Delphi or extrapolation. Robert Kennedy said:

Some see the world as it is, and explain Why
Some see the world as it could be, and ask Why Not?

Chapter 9

Computer Models

Previous chapters have emphasized that all forecasting methods are inevitably imprecise, and have argued that the circumstances in which a given method is most appropriate depend chiefly on the purpose of the forecast. For example, as the last chapter has made clear, many decisions, particularly short-term and local investment policies, are made on the assumption that certain social and economic trends or behaviour will be maintained and that these trends can often be 'satisfactorily' estimated using relatively simple extrapolation methods. In contrast, longer-term policies, which are designed to bring about changes in socio-economic trends, require a deeper understanding of mechanisms underlying their historical behaviour if greater precision and agreement on forecasts is to be achieved. This chapter looks at the applications of one highly sophisticated technique: large-scale computer modelling, which attempts to extend forecasting capability beyond that of the simpler methodologies.

The exploration of long-term social, economic and ecological trends requires an understanding of a wide range of processes. The longer the forecasting period, the more likely it is that, to some degree, a large number of diverse factors will affect a given issue, and hence, the perspective and expertise that need to be brought to bear upon it will be wider. 'World problems' in particular tend to be the concern, not of a single discipline, but of a 'hybrid' of the social, physical and biological sciences and their mutual inter-relationships. The complexity of these problems suggests that quantitative methods such as systems analysis and especially computer modelling may offer a possibility of clarifying the behaviour of 'hybrid' systems. At first sight, dynamic computer models appear to offer a rather attractive technique, since they permit time-dependent and non-linear processes (which appear to be important to the behaviour of social systems) to be represented and calculated more easily than with other methods. Many researchers are, in fact, currently attempting to apply dynamic analysis using modern computing methods. Of course, the principal function of the computer in work of this kind is to ease the load of repetitive computation. Therefore, although there are problems in making efficient and accurate use of a computer, very little will be said about this here, because of the limitation of space. Neither, for the same reason, will comment be made on the difficulty of organizing research of an inter-disciplinary nature, which applies to computer-based projects just as to any other multi-faceted project. These are discussed in Clark *et al* (1975). Hamming (1962, 1973), in a book entitled *Numerical Methods for Scientists and Engineers*, takes the motto, 'The Purpose of Computing is Insight, not Numbers'. However, in the second edition (p.504) it is suggested that the motto might be revised to 'The Purpose of Computing Numbers is Not Yet in Sight' – a view which gets some support in this chapter.

Three topics will be dealt with here. First, very briefly, some of the conceptual and technical research problems in building a complex social model will be considered, to supplement, rather than to repeat, what has been said in previous chapters and to make points particularly pertinent to a discussion of complex computer models of socio-technical systems. Second, a discussion of the uses that have been made of computer models in aiding public policy making will help to illustrate the difficulties and some of the considerations for the successful application of modelling methods. The third topic, which is particularly relevant to the kind of futures issues discussed in later chapters, is a description of some of the current activity in building world models, such as that described in Forrester's *World Dynamics*. Finally, an evaluation of the current status and role of computer models is given, particular attention being paid to the potential use of computer models of the world.

Technical and theoretical considerations

For a variety of reasons formal quantitative analysis, with or without the aid of a computer, is most appropriate to processes for which the identification and measurement of parameters is unambiguous, and ideally where opportunities for controlled experimentation on isolated simplified systems exist. Not surprisingly, therefore, the most successful descriptions are those of man-made, 'engineered' systems, actually designed according to the same principles and formulae as the mathematical model. The machine may be constructed according to a specification provided by the model.

Elsewhere, analytic methods have proved a valuable tool for explanation and prediction of restricted and well-defined effects in the physical and biological sciences, and to a lesser extent for the description of social processes. To take some examples: missile trajectories may be calculated with great precision; airframes are constructed partially empirically but largely using numerical methods; uncertainties in the result from models of river systems depend less on their inherent accuracy than on that of the data they employ. Further, it is often the case that the behaviour of the machine described is subject to external forces of climate and so on, and this sets limits on the opportunity for correct prediction. Within this constraint, however, prediction may be rather successful. The problems of building a complex model, of course, increase markedly with its size and scope. This applies even to engineering systems where, for example, a satisfactory model of all aspects of the behaviour of a nuclear reactor has yet to be made.

The calibration and testing of complex models is exceedingly difficult. For a long-term social forecasting model it is virtually impossible to calibrate a model against historical trends and even if it were not, there would, for the reasons indicated above, be no reason why the model should satisfactorily project the future. The situation is exacerbated for non-linear models, such as the *World Dynamics* models, where even fewer techniques of calibration and testing are available (see, for example, the discussion in Cole and Curnow, 1973; Naylor and Finger, 1971).

Whereas most everyday 'physical' explanation rests on well

established and widely accepted theories, the same solid empirical and theoretical base does not exist in the social sciences except in a few isolated and non-generalizable cases. Thus the social context of any model or its socio-political interpretation is inevitably subjective and ideological. What is more, the debate surrounding a model may feed back and modify the social process. This theoretical and ideological debate about a theory extends not just to the form of the relationships considered, but also to the identification of parameters and the possibility of their measurement. Economics is perhaps the only social science where the question of measurement is resolved even if the precise interpretation of the quantities obtained is not.

Dynamic models of the kind focused upon in this chapter describe 'flows' of goods, of people and ideas. In very many engineered systems the concept of a flow is explicit and unambiguous: channels and components are easily identified and measured – for example, the wires and switches in an electrical circuit. The same precision is lacking in social and many natural systems. Economic classification of industries, etc. is somewhat arbitrary; definition of social class or what is a developed or an under-developed country rather more so, as also are categories of weather systems.

In terms of the perspective afforded by consideration of social and technological elements within one framework, the following situation arises. As one moves from discussion of the technical features of the system, the ideas to be incorporated into a theory tend to become more diffuse. The spectrum from technical to social does not represent a continuum, however, and since it is the ability to identify and measure flows which is important, it is the case that, at present, many economic processes are better understood than ecological phenomena. Whether modelling flows provides the best representation of social processes remains a moot point. It is an ambitious approach in that the modeller must impute causal mechanisms between specific 'identifiable' components from which he constructs a 'circuit' diagram (analogous to that for an electronic circuit) simulating the mechanisms he perceives in the real world.

To some degree this approach stands in contrast to more conventional statistical estimation methods used in the social sciences such as factor analysis and regression analysis, which often provide clues as to the relations to be included in a dynamic model. In these statistical methods, to exaggerate somewhat, the researcher attempting to understand society takes the position of observing a 'black box' covered in dials, the accuracy of whose reading he can only guess at; he tries to spot correlations and relationships between them, and usually fails to take account of intuitively important features such as the inevitable time-lags between the operation of related mechanisms. Clearly, if the contents of the box were a complex electrical circuit, the results obtained by statistical estimation would be highly incomplete and provide quite unsatisfactory theories. Since empirical observation provides a fair degree of justification for the concept and causality in social areas besides economics, to attempt to peer inside the darkened interior of the box and understand its somewhat diffused contents must be considered a reasonable approach, at least for a wide range of applications, some of which we now consider in greater detail.

Models in application

One major function of a forecasting methodology is to improve the precision of discussion about the future. The ideal sought by computer modellers is a method which would permit policy outcomes, relevant to the issue under consideration, to be explored with a minimum of uncertainty, so avoiding risk of damage to the real world in economic, social or environmental terms. Although an appropriate criterion against which to assess modelling methods might be how closely they approach this objective, a less onerous and fairer criterion is whether models provide an input to policy makers' understanding. The main constraints for modellers to overcome in order to achieve the former are the theoretical and technical issues briefly discussed above; the main problem in connection with the latter is the institutional one of integrating modelling methods into the policy structure, and this will now be considered.

The kind of 'social' models which have been most successful in terms of both these issues are 'queuing' theory models and traffic control models generally. However, these deal with relatively straightforward systems compared to world systems, or even urban systems. The most common attempts to use large-scale computer models in public policy have in fact been in national economic planning and urban planning. The former has been moderately successful, the latter far less so. In attempting to assess world models later, it is useful to understand the reasons for the fortunes of these other models.

To consider economic models first; although they are increasingly used in the drawing up of short-term national economic plans, they are clearly far from perfect. Strictly speaking, the models which are employed are rather different from world models. They employ an input framework which provides a convenient means of accounting for flows of goods but often little more. Even so, the importance of this is not to be underestimated, and much of the art in this kind of modelling, as intimated previously, is in the identification of the best elements and parameters to use in the matrix. For example, much attention is now being paid to the inclusion of 'disbenefits', such as environmental pollution costs, into established accounting procedures in a consistent manner. Beyond this, various economic models of a greater sophistication are built up from sets of relationships based upon statistical estimations from time-series and cross-sectional data. The individual relationships in these models are often sound with apparently little error, although the total model is usually far less satisfactory. (See, for example, Ball, 1968.) Typically, their useful performance, in terms of predictive power, is restricted to only a few quarters ahead, despite their being based on at least a ten-year period of the best social data available. (See for example, Ash and Smyth, 1973.)

Because a complex economic model is so extremely difficult to calibrate and test, it tends to be judged on its proven 'forecasting' ability. Projections of different models for a given country, both in government and outside, often disagree. Thus, for example, the models of the London Business School and the National Institute provide a useful check on the performance of the U.K. Treasury model, and allow some public academic discussion about the methods used. In particular, because the methods of the National Institute model and the Treasury model are so similar, the former provides an insight, by implication, into the assumptions underlying Treasury thinking. In the United States there are at least eight well-known regular economic forecasts to be compared (and averaged in the American Statistical Association Consensus Forecast). Although models sometimes disagree, economists on the whole tend to comply with the theoretical structure incorporated in them (although by no means universally, as is illustrated by the current Cambridge debate between the 'New' and the 'Old' Schools or the debate as to the 'causes' of inflation). Agreement about theory is important to the success of the models in terms of their use and acceptability, as well as in terms of their ability to explain economic trends. Also in this respect it is noteworthy that most national economic models exist within a politically inert environment, in that the assumptions underlying the models fall within the value framework of the major political parties and permanent government officials. It is therefore possible to explore a full range of policy options without major modifications of the model and for confidence in the model to be established over a period of several years' experience. Nevertheless, although economic models do have an advantage in terms of predictive performance over 'naive extrapolation' (Ash and Smyth, 1973), turbulent world economic conditions such as those existing in 1974 seem to favour expert 'guesses' based on a reading of the leading economic indicators (*Business Week*, 1974).

Like their industrial counterparts, national economic models are increasingly part of a style of planning with relatively few more or less clearly stated objectives. Kaldor (1971) has pointed out that post-war governments in the U.K. have consistently come to judge economic performance in quantitative terms and that this has led to a managerial approach to government handling of the economy. He notes that economic policy objectives are more and more expressed in management terms of economic objectives and that successful management is the achievement of these objectives. Some aspects of the 'social' indicators movement might also be viewed as an extension of this trend providing social objectives to fit in with the needs of a management philosophy. However, this is not universally the case and there is a broader discussion of how these changes can be avoided elsewhere in this book.

Institutional considerations involve not just matters of organization but relate to the compatibility of formal modelling to the present form of the political process. For example, it is typically claimed by modellers that one of the benefits of formal modelling is that it *does* require a precise statement of problems and objectives (see for example, Forrester, 1968). However, as for example Maestre and Pavitt (1972) have pointed out, it is often precisely because objectives are *not* clearly stated that compromise is possible at all. Whatever the case, it is probably true to say that the existence of a managerial style of planning is almost a precursor to a successful public policy model.

The situation of models of economic development and similarly complex models of international economic relationships is therefore less favourable than for national economic models. To achieve comparative success the theoretical structure of a model would have to be agreeable to an institutional structure representing a wide spectrum of ideologies. Even in areas where there might be a consensus as to the best theoretical foundations for a model, as for example in the use of a production factor for economic sectors, parameters are extremely difficult to measure and interpret. Data on an international scale are of considerably less reliable quality than for many single countries and are often not strictly comparable between countries. Data on trade may be excellent in some cases, but theories of development depend on much more than this. Accurate information on ownership and foreign investment is hard to come by: theories of research in relation to development needs are the subject of extensive debate and controversy.

Similar considerations go some way towards explaining the relative lack of success of large-scale urban models. These models have taken a variety of forms including input–output and simulation models. After a decade or more of considerable expenditure and effort, little has been gained either from the point of view of the city or regional planner, or, worse, according to Lee (1973), even in terms of understanding of the working of the urban social environment (see also some fascinating discussions in *The Planner* and the *Journal of the American Institute of Planners*, 1973–74). Those authors such as Lee who have examined the reasons for the failure of large-scale urban models are almost unanimous in recommending a return to small-scale models. Whether or not Lee's view is exaggerated, it seems to have wide support and, though others have countered his pessimism, there is a general unease as to the value of very big urban models. Sears advocates 'midscale' models pointing out that the empirical models are irrelevant to current planning problems. However, there are exceptions; for example, Kajanoja (1973) considers that only through disaggregation can the necessary relevance be obtained. One problem with urban models is that they are rarely subjected to a critical evaluation and assessment by other modellers. Brewer and Hall (1973) note that the only model in the U.S.A. to receive detailed critical appraisal was Forrester's *Urban Dynamics* model. Even so, for this model the spectrum of views expressed by critics was so wide as to make any kind of definitive evaluation impossible.

Urban modellers in particular, but systems analysts in general, have come in for considerable criticism for overselling their product and then not delivering the goods (see again Maestre and Pavitt, 1972). Lee gives some examples of gross exaggeration by modellers. He cites the San Francisco model which was delivered 'tested and proven': true the estimates for *total* housing requirements in the city fitted reasonably to those recorded, but in later looking at the breakdown into different dwelling types, some figures were out by 1000 per cent, hardly providing a basis for policy! Brewer (1973), investigating the motives behind the construction of this model, shows that the construction of a useful planning tool did not figure very largely amongst them.

In the main, the urban models which have been used regularly because they are comprehensible to planners are the simple empirical 'gravity' models used to estimate trip densities, retailing potential and so on, and the even more straightforward input–output models. However, even these simple models have encountered considerable criticism, on the grounds that they have little behavioural content. Despite this, the results of simple empirical models often form a basis for discussion at public enquiries, and criticism tends to be reserved for the antiquity of the data rather than the model itself. Although real progress in urban models probably awaits the emergence of better social theories, one advantage in modelling urban systems is that there exists a large empirical base against which to test theories.

From the above discussion it is apparent that 'success' for any type of model will ultimately depend on whether it is well adapted to the institutional demands of the relevant policy body. Even so, a reasonable level of professional agreement as to the status of the theory used in the model determines the likelihood of its being considered as a basis for policy decisions. Three broad classifications of models in relation to their degree of 'acceptance' and hence policy application can usefully be distinguished:

(a) In some circumstances, it is possible that a given model may accommodate the views of the majority of interested parties to a discussion. Such a model may be called a *policy model* since it may be used to test some aspects of policies in a more or less non-controversial manner agreeable to all. Examples are the most successful economic and industrial models, and meteorological and other models of a physical nature.

(b) In more controversial issues several models may be employed, their use being to assist each party to a debate to understand more fully their own, and others' points of view and their consequences. These may be called *viewpoint models* and most models used in policy fall into this class. Examples are economic development models, conflict models and most urban models.

(c) Finally, there are *experimental models* which contribute in an indirect manner to the least well understood policy issues. These help to establish general views and suggest broad strategies for dealing with issues. All models pass through this stage.

Models and theories

It cannot be emphasized too strongly that computer models are only as good as the theory and data they contain. The fact that the social sciences do not at present have a solid well-accepted theoretical base is a major factor militating against the effectiveness of models both as forecasting devices and as aids to policy making. A claim frequently made for models, however, is that they can, in a number of ways, assist the development of understanding of social processes and lead to an improvement in theory.

This claim is based on two features which computer models are perceived to possess which are not present in most other techniques, particularly those involving 'literary' approaches. The first is that, unlike 'mental' models used in verbal and written discussion, a mathematical model is clear and unambiguous. It thus forces a researcher to make his assumptions explicit and reveals any inconsistencies in them. The second is that the computer, unlike the human mind, is able to manipulate a large number of variables simultaneously, and thus can trace, with high accuracy, the implications of a large number of interlinked assumptions. Forrester (1972) contends that this process frequently leads to surprising or 'counter-intuitive' results which vindicate the suggestion that computer models can provide new insights into the behaviour of social systems. For these reasons, it is maintained that computer models serve a particularly important role in clarifying and articulating theoretical ideas.

On the question of clarity, it is true that a full presentation of a model enables a group unconnected with its constructors to analyse the work in a less ambiguous way than is possible with a verbal treatment. Thus the risks of misunderstanding and misinterpretation are largely overcome. However, in two other ways, full clarity has not been achieved. First, there is the problem to which we have already referred, namely that of comprehension by those not familiar with mathematical notation; they would scarcely be persuaded that models afford a clearer presentation of ideas, and may complain that an attempt is being made to 'blind them with science'. This problem is particularly acute in those cases where models are expected to be of use in public policy, both because the policy maker is unlikely to put trust in a model he does not understand and because public debate is likely to be restricted. Secondly, it is doubtful whether many mathematicians, used to studying equations written in closed form, would regard a large-scale computer model as 'clear'.

Indeed, it seems that to check out even some of the implications of a large-scale model requires a great deal of work, and even then one is left with the feeling that full understanding has not, and cannot, be achieved. It may not be enough to understand in isolation the individual relationships comprising the world; the connections between these relationships are profoundly important to model behaviour and it is extremely difficult totally to grasp their effects.

Whether these disadvantages outweigh the advantages depends on the type of model and the use to which it is to be put. Loss of ambiguity may be of first importance in testing consistency of theories; lack of public comprehension may be fatal for policy making.

The second contention is that computer models can indicate that social systems behave in a 'counter-intuitive' way, and that the most appropriate remedies to problems are often not those which seem intuitively obvious to decision-makers. This assertion is based on the fact that a large model treats the interactions between a number of variables simultaneously; it is claimed that only such an overall view can reveal the true consequences of policies which are often implemented from a much narrower perspective, without a full awareness by the decision-maker of possible ramifications in parts of the system with which he may not be familiar. If a given policy directly improves a particular situation A, it is often implemented, despite the fact that it also causes changes in a part B of the system, which in turn cause a worsening of A, which may be more significant than the direct improvement. As a particular example, Forrester, in his *Urban Dynamics* (1969), quotes a policy frequently adopted to ameliorate urban decay – the provision of low cost housing, whereas his own model indicates that this merely causes a migration into the city of more people; this exacerbates the unemployment problem and eventually worsens the urban problem as a whole.

This argument is really nothing more than an emphasis on the need to take a holistic view; it simply asserts that, by so doing, one obtains different results from those obtained by a more restricted viewpoint, and that the former are more likely to be valid. As with the 'clarity' argument, it seems to us that generalization is difficult. In theory the argument is convincing; in practice, bearing in mind that a holistic representation demands complexity and the use of theoretical ideas of varying quality, it is quite possible that 'noise' may be introduced and that the results may be entirely spurious. Forrester's conclusions on urban problems depend on the quality of the assumptions he used, and are highly controversial. (His most drastic proposals arise because he fails to take proper account of the regional environment of the single city he considers.) Furthermore, it seems that, even in a large-scale computer model, behaviour is often dominated by one or two key assumptions which make the likely results clear; given these assumptions, the results are not at all surprising. Nevertheless, computer models can aid theory development in a less direct way, by indicating those parts of a system where theory is weakest. If model behaviour is found to be dominated by a sub-system about which great uncertainty exists, it is clearly an indication of the area in which future research effort is likely to prove most valuable.

Global models

Global models are a very recent development in large-scale modelling and are especially relevant to the major issues dealt with in the last part of this book. In view of their short history it is not possible to evaluate global models in the same way as other models, although experience with other models may provide some useful basis for discussion. One of the particularly interesting features of global models is that they attempt to combine within a single model many factors pertaining to a specific issue or set of issues. Thus they contain social and economic factors together with ecological and physical constraints.

At least four new models are currently being constructed at institutes in Europe, America and Japan. These projects attempt to improve upon the original work of Forrester and Meadows, discussed in earlier chapters and in *Models of Doom* (Cole *et al*, 1974), and to overcome criticisms of the *Limits to Growth* models. One significant common change is that they do not treat the world as a single homogeneous unit, but recognize the physical and societal variations across the world and try to account for these in the models. There is also an attempt to leave the less measurable relationships out of the formal model and instead to arrive at 'realistic' values for parameters through discussion with relevant social scientists, policy analysts and so on.

A number of comparisons can be made between global models and economic and urban models. The problems with regard to data and theory are similar, only worse, to those of the development models. The quality of the theoretical foundation of global models is highly varied, much of it being straight speculation; some of it is more or less agreed although even here the margins of error tend to be wide. The models contain such a variety of factors that many of the relationships and concepts fall outside or between the traditional academic disciplines.

Since most global models look at long-term rather than short-term possibilities, the difficulty in calibrating and testing the models is magnified beyond that of an economic or urban model of similar complexity. As explained earlier, in addition to a high level of complexity, the models are non-linear and those involving non-linear relationships are exceedingly difficult to calibrate even in the most favourable circumstances, whereas with short-term models, such as national economic models, each relationship is substantiated separately and then the predictive power of the model as a whole is checked empirically. For long-term models this last check is available only in a very limited manner.

For reasons of space, only a short description of some of the newer world models will be given here, sufficient to provide a comparative discussion of their contribution to our understanding of the global system. The models are described and reviewed in more detail in a recent report to the U.K. Research Councils, entitled *Application of Dynamic Analysis to Forecasting and World Problems* (Clark *et al*, summarized in Cole, 1974), and in a recent book, *Global Simulation Models* (Clark *et al*, 1975).

Most of the current projects are less pessimistic than *The Limits to Growth* model concerning *global* physical limits. They are more concerned with resource location, the technologies of extraction and production, and socio-political interpretation. 'Playing safe' on the future of technology, most projects assume current best practice since they are designed to show possibilities rather than probabilities. Of these, the one which might quite fairly be called the most determined attempt to 'do Limits right' is the Pestel-Mesarovic 'Strategy for Survival' model (Mesarovic and Pestel 1974). This is the largest of the new models, and is some two hundred times larger than the 'Limits' model.

The 'Strategy for Survival' model considers five world geopolitical regions: North America, Western Europe, Japan, North Africa and Middle East, two socialist blocs, Latin America, Australia and South Africa, the remainders of Africa and Asia.

The goal of the project is to 'indicate' the time and nature of the specific different crises to be expected in the seven regions in various circumstances. As the simple two-region model of the Sussex critique demonstrated, division into linked regions can produce quite significant changes in the pattern of stability of a global model. Thus the 'Survival' project will examine the shortages in materials, energy, food etc., which could appear, paricularly in Europe and North America, as world demand rises.

In contrast to the 'Strategy for Survival' project, *The First Alternative World Model,* which is a Latin American project (Herrera, 1974), will postulate that constraints upon the development of the Third World do not arise as a result of physical or technological limitations. The Bariloche team intend to demonstrate that the real constraints on possibilities for development, both internal and external to the Third World countries, are socio-political in nature, arising chiefly from trade and technological restrictions being imposed by the developed world. The kind of questions that will be examined with the model are whether the developing countries could achieve a satisfactory living standard, more or less independently of the industrial world, by trade exchange between themselves.

The Japanese global modelling effort has many facets (Kaya *et al,* 1972, 1973), perhaps the most interesting of which is an examination of the relocation of industry across the world according to some 'optimum' distribution. Besides questions of location, access to resources and markets and the availability of labour and transport, ecological factors would be important in the determination of this goal.

The main characteristic of the original 'Limits' model was that of 'overshoot and collapse', exponential growth of population and industrialization being blocked by rigid resource limits. In terms of global stability, the scenarios of the models described above are radically different both from each other and from 'Limits'. From a purely analytic perspective, the levels of stability afforded by different global structures are not easy to determine nor as intuitively obvious as overshoot and collapse. In the first place, one must distinguish between various kinds of stability; between, say, the long-term kind, apparently afforded by equilibrium, and short-term stability which mitigates against transient disturbances. Instability of the latter kind arises from changes in the number and type of linkages in a complex system. The current energy crisis is an instability which seems to fall into this category and is the sort of issue that may be speculated about, using, for example, the Pestel-Mesarovic model. In the search for a global optimum the impact of such occurrences may increase or there *may* be destabilizing factors which arise from an increased uniformity of production and markets – the possible over-reliance on relatively few major technologies and parallel changes in ecological stability arising from a reduction in the range of cereal crops grown, for example.

Regional or local self-sufficiency may give rise to greater global stability than a global optimum, although this might be traded off against long-term 'efficiency'. However, much care has to be taken with such an interpretation since, as already pointed out, stability in this case means that if one part of the system fails the rest will not be unduly affected. While this may be satisfactory in some engineering systems, it is hardly so when the 'components' are individual countries or regions.

The consequences of changes in diversity and complexity are not easily obtained from a simple calculation. The 'Limits' model only took account of factors such as those indicated above to the extent that they were considered destabilizing and 'inevitable'. Indeed, it is difficult to infer likely results from more general considerations or, for example by analogy with other systems, to show that their overall stability decreases exponentially as the number of linkages increases (Gardner and Ashby, 1970). However, care must be taken in drawing inferences from this since, in the first place, social and biological systems are not randomly connected and, secondly, one is not concerned only with global stability. Examination of the properties of simple food web models, described for example by Maynard-Smith (1974), shows that stability depends on the manner of connection and he cites work which indicates that, contrary to much conventional ecological wisdom, stability is not a necessary or even a likely consequence of complexity. But again this is by no means certain; nor does it distinguish between complexity and diversity. In addition, whereas natural systems do not appear to be centrally governed, in that each species or individual attempts to ensure its own continued existence with relatively little regard for the whole, this is not exactly the situation for human societies, especially when seeking a global optimum. Again, simple calculations indicate that the stable solutions for structurally identical systems with divergent objectives are quite different.

Even from an analytic standpoint, it is true to say that factors in the organization of structures which ensure both long-term and transient stability, in addition to global and local stability, are poorly understood. Concern with stability (and equilibrium) is central to many areas of understanding of social and ecological processes and, as experience with theories of relatively straight-forward physical systems shows, the problems are exceedingly difficult. Researchers such as Prigogine (1972) have developed models from physical theories of ideal systems fluctuating far from equilibrium, and their results indicate that spontaneous deviations from macroscopic behaviour are critical to the long-term development of the systems.

Unlike the relatively simple 'Limits' model, the properties of more complex (and arguably more realistic) models are not intuitively clear, and it may well be that a better understanding of the question of global stability which is of use to empirical application will emerge from further studies using dynamic modelling methods. This may be one area where relatively large models are essential.

Translation of theoretical insight into policy recommendations always has to be treated with caution. For example, concern that the use of new strains of cereal, considered vital to the relief of hunger in many parts of the world, might create serious instabilities in the local ecosystems was to some extent mitigated once it was realized that these crops would adapt selectively to particular local growing conditions (Josling, 1973).

Conclusions

In this last section some of the considerations of the previous discussions will be drawn together. First, the position of world models will be considered and then some general issues beyond that mentioned immediately above concerning the use of all models will be discussed.

Recent activity in global modelling has sought to overcome

the principle technical objections to the Forrester-Meadows work. Consequently, current work should be considered as the second phase of activity in the area. Although the trend is towards more complex world models, some attempt is being made to make them more manageable; the success of this has yet to be proven. There may be an important lesson for global modellers in the prevalent move away from large-scale models in urban research. Indeed, already *two* of the new larger global modelling projects seem to have run into difficulty. The Linneman *Doubling of Population* study has after many teething problems opted not to concentrate exclusively on world food problems, and work on the Battelle *DEMATEL* model has apparently ceased. Although there is relatively little work confined solely to dynamic modelling of single issues, this seems to be because of the importance dynamic modellers attach to the examination of the inter-relationships between the world's sub-systems themselves, rather than because the separate issues would not benefit from a similar examination.

The information demands which would be placed upon a long-term world model would probably not be as relatively severe as those placed on either urban or short-term national economic models. Indeed, global models would be indirectly useful to policy if they could provide even a marginally clearer picture of future global trends than are provided by other methods. 'Viewpoint' and 'experimental' models can play a useful catalytic role in stimulating and structuring debate, in indicating gaps and shortcomings in theory, in facilitating interdisciplinary communications and in improving fundamental understanding of issues. Any significant reduction in the uncertainty of policy repercussions is likely to be welcome. Certainly, the chances of reaching a high level of precision in anticipating the long-term future are low, using models or any other method. The performance of models would obviously improve as data and theory are mutually improved. But as noted above, full calibration and verification of complex models is exceedingly difficult at the moment and in the case of long-term models is virtually impossible. Consequently, a high level of confidence in the results of global models would almost certainly be misplaced and it is always a pertinent question to ask, therefore, whether a more straightforward method would not serve as well.

From the earlier discussion about theory and application it

might be argued that world models such as those mentioned above, whose results are critically dependent on their 'non-physical' context, are unlikely to be counted as pure policy models. Modelling goals which emphasize 'survival' or 'development' or 'equality' are likely to suggest very different solutions. But even so, the various projects may make a collective contribution by providing a range of insights into questions inherent to the debate of important global issues. Currently, we are probably at the stage where, apart from the point of view of experiment, any possible advantages of a 'general purpose' global model are outweighed by the additional technical and manipulation problems involved in such a model. Our ability to make a long-term forecast of many social phenomena, such as population growth or elasticity of demand for commodities, would be poor even if the physical and technical environment were known exactly. In any case, it might be argued that it is precisely with regard to these considerations that there should be a maximum of public debate, since there is evidence to show that people are far more likely to accept the results of policies they have had a hand in formulating. For many policy purposes, current forecasts would be rendered no less reliable if a range of plausible assumptions based upon best expert judgment were made with regard to many social factors.

To some degree, the institutional framework for the use of global models, which as argued above is likely to be important to their success, already exists within international organizations. As an aside, it might be mentioned that the International Labour Organization, for example, has already proceeded some way with its own large-scale employment model which, although not a global model, contains some of the features common to these models (Blandy *et al*, 1973) and the Food and Agriculture Organization has supported a number of commodity models. Indeed it may well be that models dealing with specific global issues would be more successful than most 'general purpose' models such as *The Limits to Growth* model. For example, in the fields of ecology, including in particular meteorology and oceanography, there is already a fair degree of international co-operation and consensus (see for example, the project of B. O. Jansson, 1973). International learned societies and institutions play an important role in resolving such conflicts, and in spearheading the introduction of a united global agreement between members of the international scientific community, in contact with their own national governments. They provide a common technical basis for discussion of a number of multinational (if not truly global) issues which must be confronted if the long-term effects of industrialization are to be handled.

Despite their many failings, not least whether they were models of global problems, the MIT models certainly had tremendous impact in raising the level of public concern about particular important issues. The impact of the MIT work may be attributed to a number of reasons:

(a) It came at a time of increasing concern with issues of pollution, famine, and overpopulation, and, to a lesser extent, resource shortages on a local and global scale.

(b) In addition to this, the authority of MIT appeared to be behind the work.

(c) The use of a computer and computerized output added to the appearance of respectability of the work.

(d) The Club of Rome was an important factor in initial acceptance as an influential and active organization.

(e) Perhaps the most significant factor, apart from timeliness, was the 'marketing' of *Limits to Growth* by Potomac Associates who, recognizing a commercial product, gave it wide publicity. Moreover, even though Forrester's more dramatic model did not benefit from Club of Rome or Potomac activities, it still achieved limited front page attention in the international press.

Specific policy changes resulting from the work cannot be identified, but, in view of widespread attention at government level, some changes in policy perspective have almost certainly occurred. The work and its conclusions have had governmental supporters, if not advocates, in the United Kingdom, Europe and the United States. In the United Kingdom, for example, the degree of official interest has been sufficient to stimulate the setting up of a government research team charged with the examination of long-term global issues. So it must be said that, as experimental models, they have had exceptional influence.

Both Forrester and Meadows implied that their work could be used to some degree in the formation of public policy. However, as 'policy' models, the work fell down on a number of counts. The MIT models are certainly not non-controversial in a political or academic sense; they deal only with parameters in terms of global averages and in an extremely generalized fashion. Because of this the models might be considered naive, yet even this level of simplicity has led to a level of model complexity (especially in the case of Meadows) apparently beyond the comprehension of many academics, policy makers and laymen.

Apart from the timeliness of the effort and the inherent interest in a novel experimental approach, none of the reasons for the impact of the Forrester–Meadows work could be considered appropriate criteria for 'success' in an academic sense. It is generally accepted, however, that the role of futures research goes well beyond that of academia. The balance between the academic and 'ideological' role of futures research is a matter of diverse opinions which may ultimately be understood through 'peer group' activity as the subject develops. Finally, it should be said that although it is easy to be sceptical about current attempts at global modelling, it should also be remembered that many widely used economic models, for example input-output analysis, were highly controversial at one time; so scepticism about global models may be misplaced when viewed in an historical context. However, in view of the difficulties of gaining confidence in a long-term forecasting model the gestation period of acceptability and confidence may be many years.

In practice, it has often been the case that social issues examined using large-scale modelling methods have tended to be so complex that the methods have been unable to contribute greatly, and sophisticated methods seem sometimes to have added to the confusion. Often, as with the large urban models, there has been a tendency to attempt too much with a single model. Consequently, even the apparently reasonable claim that formally structuring a problem leads to clarification, has often turned out not to be true in practice simply because of extraneous detail. In the main, attempts to produce large-scale 'general purpose' models accounting for a large number of issues or interest groups have led to models which are both too simplistic and unmanageable. Lack of manageability manifests itself in a number of ways. Large-scale models in particular are slow to develop, requiring a large empirical base and, in principle, when details are changed they need quite extensive recalibration.

Fashions in problems change; they 'disappear' or are overtaken more rapidly than can be easily accommodated by the slow growth of theory. Again this seems to have been particularly true of urban models. As a result, it is often difficult for models to provide the degree of flexibility and confidence required of them. In the main, a successful computer model (or any analytic method) requires a good basis of theory and data normally only achieved over a considerable period of time. Thus, as Schultze (1968) has remarked, it can turn out to be the case that simply because this time has elapsed, interest groups with entrenched positions have come into being and often tending to frustrate compromise.

The question of confidence is obviously important before a policy maker will use a model, since he will not lightly risk his career. He must first have confidence in the assumptions of the model, i.e. they must reflect his own point of view, and second he must have confidence in the way the model manipulates those assumptions (see the discussion in Tanter, 1973). The first is difficult in any kind of 'general purpose' model and the second is more difficult if the manipulations are obscured by over-complexity in the model. This does not imply that a policy maker in general actually operates the model himself (although some such as the Pestel-Mesarovic model are designed to be used by policy makers directly), but he must find it credible. Essentially what most models provide is a tool for clarifying the policy maker's or interest group's own views and their consequences. It is rarely that a model accommodates the views of the majority of interested parties to discussions of policy. However, models such as those the Treasury uses are true 'policy' models since they may be used to test some aspects of policies in a way that is more or less noncontroversial and agreeable to all parties.

As pointed out earlier, the more 'engineered' a system is, the more likely it is that a satisfactory model will be made. Similarly, because the management function in an 'engineered' society would be high, the application of the model is likely to be successful and the ideas it contains reinforced. Some authors (for example, Armytage, 1965; Hoos, 1972) therefore view with suspicion the widespread adoption of a managerial approach to government, fearing that it could lead to a technocratic and insensitive style of control. Others concerned for different reasons have demonstrated that analytic methods have often led to worse rather than better plans even for the limited number of factors they were designed to improve and have resulted in considerable waste of public funds (Lindblom, 1959).

The apparent rationality and objectivity of models is appealing but can hide quite dubious assumptions concerning, for example, measurement of parameters on invalid scales or implying a consensus of views which does not exist. There is also an added danger that computer models tend to produce an atmosphere of inevitability about the forecast future in the public and policy maker's minds, so there is the danger of self-fulfilling but unwelcome prophesy. In large-scale models, these issues are all the more difficult to unravel. There is clearly a balance to be struck by the modeller between the degree of realism and completeness of his model and its application.

Present political processes with all their imperfections represent some kind of collective model of very many people which is moderately well adapted to tackling complex and finely balanced issues. The purpose of mathematical modelling of human systems is to simplify, but not to over-simplify; in essence to bring complex issues into the realm of comprehension of the political process. For this, models are sometimes considered to provide a 'framework for discussion' of issues or as a 'tool for education'. However, far more efficient techniques for both these processes are available and so ultimately modellers should aim at something better.

Avoiding the dangers and making best use of the potential of models can hardly be an easy procedure. Much experience has shown that even from the point of view of prediction there are diminishing returns to complexity. There may be systems whose behaviour is critically dependent on a large number of their component parts and which can therefore only be adequately comprehended through the conscious relating together of many of those parts. Even so it turns out that eventually these systems can often be reduced to simpler descriptions characterizing collective behaviour once their operation is understood.

Except in particular instances, there is no real virtue in complexity and since the purpose of modelling is to clarify as well as to describe, it ought to be the case that models which trade off correctly the opposing demands upon them, coupled with careful and imaginative interpretation, could be at least as useful as highly elaborate models. These somewhat smaller models can be a vital aid to the structuring and development of the understanding of complex processes. Furthermore, they are more readily related to styles of policy making which take realistic account of the uncertainties inherent in forecasting.

Chapter 10

Cost-Benefit Analysis and Technology Assessment

The aim of this chapter is to examine cost-benefit methodology and its relevance to technology assessment. Both are, in broad terms, means of attempting to assess the consequences and desirability of undertaking projects, such as building an airport or introducing micro-wave devices. We conclude that both cost-benefit analysis and technology assessment have many defects, and their best role is in raising, identifying and clarifying issues rather than in solving problems. The core of both lies in identifying or forecasting the changes stemming from a specified change. The immediate motivation may be either concern about the effects of an innovation, or a desire to indicate the extent to which an innovation is likely to satisfy a goal. These could be labelled 'technology-orientated' or 'goal-orientated'.

In practice, the range of considerations in cost-benefit studies is generally limited; important social considerations are often ignored. Technology assessment generally encompasses a much wider range, although these may still receive only scant attention.

The forecasting element in cost-benefit studies is minimal, and is hardly more developed in assessment. It is not easy to suggest how this situation may be improved, given the problems of forecasting. Some of the technicalities in cost-benefit methodology may be unnecessary, given all the other sources of error. If the quantification of many items is, so to speak, far from objective, are there not dangers that aspects which can, at times, be niceties (such as shadow-pricing and discounting) are nothing but redundant? The danger is of concentrating upon details and ignoring the difficult but fundamental issues.

Definitions

To explore the nature of cost-benefit analysis and technology assessment methodology, we need definitions which not only reveal the characteristics of each, but also their similarities and differences. Given the lack of agreement to be found in the literature about definitions – especially for technology assessment – parts of this task are hard, if not impossible. Thus, much of what follows must be arbitrary rather than authoritative. The following is a list of some of the characteristics of cost-benefit analysis and technology assessment, as defined for this study:

1) *Mutual acknowledgement:* Whatever cost-benefit analysis and technology assessment might be, their two literatures generally show complete ignorance of the other's existence. In the cost-benefit literature reviewed in this study – generally categorized as such by the titles or introductions – only one refers to technology assessment by name (Starr, 1973); similarly, we have found only four or five technology assessment references to cost-benefit analysis, either to cost-benefit analysis *per se* or to some related concept such as discounting; even when discussing the problems of quantification, cost-benefit analysis is not explicitly mentioned. This is surprising, given the potential similarities of the two approaches; perhaps it is partly due to cost-benefit analysis being the prerogative of economists, while technology assessment authors tend to come from the natural sciences.

2) *Age:* Cost-benefit analysis is commonly traced back to 1834, when J. Dupuit published, in France, *On the Measurement of Utility of Public Works.* The American government has acknowledged cost-benefit analysis since the turn of the century (when legislation required cost-benefit analysis studies before certain types of harbour project could be authorized). In contrast, the term 'technology assessment' is quite recent; it has been ascribed to Philip Yeager who, as counsel to the Daddario Committee in the U.S. Congress, used it in 1966. Depending upon the definitions used, it could be argued that technology assessment has been going on since the Industrial Revolution (if not considerably earlier). Malthus did not believe technology to be capable of postponing famine, and Marx predicted that, within the capitalist

context, technology would alienate man from both his fellows and his work (and thus increase inequalities). Spontaneous efforts by the Luddites to preserve their jobs and communities were early attempts at social control. However, formal social controls arose only much later, and were related to safety of workers and users and, still later, to prevention of pollution.

There have also been attempts to assess, and less successfully, to control, deliberate application of science and technology to the development of military weapons. The use of gas in World War I caused great public outcry. Widespread use was avoided, however, not as a result of this, but because gas was an ineffective and unpredictable weapon. Many technology assessments of nuclear weapons have been made, including the remarkable Franck Report (1945) and some social control has been achieved through the 1967 non-proliferation treaty. In spite of this, development of ever more dangerous weapons continues.

3) *Extent of the literature:* The literature on various aspects of cost-benefit analysis (such as shadow-pricing and discounting) is large; the total cost-benefit analysis literature is thus very large. Although much of it is theory oriented, there remain countless examples of applications of the technique; for instance, studies of the London Victoria Line (Foster and Beesley, 1963), on which of four sites to build a Third London Airport (Roskill, 1970), the M1 London–Birmingham motorway (Coburn *et al,* 1960), the Channel Tunnel and Bridge proposals (Ministry of Transport, 1963), etc., etc. In contrast, the literature on technology assessment is minimal, and is mostly either a plea for technology assessment and its institutionalization, or else on methodology. Even at the international literature level, there are very few examples of actual technological assessments – as defined by the original authors – and they are virtually all American (see, e.g., Coates, 1971; Bowers and Frey, 1972; MITRE 1971-2; Spangler, 1973; National Academy of Engineering, 1969; or Medford, 1973).

4) *Problems considered:* A comparison of cost-benefit analysis with technology assessment projects suggests that the former is concerned more with applications of established technologies to situations narrowly defined in time, space and other physical dimensions, while technology assessment is concerned more with new technologies – with innovations. For instance, in the case of

the cost-benefit analysis of the new underground line in London (Victoria Line), what was technologically new (e.g. driverless trains) was not important to the study; the focus of the analysis was the impact of the line on reducing travel time, increasing comfort, etc. An analogous technology assessment study would focus upon the new technology employed – the impact of the technology needed for driverless trains. A more likely technology assessment brief would be the impact of a new transport mode, such as a small, driverless bus system.

In one sense, this point permits cost-benefit analysis to be regarded as a special case of technology assessment; while technology assessment assesses, in general terms, the impact of a technology on (say) a given community, cost-benefit analysis assesses the impact of one particular application of that technology. This distinction will correlate with the relative ease of quantification in the two types of study.

It can be suggested, in passing, that while technology assessment must, by definition, consider technology, cost-benefit analysis studies can take on problems where the technological or physical side is minimal. A non-physical cost-benefit analysis candidate, for illustration, could have been the post-war debate in Brighton on what kind of tourist to encourage – the poorer masses or relatively few tourists rolling in holiday money. In principle, a study could have systematically compared the likely social and economic impacts of the alternative courses (see Musgrave, 1973).

5) *Quantification:* Almost by definition, cost-benefit analysis studies entail quantification of most, if not all, factors considered, whereas the technology assessment studies conducted so far entail minimal (if any) quantification. It would be controversial to give this as a theoretical distinction between the two, because of the calls for quantification in papers allegedly on technology assessment. However, given the preceding distinction, this one is partially implied. When considering established technologies, there is past experience to give a reasonable picture of what kinds of problem one is dealing with; although a dam has never been built on a given river in a certain area before, there have still been enough dams built elsewhere to permit answers to many questions about the impact of the new one, perhaps even to permit quantification. In contrast, there is relatively little past

experience to indicate the possible impact of micro-wave devices, and less still to help assess the impact of manned space stations.

Two footnotes could be derived from this point. One is that some of the debate between cost-benefit analysis and technology assessment (if there really is one) concerns when it is 'reasonable' to quantify in matters socio-political; this is not unadjacent to debates on mental versus mathematical models. If a quantitative technology assessment of a phenomenon cannot be produced, is it sane to try to model it mathematically? And of course, *vice versa*. The other point, which is of interest rather than importance, is that here we may have a case of an established discipline (cost-benefit analysis) moving towards a *less* quantitative form as time goes by, whereas in most cases numeracy is assumed to increase with time.

6) *Language:* A view sometimes approached, and occasionally reached, is that what Europeans call cost-benefit analysis, Americans call technology assessment. If there is any truth in this, it is minimal. Firstly, much of the cost-benefit analysis literature is, in fact, American; likewise, Europe is certainly not completely lacking in technology assessment literature (see, for example, Medford, 1973; Sinclair, 1973; French Water Control Agency in Cetron *et al*, 1973). Secondly, as suggested above, there are some differences between the two. There could also be a third factor implicit in the 'it's all semantics' view; namely, given the apparent ignorance about cost-benefit analysis in some of the American technology assessment literature, these people seem to be heading towards the discovery of cost-bent analysis. In some instances, this is probably true; but is it an entirely fair generalization? The next section outlines what seems to be a standard cost-benefit analysis methodolgy, and its relevance to technology assessment. It may be useful to round off this section with a look at a few more formal definitions.

'Cost-benefit analysis', according to Prest and Turvey (1967), 'is a way of setting out the factors which need to be taken into account in making certain economic choices. Most of the choices to which it has been applied involve investment projects and decisions – whether or not a particular project is worthwhile, which is best of several alternative projects, or when to undertake a particular project. . . . Cost-benefit analysis can also be applied to proposed changes in laws or regulations, to new pricing schemes and the like. . . . The aim is to maximize the present value of all benefits less that of all costs, subject to specified constraints.' Mishan (1970) claims that, 'As everybody knows, a cost-benefit analysis purports to measure in money terms all the benefits and all the costs to be expected over the future of some mooted project, and to admit the project if the sum of the benefits exceeds the sum of the costs by a sufficient margin.' The Congressional Research Service definition (1972) makes it explicit that, 'Benefits and costs include direct and indirect effects.'

All these definitions are lame in that they refer to theory rather than the practice, and an important word occurs in Mishan's statement '*purports* to measure'. Nevertheless, one can sense a distinction in comparison with the CRS definition of technology assessment: 'A process for the generation of reliable, comprehensive information about a technology to enable its effective social management by political decision-makers.'

The Congressional Bill introduced by Emilio Daddario described it as 'identifying the potentials of applied research and technology and promoting ways and means to accomplish their transfer into practical use, and identifying the undesirable by-products and side-effects of such applied research and development in advance of their crystallization and informing the public of their potential in order that appropriate steps may be taken to eliminate or minimize them.' Emphasis is generally upon management of technology ('to improve the management of the total technological society', etc.) and, in particular, upon the minimizing of 'unintended, unanticipated and unwanted' consequences.

Distinctions can be drawn between various types of cost-benefit analysis and of technology assessment. One of the more useful may relate to goal-orientated technology assessment, following the National Academy of Engineering (1969) pattern. This starts with an indentifiable social problem and seeks relevant technology (to reduce pollution from cars, for instance); the other starts with an identifiable social problem and seeks relevant technology seeks out the possible social consequences. This is the difference between normative and extrapolative approaches; as argued elsewhere in this book, the importance of the former should not be under-rated. It may be redundant to emphasize the related dangers of the 'technological-fix' trap – that attacks on the police can be solved by giving the police protective clothing (Etzioni, 1972).

It was pointed out at the outset that to attempt a definitive definition of technology assessment is verging on the impossible, and perhaps on the pointless as well. It could be argued – and persuasively – that *any* study which examines the link of science and technology with society is a technology assessment. Rather than pretending that there is something special about these few studies, it should instead be acknowledged that the selection criteria often used for admitting studies into the category 'a technology assessment' are highly suspect. Much of the work of, say, the Federal Drug Administration and the National Transportation Safety Board (see, e.g., Kasper, 1972) is perhaps technology assessment.

Steps in procedure

The steps involved in the 'standard' cost-benefit analysis approach are as follows:
1) Precise identification of the project to be analysed.
2) Fixing of the (alternative) time horizon(s).
3) Fiscal statement of expenditures and revenues.
4) Identification of the consequences of the project – who will be affected, how and when, together with fixing the 'cut-off' points.
5) Distinguishing between which consequences are costs and which are benefits.
6) Quantifying the costs and benefits in money terms.
7) Weighing the various costs and benefits (if not subsumed in (6)).
8) Adding the costs together and the benefits together.
9) Discounting the money sums to their present-day values.
10) Comparing the costs with the benefits.
11) Selling the results to the appropriate decision-makers.
In any specific analysis, some stages may not be relevant, and their order may also be different. Other possible variations include distinguishing the quantifiable from the other costs/benefits (and

handling the latter in a purely prose form, say) or else exploring the sensitivity of the final conclusion to changes in some of the assumptions (like the assumed discount rate).

Given the less consolidated nature of technology assessment, it is not so easy to give a parallel 'standard' procedure. From what has been said already, it will be apparent that quantification will be of less importance; this will also mean less attention to shadow-pricing, discounting and so on. There may instead be more effort put into seeking out analogous situations from the past, and into obtaining views and insights from those people experienced in related fields. However, the purpose of the rest of this chapter is to explore exactly this issue.

1) Project definition and applicability of cost-benefit analysis or technology assessment

Firstly, two illustrations of the importance of project definition. The set objective of the Roskill Third London Airport study (1970) was to decide which of four possible sites was the best. This meant that emphasis was laid on the *differences* between the sites; that the 'best' could still have been 'bad' would not necessarily emerge, as no absolute comparison of total costs and benefits was called for. Had an earlier Ministry of Transport comparison of a Channel Bridge and Tunnel proceeded similarly, it might not have emerged that, although the Tunnel beat the Bridge, the Tunnel would nonetheless have represented a net loss at certain low traffic levels.

Another example showed the alleged net benefits of eliminating syphilis in the United States (Klarman, 1965); what would have been of greater use, going by one critic (Muskin, quoted in Mishan, 1971), was showing the net benefit of various intermediary reductions in the level. Strictly speaking, project definition may not be part of the assessment process; nonetheless, it is obviously important.

In what instances the techniques are applicable is a highly debatable issue, especially regarding technology assessment: it can be argued that the problems of technology assessment are such that there is no applicable methodology. As a start, can we rule out those investment decisions which are largely political – such as the small, poor country establishing a state airline (or

European countries combining to develop a military aircraft)? We cannot necessarily rule these out if we accept cost-benefit analysis as a *part* of the input to the decision; the knowledge that such a project has not been positively evaluated by a reputable cost-benefit analysis (as against a commercial feasibility study) may have some bearing. Also, it can be useful to have a systematic way of following through the consequences of a political decision or viewpoint. Cost-benefit analysis studies can permit a wider audience to participate in assessments – as indeed Roskill showed. It may be that the only times when cost-benefit analysis studies should not be conducted (given, quite unrealistically, unlimited funds) is when the results may be taken too seriously: it is far too easy to forget the defects or arbitrariness of the technique; this applies equally elsewhere. That no such study was done, for example, on Concorde in its early days, may not be as important as it seems (Freeman, 1970), because the study could well have repeated the mistakes of those who made the actual decision – such mistakes as grossly under-estimating the development costs, and over-estimating sales. If the aim of the study had been to initiate a public debate on Concorde, it would have been only one of several possible routes to that goal.

Any present-day assessment of the applicability of technology assessment must be verging on the premature, because there is as yet insufficient hard evidence of its feasibility. When it is implied (or even stated) that technology assessment is a con trick, the point's validity cannot be denied. But neither can it be confirmed. Certainly statements such as 'technology assessment will be the salvation of our democratic, free-enterprise system' have few merits beyond quotability. The sanest stand is perhaps that of Charles Falk: 'The only way we are going to learn how to assess technology is by doing it now, with whatever tools are available and as best we can. Only then will we be able to sharpen those tools' (quoted by Kiefer, 1972) or, as might be concluded, only then will the exercise be shown to be another futures research-type fad.

The definition of a technology assessment project is likely to be much less precise and detailed – more nebulous – than that for a cost-benefit analysis, because less will be known of the former project (assuming it to be an innovation) than of the latter. Indeed, some technology assessment studies (e.g. those from MITRE or on micro-wave devices) are largely qualitative forecasts; the forecasts are needed to know the outlines of the beast being assessed.

2) Time horizon

Given that the consequences of a project will extend into the future, cost-benefit analysis is in the forecasting game. Time horizons vary; criteria for selecting horizons are not easily evolved and applied. The physical life of the construction? The period during which it is certain to be of use? The amortization period? The period over which costs and revenue forecasts are likely to be within certain error limits? However derived (and it is often arbitrary), the answer is usually decades rather than years – both the Victoria Line and Channel Tunnel studies have taken the round figure of fifty years.

Two points are worth making. The first is that long-term forecasts become less certain the further away the time horizon lies; although there will be uncertainties relating to the first five years of a fifty-year forecast, they are likely to be insignificant compared to those of the last five years. This is compensated for if discounting is applied; the discounted, present-day value (PDV) of the last five years is insignificant. As Figure 10.1 shows, the PDV of a sum twenty-five years ahead is under 10 per cent of its monetary value, using a discounting rate of 10 per cent or over, and even a 5 per cent rate reduces it to around a quarter. The PDV of sums four or five decades away is thus so low that errors are virtually irrelevant. The Ministry of Transport Channel Link study allowed additional capital expenditure of around one million pounds for each of three years – years 12, 17 and 22. There is little point in arguing with these highly uncertain figures, because their effect upon the overall results, in PDV terms, is negligible (less than 0.5 per cent).

For this reason, it is a joke to say cost-benefit analysis is in the forecasting game. Logically, it is; in practice, the forecasts used seem to be minimal, both in extent and quantity. The general basis is extrapolation of trends (in, for example, airline and cross-Channel traffic), combined with a fair amount of guesswork. Not that the more 'sophisticated' forecasting

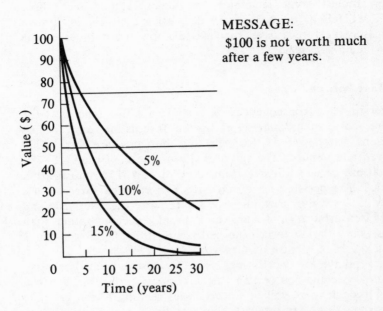

FIGURE 10.1   The Present-day Value of $100 Discounted at 5%, 10%, 15% p.a. after 1–30 Years

techniques are necessarily any better. But it does seem that cost-benefit analysis studies are not seriously interested in forecasting – in looking at changes in patterns over the decades they consider. To give but one example: the Victoria Line study argued that, by attracting travellers from road transport to the underground, conditions for the remaining road travellers would improve, and thus they would have a benefit clocked up to them. This makes sense – for the short term. But what of the long term? That underground passengers might note this improvement, and be attracted back to the roads; and that the road position could thus be helped in becoming yet worse than it was in the first place? If one is seriously interested in the next fifty years, this point should have been seriously considered. As also should other possible changes, some of which could potentially render the Line obsolete and thus turn it from an economic advantage to something London is lumbered with.

Technology assessment comes across as being much more

bothered with the changes in future patterns. The whole of the MITRE and Taylor studies, for instance, concentrate upon likely future developments and impacts. It seems that cost-benefit analysis has little to teach technology assessment on this subject; if anything, cost-benefit analysis has something to learn.

3) Fiscal statements

Even if the purely fiscal balance sheet is not of paramount importance in a project, it is nonetheless bound to be of some relevance to a cost-benefit analysis study. One key problem is likely to be the trustworthiness of the estimates involved; examples of cost over-runs are common, with Concorde, the RB211 engine and the nuclear power programme as well-known instances. Several studies reveal other examples. Estimates of revenues may also be dubious; 'Corfam' sales revenue is a well-known commercial instance. The moral could be that final cost-benefit analysis conclusions should be tested for sensitivity to such possible erroneous estimates; if sensitivity is high, there could be a problem which may or may not be solved through discussion with the source of the financial forecasts. Alternatively, or additionally, deliberate 'exaggeration' of the estimates may be tried; the Ministry of Transport added around 50 per cent to the civil engineering cost estimates of the Channel Link promotion groups.

Unfortunately there is a problem for cost-benefit analysis here: do the fiscal price statements correspond to the 'real' costs involved? If they differ, 'shadow prices' may be called in. If one of the inputs to a government project is imported, for instance, should the import duty be included in the cost of that input? If the landed price of a consignment of raw cotton is 1000 rupees, but it carries a duty of 20 per cent, should the cost-benefit analysis take the figure of 1000 or 1200 rupees? The common answer (for example Little and Mirrlees, 1969) is that 'one should ignore duties and purchase taxes' (unless they reflect deliberate government policy to (dis)encourage the use of certain imports), the reason being that what is important (in a public cost-benefit analysis) is the cost to the economy. Regardless of the level of the import duty, the foreign exchange cost is the same. Thus, here, the shadow price would be 1000 rupees (before any other, similar corrections were made). The idea of shadow-pricing applies not only to imports, but also to exports and to goods and services traded entirely within the country. The 'cost' of labour can form a thorny problem, especially when there is high unemployment.

The point is, then, that fiscal statements are relevant in cost-benefit analysis studies, and that corrections may be needed to the figures provided. Is this relevant to technology assessment?

The errors in costing applications of established technologies are generally much lower than those found in costing the kind of project susceptible to technology assessment; indeed, costing such items as manned space stations or ocean farming may be virtually impossible. On the other hand, this point is not important to some views of technology assessment: the commercial viability of projects will be looked after by industry, and the assessor should keep to the 'secondary' aspects – the consequences. Thus it would be surprising to find a technology assessment study in which the balance sheet was important, let alone corrections to it.

4) Identification of consequences

This is where the more interesting problems begin. How is one to identify, initially in qualitative terms, the consequences of a project? There is no simple answer, either in general or even as regards many specific projects. It is in fact hard to see how one would produce a model of change (of the consequences) which, while being generalized and thus applicable to many very different situations, still generated a list of all the consequences in a given situation – what would happen, to which parties, when? 'Automated' identification of consequences is just not on. Possible considerations in identifying consequences include:

(a) *Political*. There are projects which, during the mid-1960s in Britain, would have been seen as having one very important consequence: helping the British balance of payments. The impact upon imports of a mining project, for instance, would have been one of its major aspects. The balance could be reversed: environmental aspects might gain in importance, balance of payments lose importance. The project itself need not change; what is viewed as important about it has changed. Again, the Third London Airport Enquiry could not afford to brush aside the noise issue, because of the apparent public concern with noise; however, the impact of the new airport upon income distribution or upon employment of migrant labour was not featured in the enquiry. This is nothing to do with the physical facts of the issue; it is to do with politics.

The same clearly applies to technology assessment. That the electric car is seen as having an impact upon pollution and fossil fuel usage is because of the political/moral perception of the pollution/health issue, and the depletion of fuel reserves which may be needed by later generations. The impact of communications satellites upon developing countries is important to one group because they see it as important, while it is not so important to the politically/socially defined role of the British Post Office. Indeed, the very existence of cost-benefit analysis and technology assessment has a political overtone; the questions it poses are seen as worthy of attention. What is important in any instance is to be clear about the political values involved.

It is worth making the point that these political considerations make it all the harder to devise a general model or framework which will direct the search for the 'right' consequences; such consequences are not necessarily to be defined by objective means. 'Will independent scientific study groups in different [U.S. Government] agencies using the same methodology and science come to the same conclusions [on any given technology]?' (Carpenter, 1972).

(b) *Formal theory.* This is deliberately placed after political considerations: the latter may influence the use of formal theory. The theory may be to do with things physical; if you build a dam there you will get a problem with silt, or if you stand in front of a micro-wave transmitter long enough you will die. Generally speaking, such physical components in an analysis are minimal; the Channel Bridge analysis was not concerned with the impact of the bridge supports on the water flow or the seabed; the study on eliminating syphilis was not interested in the medical aspects of the disease, etc. The big advantage of this category of consequence is that, in some respects, it is entirely apolitical and value-free. Whatever your politics, silting will occur, or a certain chimney will produce tons of sulphur dioxide. It may be useful to single out explicitly these consequences from the more value-laden category. At least, that makes sense super-ficially. But is this in fact true? Evaluating the consequences of the consequence – the consequences of the silting – may involve very definite value questions, as does the related activity of looking at silting in the first place. Conclusion: it is very easy to assume things physical to be purely physical when they are really very enmeshed in things political. The process is physical, its consideration is political.

Formal theory is more often called in on the socio-economic side. The effects of a project upon income distribution between regions or social classes may be explored through established economic theory (or, at least, techniques of analysis); sociological theory can indicate how an investment in a rural area will affect urban migration. The danger here is that of placing undue trust in some of this body of social knowledge, and the problem is that, in many cases, there is little theory to be drawn upon. There is, for example, a literature building up on the impact of alternative transport systems upon traveller behaviour, but it might be an exaggeration to describe it as forming a theory (see, for example, Harrison and Quarmby, 1973; Ray and Crum, 1963; Moses and Williamson, 1963; Foster, 1963).

(c) *Historical analogy* is rather a hobby-horse of Raymond Bauer (1969b) and Bruce Mazlish, both associated with the American Academy of Arts and Sciences. The Academy has used analogy in what could be described as a pilot technology assessment of the American space programme (Mazlish, 1965), in which a comparison was drawn with the development of the American railways. As they point out, analogy is useful in generating hypotheses about potential consequences (for which science fiction has also been tried), as a 'source of general state-ments about social affairs' (if used with extreme caution), and, lastly and slightly differently, as a means of communicating. (Do such advocates tend to forget that applying formal theory to a situation is but to make an analogy between it and, on the other hand, many similar situations whose characteristics are summarized in the theory?)

(d) *Imagination.* 'The actual anticipation of a specific future state that may follow from a given technological change is a work of imagination' (Raymond Bauer, 1969b). This is perhaps the most important point in this section, given the state of alternative means of identifying consequences. Three sentences hardly do justice to this point – but perhaps several pages would not either.

(e) *Asking people.* At one level, this simply means that the analyst seeks views from his colleagues, and makes use of their experience. It can also mean approaching a wider range of people (most likely experts) working in other organizations, but in an equally unstructured manner.

This also means a formal approach to larger groups, such as those people likely to be influenced by the development. Survey research and sociology have a wide range of tools to offer, including surveys based on questionnaires (as used by Roskill, for instance) or, as used in some large construction or mining projects in developing countries, commissioning field studies by sociologists and anthropologists. In 1970, the U.K. Ministry of Technology drew up a series of questions to use in evaluating major projects. The list included the following (selected to serve as illustrations):

> Would your project – if carried through – promise benefits to the community, and if so, what are these benefits, how will they be distributed and to whom and when would they accrue?
>
> What disadvantages would you expect might flow from your work; who would experience them; what, if any, remedies would correct them; and is the technology for correcting them sufficiently advanced for the remedies to be available when the disadvantages began to accrue?
>
> If your proposition is accepted what other work in the form of supporting systems should be set in hand simultaneously, either to cope with the consequences of it, or to prepare for the next stage and what would that next stage be?
>
> If an initial decision to proceed is made, for how long will the option to stop remain open and how reversible will this decision be at progressive stages beyond that?

The actual approaches used to identify likely impacts vary considerably. The assessment of manned space stations, for instance, is strongest in discussing impacts on affairs closely related to the possible activities of such stations: astronomy, physics, bioscience, oceanography, industrial applications, etc., all items which would come to mind to anyone acquainted with the literature. Items more removed from the stations (housing, transport, etc.) form a more random list whose basis is unclear and they are discussed only briefly; equally plausible items (educational teaching aids, mechanical engineering) are not mentioned. Bowers uses an historical analogy to suggest band allocation problems for microwave, and other literature to reveal a possible health hazard. The MITRE studies employ literature searches and interviews, together with a hefty sprinkling of imagination.

Unfortunately, the cost-benefit literature does not have much to add to this qualitative side. London's Third Airport is obviously going to affect actual and potential travellers, those people living near the airport, the airlines and auxiliary services, and 'the public at large'. The Channel Tunnel will influence travellers again; while eliminating syphilis has a bearing on doctors, patients and time lost by suffering employees of companies. If anything, the cost-benefit literature is less impressive in this particular respect than is that on technology assessment.

What can be done to improve this situation; to improve the ease of identifying consequences? Firstly, we might try to establish the merits of present approaches – are literature searches and imagination, for instance, all that bad as an approach? (Assuming, that is, that enough people have access to the reasoning and conclusions, and thus, to a greater or lesser extent, place assessment in the political bargaining arena.) Secondly, we can forget ideas of 'automated' methodologies, meaning a methodology in which you basically insert the problem in question, and out come the answers. If we accept this, we should beware of the danger of spending much time and money on seeking the impossible. Lastly, it is difficult to see short-cuts to greatly improved methodology; one can expect a 'natural evolution' as, bit by bit, more knowledge is acquired on how society and technology are related, leading slowly to better forecasting and consequences. Recent events have shown the dangers of seeing model building as such a short-cut – the (implicit) hope that, if numbers are inserted into guesses and hypotheses and then fed into machines, they will produce a representation of the real world, which will enable identification of the effects of changes.

For details of the present state of the art in forecasting, the reader should turn to the other chapters in this part of the book. Their message is not reassuring: formal techniques, such as Delphi, extrapolation, modelling, etc., will not provide accurate and trustworthy pictures of the future which would follow from stated decisions or events. This reinforces the need for exposure of reasoning and conclusions to as wide and as heterogeneous an audience as possible.

Lastly, we have the further issue of whether an item should be counted as a cost if it *could* be averted. Example: a project brings a benefit to one group (such as mechanical potato digging to farmers) while bringing a cost to another (those displaced, unemployed farm workers). On balance, is the change for the better or the worse? There is the argument that, if the benefit is so great that the gainers *could* afford to compensate the losers, the change is for the good. A controversy exists over whether this ability has to be realized or not, a controversy perhaps not entirely devoid of political content.

In conclusion: Until forecasting techniques improve, both cost-benefit analysis and technology assessment can have only limited trustworthiness. A suggestion worth considering is that a hindsight study be done on big projects (e.g. construction projects), to take the consequences anticipated by the original advocates of the project, and see if things turned out as expected. A number of interesting lessons could be learnt from such a review.

5) Distinguishing costs from benefits

The point here is that costs and benefits are not necessarily 'objective' terms, but value-laden. To good, liberal, enlightened citizens, eliminating syphilis would be a good thing – a benefit. It would not be impossible to find people who regard it as a bad thing – who see syphilis as the Just Outcome for doing Wicked Things. It would be easier to find people who regarded aborting an unwanted pregnancy as an even worse move than eliminating syphilis. What is good and what is bad is subjective; what is a benefit and what is a cost is subjective.

The economics literature would not be a good place for deciding such issues, which is perhaps why there is little discussion of the issue there. Technology assessors would be equally ill-advised to answer the question. But, on the other hand, if a study is to proceed, items must be classified and, in the vast majority of cases, it seems there is little disagreement between authors, decision-makers and that part of the public joining in the discussions (which is not to say that major arguments do not arise over which items to include and how they should be weighted). Nonetheless, problems do arise. Steiner (1959) wrote about 'Choosing among alternative public investments in the water resources field'. One of his basic premises is that, when government does a job which could be done by the private sector, there is automatically a cost involved; public projects 'displace' private projects, involving 'the loss of those public benefits that would arise through private endeavour'. Our complaint – if we complain – cannot be about the introduction of values, but only about those specific values being reflected. It is also worth noting that what is to be regarded as a benefit at one point in time may be seen as a cost at another point. Cars were a benefit when they reduced the health hazard from horses in urban areas; they are now seen as a cost by many groups. Again, multi-storey car parks are perhaps a net benefit to the community now, but will they still be so in fifty years' time if their highly strengthened building blocks turn out to be virtually impossible to demolish? Another example: take the view that one of the major sources of income redistribution in developing countries is theft. Is an improvement in the police force, which reduces the theft rate, to be regarded as a cost or as a benefit? (For whom are you doing the assessment?)

6) Quantification

For cost-benefit analysis, the consequences of the project having been identified, have to be measured in terms of a common unit. Many different units could be used, ranging from arbitrary 1 to 10 scales for rating consequences, to possible changes induced in birth and death rates, or anything else which could be bent to form a measuring unit for a given situation. The unit generally – perhaps always – taken is called money; it has the advantages of meaning something to people, of having ordinate properties (or, at least, so it is usually assumed), and of already being used to measure some characteristics of countless diverse objects. It remains an open question whether money is necessarily the best measure in all cases; alternatives may be worthy of consideration in some instances. For example, some (non-cost-benefit analysis) studies are using energy as their unit.

A related point is the argument that, to compare items, they must be expressed in the same unit – you cannot compare apples with oranges, and things can be as different as chalk from cheese. All this is blatant nonsense. Among a small sample of respondents, all were perfectly capable of making a choice between various quantities of apples and oranges, and only one stated a preference for chalk over cheese. The serious point is that it is not necessary to provide an explicit common unit to those people one is asking to make choices; indeed, the political process is largely to do with such choice situations. Thus, although units should perhaps be kept to a minimum, it would seem sense for cost-benefit studies to contemplate other units, such as jobs produced, energy consumed, or quantities of food arriving at the market. Sometimes items will start in a quantified form; for instance, construction costs or sales revenues. These have already been mentioned.

How far can technology assessment follow cost-benefit analysis in quantification – a path which many technology assessment advocates recommend? How successful is cost-benefit analysis itself in quantification?

Key theoretical concepts in cost-benefit quantification are the 'consumer surplus' and 'willingness to pay'. These say that, if you are willing to pay (say) $100 for a goods or service, and you are charged only $60, you are gaining; you have a surplus of $40. That you are, in principle, willing to pay $100 may have been borne out by that having been the previous price, which has been reduced, perhaps as the result of an investment in new plant by the supplier. Thus we have a way of measuring the minimum benefit of a change in price; it is a benefit in that the reduction releases funds for spending or investing elsewhere.

The problems of applying this approach may explain why it is rarely used in practice, even if often referred to. Estimating the price people are willing to pay is sometimes hard, sometimes virtually impossible; how much would domestic consumers be willing to pay for their water, for instance? Secondly, the derived minimum benefit may bear little resemblance to other estimates; that a couple may pay $1 a month on contraceptives may certainly prove that the disbenefit of an unwanted child is more than the $1 a month – but how much more? Again, the 1972–3

outcry against museum and art gallery admission charges implied
– using this specific argument – that such facilities have (nearly)
zero value to certain groups. Lastly, little idea may emerge
regarding which groups benefit – is it the rich or the poor, for
instance? A national reduction in the price of milk will produce
a computable minimum consumers' surplus (i.e. surplus in
relation to the previous price); how is this surplus spread over
the population? Note also that measuring impacts does not
necessarily imply a need for a qualitative picture to come first –
unlike the impression probably conveyed by the previous section.
Quantification may be possible without complete previous
qualification.

There is at least one other conceptual advantage of the consumers' surplus: that releasing funds for use elsewhere is, in
itself, a benefit. This aspect can be elaborated on by considering
opportunity costs, something rarely tackled in technology assessment studies in any systematic manner. An assessment of manned
space stations, for instance, should try to examine not only the
value of the project sub-components (such as the various classes
of research which could be undertaken in space), but also the
value of the overall project and components in comparison to
other possible ways of spending funds. This is certainly not an
easy undertaking. A possible defence is that technology assessment is mainly concerned with identifying the undesirable
consequences (and the means of controlling them), as market
forces will ensure the eventual appearance of many of the
benefits. Is this true in a government-financed space programme?

There are, of course, many other ways of measuring benefits.
Intermediate units may be employed (working hours lost through
illness or gained through travel, for instance) and then expressed
in money terms. But if a journey takes half an hour rather than
a full hour, is an employee going to do an extra half-hour's work,
or will he stay in bed longer? And is 10,000 people saving half
an hour equivalent to 5000 having a full hour? (A literature is
slowly building up on this issue of travel time.) Social surveys
have been used to help quantify certain costs. The Roskill
Commission wanted to know about the costs involved through
airport noise driving residents away from the area. The loss to
the household caused by moving elsewhere was taken as '(a)
estimated depreciation of their property, plus (b) removal

expenses, plus (c) "consumers' surplus"'. Problem: how to measure the consumers' surplus? (Meaning that, if the house cost $10,000 initially, but the new owners would have been willing to pay $12,000, the surplus is $2000). The Roskill solution was to ask the following question of residents: 'Suppose your house was wanted to form part of a large development scheme and the developer offered to buy it from you, what price would be just high enough to compensate you for leaving this house and moving to another area?'

The question could well be taken to imply a small development (a supermarket?), and so moving 'to another area' could mean the other side of town. Does it imply finding a new school, new shopping centres, and perhaps even a new job? Secondly, is there any similarity between talking to an interviewer (note: 'your *house*') and haggling with a developer when you are about to be evicted (when it becomes 'my *home*')? The problems of surveys are well-known, it being suggested that bad surveys substitute collective ignorance for personal ignorance.

A final – and, say some, the most damning – comment on cost-benefit quantifications is that, despite the protests to the contrary, they tend not to quantify many important consequences of changes. A study of the impact of mechanized potato digging ignored the fact that the innovation displaced one-third of the workforce (over eight years) from the land, and they were not a group which easily found work elsewhere. A similar study of the U.S. cotton picking scene ignored the same problem – the displaced workers. If such major items are totally ignored, the conclusions of the analysis may be highly suspect; major omissions should be brought to the user's attention.

7) Weighting

Little need be said about this. The various costs and benefits may have already been (implicitly) weighted in previous stages; they may not have been. Points could be made about, for instance, the need to ensure that, if different projects are being compared, the same items are given the same weighting when they arise. But in the context of technology assessment, the point to make is that the weighting reflects, once more, political values.

8) Adding the costs and adding the benefits

Little need be said on this. If all the items in each category (cost or benefit) are expressed in the same unit (namely, money), and the unit is assumed to have ordinate properties, then the addition must have arithmetic validity.

One can observe that the totals may well be of less importance than the items making them up. That the total net benefit of eliminating syphilis is estimated at $3.1 billion may be important to a decision-maker; he should also have made clear to him that one item constitutes 40 per cent of the benefit, that item being elimination of the 'stigma' associated with the disease. Also the question was raised above about whether decision-makers can, after all, add apples to oranges.

9) Discounting

The principle of discounting is that money received now is worth more than the same sum received in the future. Two related reasons justify this. One is that $100 received now could be invested and thus changed to, say, $121 in two years' time; the alternatives one would be indifferent to are $100 now or $121 in 1977. The second reason is that consumption now is preferable to the same consumption in the future (and, in some economic theory, the interest paid to savers – the $21 in this case – is the reward, the compensation, for postponing consumption).

The consequences of discounting are problematic; what bearing does it have on technology assessment, in either a conceptual or even quantitative respect? The two main problems, for our purposes, are: (a) What kind of item can be reasonably discounted? (b) The strong, resulting bias towards the present day and away from the future.

I would prefer $10 in 1976 to $10 in 1977; I would prefer $10 worth of pram in 1976 to $10 worth of pram in 1977 – if I could promptly sell it for that sum; as a non-parent, I would find $10 worth of pram which was not convertible to cash (or other goods or services) a downright burden at the moment; by 1977, there is a chance that it will be just what I need. The conclusion is that, if an item cannot be converted to cash, I may prefer to *postpone* consumption. A favourite illustration of some economists concerns Robinson Crusoe on his economically isolated island. Under some circumstances, Crusoe would indeed prefer 100 barrels of wheat now to the same 100 next year; if, however, he was unable to store the wheat in satisfactory conditions, he might rather postpone consumption of at least part of it for the year. A more cost-benefit orientated instance is the validity of discounting passenger 'comfort and convenience' or discounting the 'pain and discomfort' associated with syphilis (which was discounted at 4 per cent p.a.) (Muskin, 1971). The fact that analysts can put a money value on such items does not mean that they can be discounted with meaning.

The other related point concerns the relative weight of the future as against the present. Taking the weighting implied by discounting to its extreme, future events would have no present-day value – so why bother to look ahead? This is counter to the whole concept of assessment and the anticipation of possible future costs and benefits. This may help explain the virtually total blank on discounting in the technology assessment literature.

The National Academy of Sciences report (1969) comments: 'In the consideration of costs and benefits, [studies] ascribe too little significance to the preservation of future options.' This is a key point, and has already been discussed.

10) Comparing costs with benefits

If the benefits outweigh the costs, the project is worth undertaking. There is only one important qualification; are the available funds unlimited? Clearly, not all projects can – in practice – be afforded, and so a minimum level of benefit (perhaps a minimum benefit-cost ratio) is required. (This assumes that opportunity costs have not been fully incorporated into the analysis.) It may not be possible to complete the comparison, because some items may remain unquantified or, at least, not quantified in money terms. The decision-maker has to weigh them up for himself.

The comparison may not be relevant to technology assessment if the exercise was deliberately biased towards the undesirable consequences.

11) Selling the results:

This is not an aspect generally considered in evaluating methodologies. Nonetheless, we can assert the importance of using a methodology which permits the conclusions to be sold to the audience. The analysis must reach, and be understood by, the people for whom it is intended. Otherwise the exercise will verge on being a waste of time and resources. How the two techniques compare, we can only speculate; so can others.

The extent of the impact should not be over-anticipated. As Carpenter says of his context, Congress wants information, not advice; and certainly not analysts who may presume to have demonstrated what the 'correct' decision should be. Neither technology assessment nor cost-benefit analysis are decision-making procedures; they are inputs.

Chapter 11

Survey Research and Psychological Variables

Survey techniques

This chapter sets out to analyse the contribution that survey research may make to long-term forecasting, especially where it is applied to the study of such psychological variables as values, aspirations, attitudes, beliefs and expectations. While such variables are often conceded to be of great significance to forecasting – whether as the causes of social or technological change, as intervening influences which may interact with, and perhaps shape the course of, some plan or development, or as important aspects of the outcome of social change, planned or unplanned – little use has so far been made of existing research dealing with them.

The origin of much futures research and many futures researchers in technological forecasting has probably been partly responsible for a casual attitude to social science data. Social factors are fluid and evasive, unlike the solid and objective products of technology. Such an attitude is not only a poor basis for forecasts of the future of social institutions; even forecasts of the development of U.S. space technology have been repeatedly invalidated by changes in public opinion and policy towards space exploration. The role of human values and aspirations is an essential factor to be included in a complete analysis of the futures of a social system.

Mainstream social scientists themselves have done little to alter this state of affairs, although a few useful contributions have been made. (The annotated bibliography by Huber, 1971, is a convenient guide to sociological sources.) Social scientists may be deterred by the downgrading of social factors in much of the forecasting literature, as well as by the somewhat naive use of forecasting methods best suited for limited predictions of technological change when all other factors stay constant. Thus trend extrapolation is a potentially misleading exercise when applied to even such 'hard' social variables as population size and composition, as the history of demography shows. Again, Delphi procedures when applied to forecasting scientific and technological developments rely upon the judgment of experts who are often involved in making these developments happen: there are no social experts in this sense – certainly academics are not such experts! – and the use of Delphi in social forecasting is likely merely to distil journalistic impressions about social change in the élites consulted. A further reason inhibiting social science's contributions to futures research is the relatively closed disciplinary nature of much social research, when forecasting calls for the synthesis of perspectives from many disciplines.

Survey research is a particularly useful tool of the social scientist. Its distinctive feature is the simultaneous focus upon both the individual and the population from which he is drawn. Survey research usually deals with a sample drawn so as to represent the population of interest, whether this be an entire nation or some particular group in a society. (Discussions of sampling methods are presented in such texts as Moser and Kalton, 1971, and Hyman, 1955.) By sampling from an entire population it may counterbalance the focus of the media and élite opinion on the most newsworthy attitudes and trends in a population.

Of course, survey research is not a forecasting technique in its own right. Some attempts have been made to gauge public views of the future; for example Abrams (1971) describes a study in which a Dutch sample was asked how likely and how desirable it was felt to be that each of nineteen possible social changes would occur within the next decade. It was generally expected that most of these changes would come about, which is not surprising since these were mostly merely continuations of present trends or images of the future prominent in the mass media, such as more leisure and easier divorce. However, the reduction of social class differences, the change felt to be desirable by the largest proportion of people, was one item about which there was considerable disagreement concerning its likelihood. Abrams concludes that the Dutch appreciate improvements in their living standards, but are concerned about lack of progress and possible deterioration, or at least persistence, in conditions of pollution, inequality, political alienation, etc.; he also finds working-class Dutch respondents to be relatively more pessimistic, defeatist and frustrated. A similar survey carried out in Britain (Research Services Ltd., 1970) revealed a general expectation of increasing affluence and technological progress but also of deteriorating moral and environmental standards over the following fifteen years. Upper-class and élite respondents tended to be more pessimistic concerning the former type of change, and more optimistic concerning the latter.

These surveys have more to say about the dynamics of public opinion than about the future, although some useful information arises from them. For example, it is clear that these publics have been led to expect continuing material affluence, and it is thus possible to speculate about consequences of a cessation of economic growth. The social class differences point to a differential experience of social trends in different parts of society, and also to the existence of alternative mental models of past and future social change. Understanding of such models should throw light on public demands for, and reactions to, particular policies.

Survey research typically suffers from a number of limitations, however, which must be overcome if it is to be of maximum use to forecasters. These may be described as the limitations of history, geography and psychology. Firstly, as with many areas of social science, there is little time-series data available. The relative recency of survey methods makes it difficult to find information on public attitudes and behaviour extending more than a few years into the past. Much research deals with transitory issues and is never replicated: even when similar issues have been investigated at different times there has often been no attempt to employ comparable instruments or samples. Thus much information is strictly limited to a particular occasion, and the stability of the relationships reported may be open to question – for example, the public views of the future reported above may be peculiar to the current decade. It is to be hoped that more longitudinal data will become available as research is replicated more often and as computer technology makes possible more sophisticated data storage, retrieval and analysis. Such comparative research is likely to be stimulated by volumes such as that in which Hyman (1972) sets out principles of secondary analysis of surveys.

The limitations of geography are also cultural limitations. Most research is conceived by and carried out on Westerners, with American sources predominating. This is true of most of the work reviewed in this chapter. Conclusions based on such a small sample of humanity may have no significance at all for other societies and members of other cultures. Again, there are signs that this situation may be remedied, for in recent years a number of journals devoted to comparative and cross-cultural studies have appeared, as have textbooks in various disciplines. At present, however, cross-cultural replications are rare, and typically confined to a small range of issues; the origins of much social theory in the United States are likely to continue to flavour the social sciences for a long time.

The third type of limitation is a matter of psychological depth and of artificial rather than naturalistic methods of investigation. Psychological variables are notoriously difficult to measure, so that there are difficulties in distinguishing between a person's central and relatively stable values and beliefs and his more superficial and transitory opinions and responses, and there may be problems in relating verbal reports of attitudes to a person's actual behaviour in real-life situations. Most of the research reported here has been carried out using structured interviews, the data from which are basically the respondent's answers to a number of prepared questions posed by a trained interviewer. While a strong case for greater use of non-verbal and unobtrusive approaches in social research has been made (e.g. Webb *et al*, 1966), use of such techniques has been restricted for reasons of convenience and conservatism; thus studies relying on such approaches are mostly exploratory. Once more it may be optimistically reported that there are signs of growing discontent with this state of affairs, but at present most research employs verbal assessment of attitudes with little attempt to validate these reports against behaviour in everyday situations.

In this chapter the potential contributions of survey research to social forecasting will be illustrated with reference to four main approaches to forecasting: extrapolative and statistical analysis, the location of structural regularities and constancies, formal modelling of social systems, and the assessment of the impacts of predicted social and technical change. Examples are chosen so as to demonstrate something of the range of available material, rather than to build up a scenario of the social future or exhaustively review the place of survey research in the social sciences. Nor is there any attempt to argue that survey research is the only valid way of indexing psychological states. Content analysis, for example, has been used extensively and creatively as in McClelland's studies of achievement motivation, culture, and economic development (McClelland, 1961) and Namenwirth's study of trends in political values in America, which includes some interesting forecasts (Namenwirth, 1973). However, the documentary material that forms a basis for content analysis is generally only representative of a select portion of any society. The same criticism may be levelled against attempts to index a population's 'mood' by social indicators based upon aggregate data (such as suicide or crime rates).

Extrapolative and statistical forecasting

Statistical approaches to forecasting are basically extrapolations, continuations of present trends (see, for example, de Hoghton et al, 1971). Sophisticated forms of curve-fitting may be employed to take into account the fact that accelerating growth rarely proceeds unchecked for long periods: the S-curve, for example, takes into account the damping and levelling off of many growth processes. Survey data are rarely extensive enough to permit any detailed extrapolation; the shortage of longitudinal research has been remarked upon above. Some topics have, however, been the subject of surveys since the early developments of the technique. These are often related to social problems or continuing controversies, and for some such topics fairly frequent replications have been performed.

Schwartz (1967) analyses surveys carried out over a span of

twenty-three years concerning the attitudes of U.S. whites towards black people. Her book is noteworthy not only for these secondary analyses and the conclusions reached about trends in attitudes, but also for its venture into social forecasting. Taking eleven attitude questions which were repeatedly asked over the period 1942–1965, and where possible studying the responses obtained in different social groups (classified according to region and educational level), she found that most measures revealed a linear trend towards a greater proportion of respondents expressing unprejudiced attitudes about negroes. On this basis she engaged in an imprecise extrapolation of each trend in order to predict the year in which 90 per cent of each white social group will have adopted an unprejudiced attitude.

In the absence of time-series data, some authors have attempted to extrapolate from cross-sectional analysis of data gathered at one time only. Differences between age groups may provide a basis for prediction, with it being assumed that the characteristics of younger people will predominate as older members of the population are replaced by younger members; the underlying assumption is that differences observed at one time between age groups reflect stable features of the individuals concerned, rather than particular moments in a process of maturation or change in these features over the life cycle. This assumption may finally be validated only against truly longitudinal evidence, although it may be buttressed by theory, laboratory experiment, or research into social change conducted with techniques other than surveys.

Inglehart (1971) provides an interesting example of this mode of analysis. He hypothesizes that individuals whose childhood is spent in periods of hardship and war will tend to be relatively more concerned with ensuring that their basic material requirements are securely met, while those who grow up in periods of security and affluence will be less troubled by fears of hardship and relatively more concerned with creating suitable conditions for personal growth and self-expression. This is loosely derived from Maslow's (1954) notion of a hierarchical structure of human needs, in which five levels of need are distinguished, ranging in order from physiological, safety, social, and ego, to self-actualization needs. (More broadly, the lower stages of the hierarchy are termed deficiency needs, the later levels abundance or growth needs.) Maslow postulates that the emergence of concern with a need depends largely upon the degree to which prior needs have been satisfied, and that neither needs of levels higher than those at which dissatisfaction is felt, nor lower satisfied needs, are motivators.

Inglehart relates these need levels to political values, stressing safety or individual expression, and operationalizes these in a very direct manner by presenting a choice of two out of four political goals: maintaining law and order, fighting rising prices, giving people more say in decisions, and protecting freedom of speech. Respondents selecting the first two items were labelled 'acquisitive', those selecting the last two 'post-bourgeois'. Surveys carried out in six Western European countries confirmed his predictions: younger people, brought up in more secure and prosperous times, are more likely than older people to make post-bourgeois choices. This is particularly true for the youngest age-cohort, reared entirely in the post-war era, and for countries where economic growth has been greatest since the 1940s. Least intergenerational difference is found in Britain, the country with the lowest rate of growth in this period. Inglehart devotes little effort to formal projections from his data, but concludes that, assuming stability of values, the post-bourgeois proportions of the populations will be as large as the acquisitive proportions within two decades in Continental Europe and three decades in Britain.

These two examples of extrapolative social forecasting based upon survey data raise a number of general issues about both forecasting and survey research. Extrapolation of a trend or supposed trend requires some model of the processes giving rise to that trend: to extrapolate without setting out a model is essentially to adopt a model of that trend as being in some way self-reinforcing and generative of its own momentum. Of more use is a statement of circumstances under which the trend may or may not be expected to continue, of factors which maintain or alter its direction and pace. In survey research it may be useful, for example, to compare trends in different populations or sub-groups exposed to different conditions, to study deviations from an established trend and to look for deviations where they might be predicted on the basis of associated social change, and to compare trends in measures tapping different aspects of a phenomenon.

Schwartz's study provides information relevant to these points. For example, she finds that opinion changes are cumulative over the period studied rather than widely fluctuating in response to immediate events. This finding is supported by later work; for example, Greeley and Sheatsley (1971) found the trend towards increasing white acceptance of blacks to be continuing, and not to have been affected by the racial strife of the late 1960s. Schwartz ascribes these trends to a cumulative process of liberalizing policy decisions, stronger black demands, and increased contact on a basis of equality between races. Psychological theories of attitude consistency imply that as such contact breaks down racial stereotypes, related attitudes will change; this implication receives empirical support from the work of Pettigrew (1969), who finds that Americans (of both races) who have experienced such contact are more favourable towards integration. Schwartz reports that Southerners, living in a culture where opportunity for contact as equals is not high, were consistently more prejudiced than comparable Northerners. In other comparisons of population sub-groups it is found that in each period the younger and the better-educated respondents tend to be less prejudiced: the relationship of education to tolerance is most marked among Southerners. Some of the trends reported may, then, be accounted for by increasing educational levels and the displacement of older, more prejudiced individuals whose stereotypes have never been seriously challenged.

Inglehart's use of a need-hierarchy model enables him to predict several differences that should emerge between populations and population sub-groups, although he is inferring dynamic changes from static information derived from the comparison of different age groups. While the national differences in divergence between age-cohorts are in the direction he predicts, it is easy to think of reasons for this divergence being least in Italy and Germany and greatest in Britain – for example, the war experience itself.

Turning to national population sub-groups, he finds that the relationship between age and acquisitive versus post-bourgeois value choice still exists within different income and educational attainment groups, supporting the idea of a general social trend. In each age group, people earning more are more likely to choose post-bourgeois goals, which would be expected on the basis of the close correlation between childhood affluence and later income; increased education is also associated with post-bourgeois values, even when income and age are controlled for, suggesting that education itself may have an impact upon the value choice. This latter possibility goes against need-hierarchy theory, but given rising education levels leads to the same conclusion: that post-bourgeois values will increase in prominence in the future.

Inglehart is in fact able to cite some time-series data supporting his case. In a series of surveys in Germany respondents were asked which of four freedoms they considered most important. From 1949 to 1963 the proportion choosing freedom from want decreased from 35 per cent to 15 per cent, while that choosing freedom of speech rose from 26 per cent to 56 per cent. However, while this is evidence for a trend taking place, this trend cannot be entirely accounted for by the replacement of older by younger people – indeed, rather than maturation producing a shift towards acquisitive values, some Germans appear to have moved towards post-bourgeois positions as they have aged.

This raises the question of just what verbal attitude and value measures are tapping, and comparison of a variety of measures which should be related to the same underlying phenomenon is valuable here. For example, this German evidence that a simple value choice reflects attitudes which may be quite malleable over time, rather than a deeply-rooted value posture deriving from childhood experience, is potentially of great significance. If post-bourgeois values are fairly stable and central to the individual, then Inglehart's projections would imply an increasingly non-materialistic society, incorporating much of today's 'New Left' and counter-culture; on the other hand, if the value choice represents no more than a superficial response, reflecting, perhaps, current fashion, then no such forecast may be made.

Rather than use other measures with direct bearing on value trends of the sort he hypothesizes, Inglehart relates his value choices mainly to other political attitudes. Post-bourgeois value choice was associated with support for student demonstrations, for radical social change, and for European integration, and with lack of support for strong national armies and other aspects of nationalism. Post-bourgeois respondents tended to be less concerned with job security, had expectations of high future standards of living, and showed greater degrees of loyalty or shift towards left-wing parties (depending, respectively, on whether they were or were not raised in families supporting these parties). In a study of a British sample, Marsh (to be published in 1975) investigated other characteristics of acquisitive and post-bourgeois respondents, and concluded that a need-hierarchy explanation is inadequate to account for his results. He found, for example, that post-bourgeois individuals tend to be more frustrated with deficiency aspects of their jobs (such as pay, security, and working hours), while more likely to agree that these are interesting and suited to them personally, which would be growth aspects. While these respondents reported themselves to be less satisfied with Britain's level of democracy than did others, and were also less satisfied with other growth features of community and society, they were also likely to desire relatively larger income increases, and to be less satisfied than others with deficiency aspects of life such as their standards of living and their jobs.

These findings raise doubts about the speculative scenarios that might be engendered by Inglehart's work, in which a materially satiated society is foreseen, emphasizing spiritual and expressive values. While a trend towards greater desires for self-expression and participation may at present be taking place in Europe, this does not seem to imply a permanent mass shift away from material concerns. Given the evidence on the malleability of the values Inglehart has tapped, it could be argued that an economic slump would reverse this trend rather rapidly, rather than through the lengthy process of socialization of new generations.

Schwartz employs a number of different measures of racist attitude in her study, and it is significant that some of these show quite divergent trends. Her projections indicate that questions concerning the intelligence and general civil rights of blacks are likely to be those for which 90 per cent of whites will report unprejudiced attitudes soonest. Attitudes which are connected with more concrete issues however, such as those reflecting willingness to live in a fully integrated community, are lagging behind. Indeed, an increase over time in the proportion of whites objecting to their children attending schools with mostly black pupils is apparent. While prejudice and stereotypes may be diminishing, it would be unwise to predict that discriminatory behaviour will likewise decrease; apart from institutionalized discrimination, it may be that other attitudes and beliefs (such as the desire to maintain property values and educational standards, and the belief that integration will make this more difficult) can outweigh the more abstract values of equality and justice for many individuals.

The issue of non-correspondence between attitude statements and actual behaviour is a troublesome one, but while great caution needs to be exercised in predicting the latter from the former, the apparent inconsistency of attitude and action may often be comprehensible and predictable. Campbell (1963) argues that this apparent inconsistency reflects the strength of one's attitude: different situations pose 'hurdles' of different heights concerning the expression of an attitude, and the stronger one's attitude, the higher are the hurdles that one may clear. Campbell reanalysed data collected in a study of white racism in a mining community, in which more whites were openly friendly to their black co-workers in the work situation than in town. He thus argues that the hurdle in town is higher, and that those who clear it have stronger pro-black attitudes; no inconsistency is present when viewed in this light, for those miners clearing the higher hurdle invariably also cleared the lower one. Hurdles may reflect social norms concerning the appropriateness of a given attitude, or other costs of a particular behaviour. Thus a white American may happily accept integrated public transport, as long as the service provided does not deteriorate, since it continues to satisfy his travel needs while being in line with his aspirations for lessened racial conflict and inequality. On the other hand, he may oppose the integration of his neighbourhood since these aspirations are outweighed by social pressures from his fellow residents and by fears of property depreciation. Fishbein (1967) has carried out extensive research testing a more formal theory based upon similar notions.

The problem of relating expressed attitudes, or even reports of one's intentions or behaviour, to behaviour at a later point, is an important one for the study of social futures, where we are likely to be concerned with both the experience and the action of individuals, and thus need to know how these relate under different circumstances. While observation of behaviour *per se* may be laborious and call for careful assessment of ethical issues, more could often be done in terms of cross-validation of measures, checks for internal consistency, and tests of the truthfulness of statements. An example of such comparison of self-reports with real performance is provided by Inkeles (1969a), in research dealing with individual modernization that will be described in more detail later. Verbal statements of one's educational attainments and use of the mass media were validated against tests of literacy and knowledge of characters currently in the news. The necessity to develop more sophisticated while widely applicable non-verbal measures presents a major challenge to survey research.

Lest the above strikes too pessimistic a note concerning verbal assessment of attitudes, the study of Brannon et al (1973) in which attitudes measured at one time were found to be strongly predictive of later behaviour, may be cited. It was found that questions concerning support for laws on housing discrimination, embedded in an hour-long interview covering many topics, elicited responses which for more than two-thirds of the sample were consistent with their action three months later. This action concerned the signing of petitions about the anti-discrimination laws, circulated by 'concerned citizens'; consistency was still present when individuals were further asked to agree to having their names published in press advertisements concerning the petition.

This review of two extrapolative studies based on survey material has demonstrated both the feasibility and some limitations of this approach. It is rare to encounter formal attempts at extrapolation of psychological variables. (Even Schwartz uses crude techniques of projection, assuming that linear trends will continue. This may be doubted since such trends are likely to be damped as the proportion of the population holding a particular attitude approaches 100 per cent. Some of the trends she considers are estimated from only two data points, which makes the assumption of linearity in these cases suspect. It may also be argued that when estimating trends in the total population, the best approach would be to compute the distribution of attitudes on the basis of a weighted sum of the trends within different social groups.) Where longitudinal evidence exists, it is often the case that trends in opinion and behaviour are by no means as clear cut as in the case of racist attitudes in the

U.S.A. For example, despite the popular notion of a secularization of modern society, no long-term decline in religious belief or in estimates of the influence of religion has been established in the U.S.A.; rather, a peak in the latter attitude seems to have been reached in the late 1930s (Demerath, 1968). Some reasons have been set out earlier in this chapter for expecting the quantity and quality of longitudinal survey research to increase in the future, whereupon it may be expected that such material will be increasingly applied to forecasting problems.

The identification of structural regularities

A second approach to social forecasting involves the extrapolation of relationships rather than trends. If relationships between variables, such as aspects of social structure and the prevalence of given attitudes or behaviour, repeatedly occur across a wide variety of social settings, then it is assumed that such relationships may continue to hold in future settings. As with trend extrapolation, this assumption requires the support of a model of the underlying processes. In social science it is rare to find a regularity with no deviating cases, and such exceptions provide valuable insights into the causal structure of a regularity and the degree to which it may still be apparent under different circumstances.

The course that social change takes in one aspect of society is usually dependent upon the stability or change of other aspects, so that the task of identifying regularities may be of great value to forecasting. The chief data requirement involved in such a task is the availability of survey material which is suitable for comparison of different cultures or times. Examples of this approach are described here; they are drawn from a review of studies of wants and aspirations, political attitudes and political behaviour, in order to investigate the contribution that this literature might make to social forecasting.

1) Happiness and satisfaction with life

A large number of studies carried out in various countries (all of which have had prolonged contact with Western civilization, however) point to the conclusion that the more privileged a respondent is, in terms of such attributes as education, income and occupational status, the more likely he is to report feeling happy, or more satisfied or less troubled with his life, than a less privileged respondent in the same country.

This conclusion was reached by Inkeles (1960), who compared survey results obtained from fifteen industrial countries. Respondents had been asked various questions, including the degree to which they felt happy, joyous, free of sorrow, or satisfied with the progress of their lives, how often they laughed, etc. In no case was the tendency for the more privileged to report more positive states reversed; the emergence of this consistent pattern, despite the variety of measures employed, strengthens the case for this relationship deserving the title of structural regularity. Many later studies support this generalization, with recent British and American studies exploring the use of alternative self-report indices of happiness and satisfaction (Abrams, 1973; Hall, 1973; Robinson, 1969).

The most systematic comparative study is presented by Cantril (1965), who applied the same interview procedure in fourteen countries. These countries varied in wealth from India and Nigeria to West Germany and the U.S.A., and also included four Latin American, two Eastern European, two Middle Eastern and two Far Eastern nations. Satisfaction was assessed using the 'Self-Anchoring Scale', in which the respondent is asked to indicate the rung he feels describes his position on an eleven-runged ladder of life, imagining that the top rung represents the best, and the bottom rung the worst possible life he might lead. In eleven countries where appropriate tabulations are given, socio-economic status and ladder ratings are clearly related in the expected direction; in twelve of thirteen cases (the exception being Nigeria) higher educational attainment is likewise linked to greater satisfaction.

This regularity may appear obvious in restrospect: perhaps one reason for little effort having been put into finding regularities is a fear of their proving 'obvious'. On the other hand,

Western élites look romantically to the simple and fulfilling pleasures of those who do not bear the white man's burden, and the wealthy assert that money can't buy happiness.

The regularity pinpointed above is open to two related misinterpretations. Firstly, since these relationships are based on cross-sectional data, they should not be viewed as necessarily paralleling dynamic relationships across time: it does not follow that because the wealthiest are at present most satisfied, then the average level of satisfaction will be increased by increasing the average level of wealth. This is illustrated by American data: Gurin et al (1960) report first an increase and then a decrease to a new low of avowed happiness over the period 1946–1957, and studies using the 'Self-Anchoring Scale' (Cantril and Roll, 1971; Watts and Free, 1973) reveal a similar fluctuation over the period 1959–1972. Secondly, the regularity refers to differences within nations, and it does not follow that when nations are compared the most privileged will possess the most satisfied inhabitants. Cantril (1965) does find a slight trend for wealthier countries to produce higher average satisfaction ratings. However, while statistically significant this trend is weak and less impressive than the within-nation trends; it is probably due to the presence of larger proportions of less privileged, less satisfied respondents in the poorer countries, where social inequalities are more marked. The distribution of wealth, as well as its absolute level, appears to be an important determinant of satisfaction within a society.

These findings give some clues as to the causal basis of this regularity. It certainly does not seem to be the case that satisfaction with life is simply a product of the degree to which a fixed set of needs has been met. These findings suggest instead that what Pettigrew (1967) calls social evaluation (man's tendency to evaluate himself and his condition by comparison with others) is involved here; thus a poor member of a wealthy society may be dissatisfied with a level of living that would represent an eminently satisfying achievement for someone from a poor country. The most familiar concept that has been employed to account for social evaluation processes is relative deprivation, a term introduced by Stouffer et al (1949). This refers to the state of somebody who finds that his attainment does not match up to the expectations he had formed for himself by comparing himself with a reference group or person. The concept was used to account for such puzzling findings as the discovery that more dissatisfaction was felt amongst a group of soldiers with a high promotion rate than amongst a group with a lower rate; it was argued that relative deprivation was experienced by the non-promoted members of the former group, who had higher expectations of promotion. This concept has been employed extensively, as Pettigrew's review shows. It may account for more detailed relationships between life satisfaction and privilege than those captured in the structural regularity, and thus point to situations in which this regularity might not persist. For example, Robinson (1969) reports studies indicating particularly high levels of happiness among wealthy individuals of low educational attainment – this may represent the effect of relative gratification, the opposite of relative deprivation. Kleiner and Parker (1969) found among respondents in Philadelphia that, within a given occupational group, those whose vocational level was lower than their parents' tended to place themselves on lower rungs of the ladder of life than others – this suggests that higher expectations derived from childhood had been frustrated for these individuals.

2) Economic wants and satisfactions

In the cross-national research of Cantril (1965), respondents were asked to state their hopes and fears for the future. It was striking that economic concerns predominated in each national sample. In each country the most privileged respondents were least likely to express such concerns, with poorer respondents mentioning them frequently. Many aspirations were found to be expressed in terms of hopes for more money: in poor nations money may be needed simply for food or education, while in rich nations aspirations are directed towards luxuries.

Further confirmation of greater economic concerns being felt among the less privileged comes from various sources. Katona, Strumpel and Zahn (1971) present the results of surveys carried out in four Western countries: there is a strong inverse relationship between one's actual income and the desire to work for more hours to earn more money. Studies in Britain (Abrams, 1973) and Chile, India and the U.S.A. (Fuchs and Landsberger, 1973) have investigated the relationship between respondents' incomes and their desires for additional incomes, as measured by asking questions concerning the amount extra that would be needed to live comfortably. In each case, poorer respondents are likely to desire a greater proportional increase than richer respondents.

Although poorer people want greater proportional increases, it is not necessarily true that they desire more in absolute money terms. Of the studies referred to, this is only true of the Indian sample. In Britain and the U.S.A., at least, the pattern seems to be for those with more income at present to desire most extra in absolute cash terms. Although a smaller percentage increase is wanted, aspirations are still greater than one's circumstances. In West Germany, Schmoelders and Biervert (1972) found, as they considered the household equipment of families of increasing wealth, that while wealthier families possessed more, and thus cited fewer items as necessary to attain their desired living standards, these standards also became progressively higher. Freedman (1972) reports on similar increasing consumption aspirations related to income level in a Taiwanese sample.

Taken together, these surveys portray a fairly consistent picture – a structural regularity of the less privileged feeling stronger economic wants than the more privileged in a society. There is meagre evidence for the notion that material desires may be satiated among the wealthy; however, although aspirations seem to be continually raised, it is the poorer people who are most concerned about their financial condition and who desire proportionally greater improvement and are more eager to work to attain this.

There is considerable evidence for the operation of social evaluation processes with respect to income satisfaction. Among the more notable findings are those of Bradburn and Caplovitz (1965) and Runciman (1966). The former authors found evidence that people with low incomes tended to be more dissatisfied if they lived in a prosperous rather than a poor community, while Runciman found that English manual workers earning relatively high wages were more satisfied than non-manual workers on similar incomes; thus people may choose to compare themselves against their neighbourhood or against those with similar occupations.

3) Other wants and satisfactions

While there is as yet no generally accepted taxonomy of human needs (indeed, if feelings of want can arise from social evaluation processes, it may be that such a taxonomy is unattainable in an empirical sense), a structural regularity may be identified for some non-economic aspirations, broadly grouped together. The more privileged members of societies tend to express stronger wants concerned with individual competence, of acquiring social status, political influence, and education for oneself and one's children.

The work of Cantril (1965) reveals a great degree of similarity between nations in the relative emphasis put upon different hopes and fears. In all national samples deficiency concerns predominate – economic hopes alone are mentioned by over 60 per cent of each sample – with the emphasis on financial security and maintaining good health. Concerns for one's family are next most frequent, followed by those relating to one's job and character. Among twelve countries for which data are available, social, political and international affairs are of least concern in ten cases. It seems that these latter only gain prominence when wider affairs are seen as engaging more personal interests, for the exceptions are countries which had recently undergone or were poised on the brink of major political change. When respondents were asked about hopes and fears for their nations, concerns for improved living standards were common in all countries, accompanied in many cases by hopes for technological advance, improved education and reduced unemployment. In the wealthier countries concerns about war and peace are frequent, and in some poorer countries agrarian reform and political instability are mentioned by many respondents.

Analysis of the distribution of concerns within nations reveals that in general more concerns are expressed by the more privileged, especially the more educated, members of a society, although economic concerns are more common among the less privileged, as has been described above. In particular, the more privileged express more hopes and fears for their nation, suggesting that these groups identify their own needs more closely with national affairs. Some of the evidence lends itself to interpretation in terms of a need-hierarchy model – in at least eight of eleven comparisons there are tendencies for the better-educated to display less concern about economic, health and job issues, and to have more hopes concerning family, political and social affairs – but the cross-sectional nature of the data, as well as the absence of clear-cut trends across nations, makes this doubtful.

Several studies of more restricted scope bear out the suggested regularity. Inglehart's (1971) work, described above, shows that in Western Europe the wealthier and better-educated are more likely to place issues of political freedom and participation above security and financial concerns. American surveys by Rokeach and Parker (1970) found that when respondents were asked to rank a set of values in order of importance, poorer respondents tended to assign relatively more importance to conformity, less to individual competence and self-expression. A poll taken by the Japanese Prime Minister's Office (no date) reveals that poorer Japanese are more concerned about poverty, housing shortages and household hardship, while wealthier respondents are more irritated by lack of leisure and uncomfortable aspects of industrial society such as crowding and pollution. Studies in various countries (e.g. Briones and Waisanen, 1966, in Chile; Kahl, 1968, in Brazil and Mexico; Rogers, 1969, in Colombia; Shubkin, 1966, in the U.S.S.R.) show that parents and children of higher social strata desire and expect greater educational attainment than less privileged respondents. Further evidence relating to these themes is presented by Inkeles (1960), who looks at cross-national survey evidence relating to parents' occupational aspirations for their children, to childrearing values, and to workers' attitudes towards various aspects of their jobs.

So far a case has been made for the existence of three structural regularities relating wants and satisfactions to social status. It is in order once more to warn against the inference of dynamic relationships from such cross-sectional results. For example, working-class people should not be expected necessarily to move towards middle-class values if they become affluent, as Goldthorpe et al (1969) have demonstrated. It is also in order at this point to emphasize the fact that while these regularities emerge from the data, they by no means provide a total account of the genesis of aspirations amongst a community. Although average levels of satisfaction are indeed higher among more privileged groups, there is much individual variation within each group. Studies of life satisfaction (Andrews and Withey, 1974; Hall, 1973) have shown that it is possible to account for a good proportion of the variance between individuals in their overall level of satisfaction in terms of a linear combination of levels of satisfaction with specific areas of life. Similarly a study of job satisfaction (Barnowe *et al*, 1972) reveals that while it is possible to predict an individual's level of satisfaction on the basis of his occupational status, much more of the variance in the data is accounted for by using measures of the quality of working conditions as predictors. What predictive power occupational status possessed was largely due to its association with these latter variables. It would seem useful for future investigations of structural regularities to investigate specific relative deprivation in relation to the social order.

4) Political beliefs and behaviour

The research to be briefly reviewed here takes as its focus political attitudes and behaviour, where 'political' is taken to refer to institutional politics. A clear structural regularity may be pointed to with respect to political attitudes: in general, more privileged individuals tend to feel more capable of exercising an influence over political processes.

This regularity has been borne out by surveys in several nations, although it may be limited to societies which are nominally Western democracies. Various measures of subjective political competence or efficacy have been employed. Almond and Verba (1963) in studies of Italy, Mexico, the U.K., the U.S.A., and West Germany, found that the wealthier and more educated a respondent, the more likely he was to feel able to have some effect on policy makers; similar findings have been reported for various other countries – for example, Bonilla (1970) and Greene (1972) in Venezuela and Guyana respectively. This regularity may reflect a fairly realistic assessment of the relative attention politicians pay to different interest groups, the effects of education and exposure to the mass media and informed discussion in making politics more intelligible, or be a specific example of a generalized sense of competence felt by the more privileged and less deprived; evidence may be cited in favour of each explanation, and they need not be mutually exclusive.

Feelings of political competence are of interest since theories of the relationship of attitudes to behaviour would predict that people are most likely to choose political activity as a way of bringing about improvement in their circumstances when they believe that such activity may be efficacious. Thus, it may be expected that the more privileged will participate more in political activity, and their concerns be expressed more often. However, the role of other 'hurdles' relevant to the political expression of needs and dissatisfactions may mask such a regularity, although it may generally be expected that the less privileged will experience more obstacles (e.g. lack of free time, of money, and other resources) than the rest of society.

Much research by political scientists has supported a socio-economic model of political participation, in which higher social status is related to feelings and perceptions (e.g. political competence, knowledge about political affairs) which in turn predispose individuals towards higher levels of participation. Almond and Verba (1963) and Inkeles (1969b) present results in line with this model drawn from, respectively, five developed and six developing countries.

However, other findings qualify this view. In particular, the work of Verba (Verba, Nie and Kim, 1971; Verba et al, 1973) shows that while there does appear to be a general syndrome of political participation – someone who reports having taken part in any one of a number of different political activities being more likely than someone who does not to have also taken part in each of the others – a number of quite distinct clusters of activities, or modes of participation, were discriminated using the technique of factor analysis. In Austria, India, Japan, the Netherlands, and the United States, these modes of activity were labelled: campaign activity (doing party work, attending meetings), voting (both elections and referenda), communal activity (working in local organizations, attempting to influence officials about local affairs), and personalized contacting (contacting officials about a personal need or problem). In Nigeria and Yugoslavia, where there was no party competition, campaign activity could not occur; in the latter country a further mode of activity, self-management (relating to participation in its system of localized self-government by workers' and house councils), was apparent. It appears that less conventional forms of political activity, such as signing petitions and taking part in demonstrations, represent a further mode of participation, since they form a separate cluster in the Dutch sample, the only sample to report about them.

Verba, Nie and Kim (1971) found that the socio-economic model of political behaviour was of most relevance to campaign and communal activity, less so to voting, and least of all to personalized contacting. A number of other studies suggest that voting may not be a good measure to employ in searching for structural regularities in political behaviour. In India, for example, Goel (1970) finds curvilinear relationships between education and voting and between education and support for government institutions, although interest in politics and attempts at direct political influence are directly related to educational attainment. Voting may be carried out as a duty rather than as a means of influence: thus Richardson (1973) reports that rural areas of Japan compete to attain the highest turnout at elections, while Mathiason and Powell (1972) show that in their near-feudal circumstances, Colombian peasants find voting an obligation. Personalized contacting is likewise a poor candidate for structural regularities, since it appears that less privileged groups are more likely to view their problems in personal terms and thus seek help on this basis (e.g. Verba, Ahmed and Bhatt, 1971). And yet, there is little comparative survey research which may be consulted concerning unorthodox political activities. It may be concluded that there is some evidence for the existence of a structural regularity whereby political activity (of the communal and campaign modes) is likely to be more prevalent among the more privileged members of a society. One consequence of this is that the pressures exerted upon the policy makers do not mirror the distribution of concerns in the population, as has been shown by Verba (1971).

These illustrations of the identification of structural regularities suggest that a number of trends in current survey research – for example, the trends towards comparative research and multivariate analysis – will make such research of greater utility to forecasters in the future. Computerized statistical analysis, in particular, makes it possible readily to investigate the interactions of a number of variables, for example in the genesis of job satisfaction or political participation, and thus more depth may be attained in understanding the underlying causes of regularities, with concurrent gains in our confidence in extrapolating these regularities into different circumstances. It may be hoped that broad concepts like social status and educational attainment, which are of undoubted predictive utility at our present level of knowledge, may be broken down so that the components of each which are critical in establishing relationships may be located.

Apart from the work of Inkeles (1960), there has been little concern with systematically searching for structural regularities using survey material. Yet there are many psychological and social variables which might repay analysis of this kind, although the relevant material will rarely be gathered together in one place at present. The volume edited by Szalai (1972) is an exception: here are gathered together reports of the use of time by urban and suburban respondents in twelve developed countries, and some interesting regularities and divergences are reported. The literature on diffusion of innovations is of particular interest to forecasters, and there have been some useful reviews of the field (e.g. Rogers, 1971); some of the general statements emerging from this literature, for example that the more privileged (with greater exposure to communication, more resources, and particular predisposing attitudes) are most likely first to become aware of and adopt innovations, may approach the status of structural regularities.

Formal models and social theory

Survey data are often employed to test social theories or to provide an empirical basis for the construction of static models of social processes, although this is generally carried out as analysis of a given situation rather than with forecasting future events as an immediate motive. The economic sciences are exceptional, in that short- and medium-term forecasts often employ data from censuses and surveys, and there are even some examples of the incorporation of psychological variables into such analysis. Katona (1960) found that shifts in the proportion of people holding optimistic or pessimistic attitudes concerning the future course of business events foreshadowed booms and recessions in the U.S.A., and this work has been successfully extended to a number of other countries and to take into account measures of intentions to buy or to save. The psychological measures have been found to be predictive of the aggregate market behaviour of the population, even though the prediction of the future actions of the individuals concerned is fairly poor! Several discussions of recent developments in this area are presented in Strumpel, Morgan and Zahn (1972), and although, being concerned with the short-term, this literature is not highly relevant to this chapter, it is interesting to note that Hymans and Shapiro have been able to account for a good deal of the variance from quarter to quarter in the attitude measures in terms of changing socio-economic conditions such as unemployment trends. This explained component of attitudes proves to be as good as the actual survey results in accounting for subsequent economic shifts, and Shapiro finds that over two decades the same relationship held between attitude change and prior socio-economic events. It is thus possible that the survey data will become redundant, although it is too early to assume that this limited relationship between social changes, psychological variables, and subsequent social changes, is truly stable.

The use of survey material in long-term forecasts is much less common, and few sociological theorists have attempted to use models they have constructed to make quantitative predictions. Recently, computer simulation has become something of a vogue, and social scientists have been told that only by such approaches can the complexity of society be taken into account. It is noteworthy that what must be the most publicized simulation attempt, the *Limits to Growth* world model (Meadows *et al*, 1972), actually employs survey material: a cross-sectional relationship between national wealth and the average family size desired is employed to model dynamic changes over time in desired family size at the global level, as levels of world industrial output change.

The same procedure of translating cross-sectional relationships into dynamic longitudinal effects is used in a more ambitious attempt to include socio-psychological variables in a forecasting simulation, in a model of Venezuela (Silva Michelena, 1967). A large number of social groups, differing in status and social function of their occupations, were sampled in a survey, and among a set of psychological measures employed were measures of the evaluations of other groups and features of society held by members of each group. Regression analyses were used to determine the associations between the evaluations held by group members and their other characteristics, and within the simulation these evaluations, changing with different circumstances and policies, do provide a basis for conflict or co-operation among groups, with subsequent pressures upon the government.

These two models are open to the criticisms which befall most pioneering research: their mixture of empiricism and half-substantiated theory, premature complexity, and reliance on data with severe historic limitations lend them the status of exploratory studies rather than useful forecasts. On the other hand, at least these authors have made some attempt to go beyond the purely armchair treatment of social factors that has characterized many other attempts at developing predictive simulations. Silva Michelena does attempt to justify his application of cross-sectional relationships by citing social theories which involve the longitudinal form of such relationships, and his model might be refined with material collected at other points in time. Simulation may serve a useful function in providing frameworks within which different theories may be expressed and their consequences explored, and survey data may be used to test such predictions. At present, however, it seems wisest to incorporate quantified psychological variables into computer simulations on an experimental basis only.

Psychological consequences of social and technological change

A familiar forecasting technique consists of extrapolating one trend, and considering what impacts changes in the variable involved will have. This approach may be applied to the psychological impacts of given trends, although two cautions are in order. Firstly, the social and psychological changes may exert mutual causation on each other and thus alter the trend in question, and secondly, forecasts may actually serve a self-invalidating function by alerting society about the potential costs of a given trend in time to alter the trend. Although some trends appear to be irreversible in the short run, this latter caution implies that normative approaches to forecasting which set out the consequences of alternative trends are appropriate, while the former caution carries the implication that consideration should be given to interactions between the trend and its so-called impact.

In setting out normative forecasts, survey data may suggest social indicators against which alternative futures may be evaluated – for example, the measures of life satisfaction described earlier might serve this purpose, and the researcher may use survey archives as a source of relevant indicators. If the consequences of a change are to be forecast, then research dealing with similar past changes may be investigated. However, current survey material may be inferior to other sources of data for this task: typically the analysis of change through survey research lacks appropriate controls for particular individual and historical characteristics. Thus, the specific groups who are exposed to a social change earliest in a population may be predisposed to this change in some way and, not being a random sample of the population, it may be inappropriate to generalize from their experience. Experimental and quasi-experimental analyses are well suited to the analysis of the consequences of change in a variable (see Campbell and Stanley, 1963, for a valuable discussion of this point), but such designs are often restricted to the laboratory or classroom: society is only hesitantly moving towards social experimentation (Campbell, 1971; Fairweather, 1967). Social experimentation involves ethical problems associated with randomization and assignment of treatments, and methodological problems associated with obtrusiveness and the possible biases of governmental institutions entrusted with such research. Given that such research is in its infancy, and that the role of survey technique in it is that of one of a number of methods of gathering information on both psychological and non-psychological variables, we shall here consider instead how survey material may contribute to forecasting the likely impact of two ongoing processes of social change. The first of these processes affects many under-developed and poor areas of the world, involving modernization, industrialization and urbanization, while the second applies to the more affluent nations of the West, and involves what some authors have described as the transition to a post-industrial society.

1) Psychological consequences of economic development

A large body of survey research has been directed at assessing the personal impact of the changes attendant upon the economic development of a traditional culture. Many of the researchers involved have made use of the unfortunate term 'individual modernity' to describe one outcome of these impacts, representing outcomes in terms of a continuum of attitudes along which individuals may move from a traditional to a modern pole. This analysis obscures the diversity of traditional cultural forms and attitudes, and may lead researchers to anticipate a convergence in attitudes as economic development continues, despite the discrediting of ideas of social and political convergence that has taken place among sociologists.

The extent to which psychological convergence takes place is a matter for empirical analysis: since the study by Goldthorpe *et al* (1969) has raised doubts about the inevitability of working-class embourgeoisement in the West, we may feel cautious about readily accepting an inevitable Westernization of the Third World. The surveys available have been carried out in countries which are not only modernizing, but whose leaders often seek to Westernize them; developments in such countries as China and Tanzania where new indigenous cultural forms have been maintained or adopted, but where survey material is not available, must also be borne in mind.

In fact, several studies suggest that the individual attributes which have often been interpreted as characteristic of modernity fall into a number of clusters. Schnaiberg's (1970) Turkish study, and Rogers' (1969) survey of Colombian peasants (whose results are supported by comparison with work carried out in seven other nations) support a multi-dimensional concept of modernity – someone judged modern by one set of criteria may not be so classified by a different set. The strongest factor identified in the analyses of these authors describes a set of variables concerning exposure to mass media and communication with and knowledge about a larger world than the local community. Another cluster of items includes measures of innovation and participation in new ways of life.

Much evidence suggests that several aspects of socio-economic development have similar impacts upon these distinct aspects of individual modernism. The Harvard group, led by Inkeles, has gathered extensive evidence for this conclusion in surveys carried out in Argentina, Chile, India, Nigeria and Bangladesh. On the basis of interview items concerning knowledge, literacy, attitudes, belief and experience, administered to young men with different exposure to hypothesized modernizing influences, a scale describing a modernity syndrome was established (Smith and Inkeles, 1966). Inkeles (1969a) identifies three social conditions as being strongly associated with modernity: education, urban experience and industrial employment. Inkeles thus reasons that as these social conditions become more prevalent, psychological convergence between men of different nationalities will occur.

Inkeles' modern man is described in terms of seven attributes: openness to new experience with people and new ways of doing things; increased independence from traditional authority figures with allegiance shifted to interest group leaders; less passivity and fatalism and greater belief in the efficacy of science and medicine; occupational and educational ambition for oneself and one's children; desire for punctuality and forward planning; interest and activity in community affairs and politics; and finally, preference for cosmopolitan rather than parochial news. Some of these aspects of modernity clearly relate to the studies of values and aspirations described earlier. Among the measures of modernism are desires to earn surplus disposable income, to possess items like radios and cameras, to exert political influence, and to guide one's son to occupational and educational achievements. A further attitude associated with this syndrome is tolerance for new ways of doing things, such as employing new technologies like Western contraceptive devices.

These results suggest that the psychological impact of socioeconomic development involves raised material aspirations, increased feelings of competence and increased awareness of the social and political environment and of the value of participation in it. Such differences between individuals are not even restricted to developing countries. Sherril (1969) and Kahl (1968) find, respectively, deprived and low education groups in the United

States to show fewer modern attitudes. However, generalization from these results should not be too hasty. These results have been based on cross-sectional analysis, while longitudinal relationships may be quite different: for example, it may be that the groups who have been more exposed to modern influences were already more modern psychologically. To some extent the study by Feldman and Hurn (1966) of a small Puerto Rican sample answers this objection: respondents were surveyed in 1954 and again in 1965, and those who moved from traditional to modern occupations displayed greater increases in aspiration level for job, salary and education, and a greater sense of achievement, than their non-mobile peers. While supporting the proposed causal role of social conditions in producing attitude and value change, this study did reveal that mobile Puerto Ricans actually decreased their evaluation of the importance and availability of education. Feldman and Hurn consider this reflects a realistic judgment based upon personal experience of the roles of luck and influence in gaining social mobility, although many conceptions of modernism would include favourable instrumental evaluations of education as part of the syndrome. This longitudinal study supports the broad conclusions of work on individual modernity concerning changes in values and aspirations, then, but reminds us that the actual beliefs and behaviour resulting from these changes are likely to be strongly influenced by the local cultural and social conditions: so that in one state the individual with higher aspirations may seek education and political influence by conventional means, while in another he may employ bribery or family influence. Inkeles (1969b) reports different relationships in different developing countries between political participation and political trust. Since the former variable is linked to his modernity syndrome, the more modern individuals in different countries may be expected to direct their increased political activity along different channels, with potentially divergent effects upon the political systems of their nations.

While it seems likely that the characteristics of psychological modernism will spread with the continued growth of urbanization, industrial life, mass communications and schooling, this need not, then, mean convergence of behaviour. Indeed, increasing overt conflict may result rather than harmony – rising aspirations may become rising frustrations as they conflict with reality, and oppressed groups may gain a sense of efficacy and attempt to exercise their rightful influence. These possibilities could account for the findings of Flanigan and Fogelman (1970b) who tabulated the incidence of political instability in sixty countries over a historical period: in general, they found political instability to increase to a peak in the early stages of industrialization and urbanization, and then to drop off. Countries undergoing socio-economic development in more recent periods seem to have experienced higher levels of instability – possibly as a result of their citizens' aspirations being raised by the affluent West?

2) Psychological consequences of late industrial social change

A diverse set of trends in recent Western society has led some commentators to herald the coming of a post-industrial society, in tones ranging from the pessimism of Ellul and Mumford to the exuberance of Fuller and McLuhan. Survey techniques are limited in their projection of the consequences of such trends: the individuals who have been more exposed to new life styles, for example, are not likely to be representative of the broader population, and it is likely that social trends will interact to produce psychological consequences qualitatively different from those produced by isolated changes. These criticisms apply equally forcefully to attempts to generalize from the experiences of Americans or Swedes to the likely experiences of less affluent nations where different values and institutions may lead to a given social change having a completely different impact. The spectacular failures of some recent social innovations may lead planners to adopt a more empirical and experimental approach to manufactured change, but for unsolicited social changes forecasters must use whatever survey evidence is available with full awareness of its shortcomings.

Some research relevant to social changes now taking place in Western societies has been reviewed elsewhere (Miles, 1974) and suggests reason to be critical of several prevalent assumptions concerning their psychological impacts. The notion of 'future shock', for example, is challenged by evidence on the adaptation of workers from traditional backgrounds to advanced technological environments, and it is likewise clear that automation need by no means lead to less satisfying working conditions. Nor is there support for the notion of 'massification' in contemporary societies, a supposed psychological convergence between people of different classes, ages, regions or sex under the impact of increased mobility and mass communications. On the other hand, there is some evidence for the contention that, in American culture at least, larger scale (both of organization and community) is associated with less individual participation, interaction, satisfaction and helpfulness. (Among studies relevant to the above contentions are Form, 1971; Glenn, 1967, 1974; Inkeles and Smith, 1970; Mueller, 1967; and Willems, 1973.)

Review articles may often be found in social science handbooks and journals which are relevant to assessing possible impacts of trends, in that they can direct the forecaster to appropriate research sources. All too often this will only yield information on impacts under one particular set of circumstances, but this may often contradict assumptions about the inevitable effects of social changes and thus widen the range of considerations and deepen the analysis employed. Thus if Mitchell (1971) finds that high density housing does not have any effects on emotional illnesses or aggression (although social features of the dwelling do), it may be possible to query the general applicability of his findings, based as they are on a Hong Kong sample – but the forecaster is forced even more clearly to reconsider the oft-cited conclusions about the destructive effects of crowding based upon animal studies.

A further focus for the investigation of potential impacts concerns changing social relationships at the interpersonal and family level, rather than in wider organizations. For example, some notions concerning the impact of different forms of family organization upon the values of children may be derived from survey research: for example, the work of Spiro (1958) on children raised in Israel's kibbutzim and a host of studies concerned with relating child-rearing styles to children's personality. The effects of changing definitions of sex roles and the trend towards greater female emancipation may likewise be considered, for instance Nye and Hoffman's (1963) study of employed American mothers, which found that participation of women in the labour force increased their independence and self-evaluations, and LeMaster's (1971) review of studies on the changing role of fathers, which concludes that fathers have become less dominant figures in families and that new child care institutions are likely to expand in Western societies in consequence of contemporary changes in values. While many commentators have viewed increasing crime roles as illustrative of social breakdown under modern living conditions, Coates (1972) points out that surveys reveal that many forms of crime are substantially under-reported to the authorities in the U.S.A. He concludes that, as middle-class values which stress the importance of deviant behaviour being dealt with outside the family context permeate society in the future, the reported crime rate will in fact increase even if there is no real 'crime wave'.

The list of studies relevant to current social changes and their long-term impacts could be expanded indefinitely. The purpose of this review has been to convey how survey material can be relevant to the forecasting of these impacts, despite the limitations both of the survey data and of the vague conceptualization of these social changes which is generally offered. While such material should never be used to justify prematurely definite predictions, it may be valuable in preventing a foreclosing of options for policy, and too limited conceptions of the outcomes of change, based upon inadequate assumptions about these outcomes – for example, that automation necessarily involves monotony, or that urban nuclear families are necessarily the best adjusted members of society.

Conclusions

This chapter has recurrently grappled with the three main limitations of most survey research described in the introduction, and cause for optimism has been found. Firstly, in that many efforts are currently under way within the social sciences to overcome these limitations – so that much attention is now being paid to demands for more investment of energy into comparative research, into ecological and situational studies, into the development of alternatives to traditional verbal research tools, etc. – and secondly, despite these limitations, available research does in many of the cases reviewed have a genuine contribution to make to forecasting.

This chapter has not been intended to argue for a psychological reductionism: other levels of society require investigation in their own right, and survey techniques will often be of limited utility. The analysis has demonstrated, however, the possibility of making greater use of survey research data in social forecasting, and it is probable that other modes of research may also make significant contributions, despite being typically overlooked in futures studies. Survey research represents one way of assessing the role of psychological variables in creating the social future, and the reality it reveals may be used to test the forecaster's own mental models of social change.

Chapter 12

Numerical Moralities and Social Indicators

Introduction

While statistics concerning many social and economic characteristics of nations and communities have been collected for centuries, it has nevertheless been the case that such statistics, compiled for particular purposes, are often only tangentially relevant to many of the most pressing concerns of forecasters, and shed little light on many characteristics of societies which are crucial to human welfare. Social indicators, to put it in crude terms, attempt to cope with these shortcomings in the present statistics by developing quantitative measures and data for monitoring social changes; in a sense they are analogous to the better-known economic indicators such as GNP. This may be seen, for instance, in the growth of 'clio-metrics'.

A number of recent projects have been aimed at assessing social trends and measuring social differences which are relevant to common conceptions of social goals, needs and welfare, and the popular notion of quality of life. To give some idea of the scope of social indicator (SI) research, Table 12.1 depicts the chapter by chapter contents breakdown of some contributions to this literature. Some further discussion of the background to these studies follows later in this chapter; with the exception of Nissel (1970) these volumes originate from the U.S.A., reflecting the interest such research has aroused in that country, although several other nations have developed knowledge and expertise along roughly similar lines.

While this breakdown by chapter headings disguises many points of convergence and divergence between these volumes, it indicates the range of phenomena that has been considered. The Ogburn (1929) and Nissel (1970) volumes represent the first of an annual series of SI publications, while the other volumes are more oriented toward summarizing current knowledge and discussing conceptual and methodological issues. The differential coverage of the different volumes reflects partly cultural changes (e.g. Ogburn's work was written in a period when rural problems were very evident to sociologists, but modern environmentalism was absent), partly different intentions on the part of the compilers (e.g. Campbell and Converse were setting out to relieve the emphasis on physical and objective aspects of social change by focusing on psychological and subjective issues), and partly indicates no more than alternative groupings of topics (thus housing is touched upon elsewhere in several volumes in which it does not appear as a heading, while conversely the 'community' label may imply a discussion of organizational structures or of the individual's participation in social life). Some issues are still remarkably absent from these lists, such as the statuses of different age groups and the sexes.

This chapter sets out to detail potential promises and problems posed by SI material to the social forecaster. By way of introduction to the issues involved, the contemporary critique of GNP as a measure of well-being is reviewed, and one attempt to modify this statistic and provide a closer approximation to welfare is described. One lesson that may be drawn from this use of GNP is particularly relevant to those working with SIs; the economists who devised GNP had no intention that it should be employed as a measure of social progress, and economists in general are aware of its shortcomings in this respect. A social statistic may acquire more significance than its creators believe it warrants.

The problem of defining just what constitutes an SI is then discussed, along with a brief account of the rise of the 'social indicators movement'. After reviewing several methods that have been employed in attempts to devise statistical indices of the 'quality of life' that might replace or augment GNP in policy making and forecasting, and reaching some rather pessimistic conclusions concerning the feasibility of developing an index

Table 12.1: Social Indicators Research: Areas Covered

Ogburn (1929)	Sheldon & Moore (1968)	H.E.W. (1969)	Gross (1969)	Nissel (1970)	Campbell & Converse (1972)
Population	Population			Population & Environment	
Natural Resources		Physical Environment	Natural Environment	Population & Environment	
Inventions & Discoveries	Knowledge & Technology	Learning, Science & Art	Science & Technology		
Production	Goods & Services: Economic Growth				
Foreign Policy					
Labour	Labour Force & Employment				Work
Wages		Income & Poverty	Employment	Income & Expenditure	
Employment & Buying Power	Labour Force & Employment			Employment	
Occupations					
Labour Legislation					
Social Legislation					
Public Health & Medicine	Health	Health & Illness	Health & Well-Being	Health	
Communication			Mass Media		
Group & Community Organization		Participation & Alienation			Alienation & Engagement
					Community Social Indicators

			Urban Environment		
Rural Life					
The Family	Family Change				Family, Kinship & Bureaucracy
Crime		Public Order & Safety	Crime & Delinquency	Justice & Law	Criminal Justice Systems
Religion	Religious Change				
Race Relations			Discrimination Against Negros		Change in Negro Population
Education	Schooling	Learning, Science & Art	Education & Learning	Education	
Government	Changing Politics		Democratic Participation		Change in the Electorate
			Electoral Participation		
			Civil Liberties		
	Consumption				Psychological Aspects of Economics
	Leisure			Leisure	Leisure
					The Use of Time
	Social Stratification & Mobility	Social Mobility			
	'Welfare'			Welfare Services	
	Income & Poverty	Income & Poverty	Poverty, Inequality & Conflict		
			Values		
			The Arts		Aspiration & Satisfaction
				Housing	
				Social Security	
				Public Expenditures	
			Social Breakdown Welfare Services		

of this sort, proposals are presented for a matrix of SIs which could prove useful in forecasting the quality of life. The role of alternative types of statistic is discussed, and a systems viewpoint presented which may help organize different types of SI. The concluding sections turn to problems and pitfalls associated with the use of SIs in policy making, programme evaluation, and social forecasting, and an assessment is made of alternative futures for the social indicators and futures research movements.

The assault upon GNP

In recent years the use of Gross National Product as a measure of a nation's well-being has been increasingly attacked by two bodies of opinion. On the one hand, the environmentalist movement, with its emphases upon the real and potential threats to ecological systems and to aesthetic aspects of the environment which may be associated with sustained economic growth, has criticized the elevation of GNP growth to a political dogma. On the other hand, the social indicators movement, with its emphases on social problems and critiques of an 'impoverished' quality of life, which do not appear to have been alleviated by sustained growth, has contributed less to a critique of growth than to a resurgence of interest in monitoring social change and making use of quantified information in the design and assessment of policy. Proponents of social indicators have raised a number of specific objections to the equation of GNP with welfare, some of which are summarized below:

1) GNP per head cannot be equated with psychic satisfaction: as reported in the review of survey research findings in the previous chapter, the course of satisfaction in a country over time by no means follows that of its economy, and only a weak relationship has been found as evidence for people being any happier, on the whole, in richer countries than in poorer countries.

2) Per capita GNP is an average measure, lacking information on the distribution of wealth in a nation; inequality may increase during periods of economic growth, as may the absolute level of hardship of particular groups.

3) The market value of goods is not necessarily related to their welfare content, for non-economic values are omitted; whether money is spent on health or on a presidential mansion is ignored in the calculation of GNP.

4) Non-market activity is excluded from GNP, so that changes in leisure time, in the availability of public capital (such as schools and parks), or in the unpleasant side-effects of industry, and the depletion of resources remain uncounted.

5) On the other hand, transformations of non-market activity to market activity (e.g. moving from home-prepared to convenience foods) or *vice versa* (e.g. marrying one's cook) do have an impact upon GNP, although qualitative changes associated with such transformations do not.

In the general case made against growth it is argued that many features of capitalist economy involve an opposition between growth and some aspects of welfare. Desires are created and manipulated by manufacturers, whilst what were once luxuries become necessities as traditional public facilities are displaced in the market. Through planned obsolescence and vicious circles set up by the competitive ethos of society, costs and consumption spiral, although it may really be the case that in the provision of many necessities of life the cheaper the better. Finally it is argued that economic growth in late industrial society is alienating man from his true nature, preventing personal growth and producing social costs in the form of crime, loneliness, political conflict and psychic stress.

Such arguments and their rebuttals have been flung back and forth sufficiently in public debate to render elaboration unnecessary. In terms of our ability to assess variations in human welfare, two main results have stemmed from this debate: there have been attempts to produce refined versions of GNP which take into account some of the criticisms above, and there have been attempts to develop more comprehensive systems of social indicators and indices of quality of life. These latter ventures will be reviewed later.

The criticisms of GNP per head notwithstanding, it may still be a useful measure for making comparisons either across time or across nations. Insofar as current political structures persist, the poorer countries of the world are almost certainly obliged to achieve economic growth in order to satisfy the basic material needs of their populations. In the absence of reliable data, GNP may provide an estimate in cross-national comparisons of a country's status on other social indicators, since it is correlated with many measures that are more obviously related to welfare. Indeed, in factor analyses carried out on socio-economic data, GNP is represented as a central variable on the most prominent cluster of features emerging. Even with respect to the distribution of income within nations, higher GNP per head tends to be associated with greater equality, although the experience of several nations shows that growth need not lead to more equality. Inference from cross-sectional to longitudinal patterns from this sort of data often rests upon the dubious assumption that nations follow similar paths of development, although the cross-sectional correlations now evident are more likely to reflect historic imbalances in power and dependence rather than inevitable laws of economic growth. Other statistics may describe the form that economic inequality takes within a nation far more accurately than approximations based upon GNP, just as measures of housing standards and nutrition levels shed more light upon the extent of satisfaction of basic needs. Thus the case for improving or supplementing GNP is strong if one wishes to evaluate real or potential societies in terms of the well-being of their citizens.

Sametz (1968) presents one approach to providing an improved measure of welfare derived from the American GNP while retaining its logic of expressing socio-economic conditions in money terms. While the nation's GNP grew by some sixty-five times over a century, when population growth and price inflation are taken into account *real* GNP per head for the same period grew by less than a tenth of this, a reduction that Sametz considers too severe given improvements in the quality of goods and decreasing hours of work. The gain in leisure time per head is converted to a monetary metric by valuing those hours of free time gained by working for less than 78 hours weekly in terms of the average real wage forgone. Although suggestions for more accurate quantification are given, Sametz uses only a rough estimate for quality improvements, which are represented by a fraction of the rise in prices of consumer goods. Aggregating these variables with GNP, Sametz arrives at an 'adjusted real per capita GNP' measure, whose growth rate over a century is twice that of conventional GNP per head. This index fails to take into account less beneficial consequences of growth, so Sametz additionally incorporates certain of these into an index of 'welfare GNP per capita'. Thus, the effects of the commercialization of non-market activities are estimated on the basis of trend data concerning housewives' services as a proportion of GNP (it is argued that non-market production a century ago was likely to have equalled market production). Social costs due to industrialization (e.g. expenses incurred in travelling to work and distributing products), and government expenditures which are not directly beneficial to citizens, were also estimated and deducted for each period. The 'welfare GNP per capita' measure displays a fourfold growth over the century.

Sametz is at pains to point out that the measure thus derived is only a poor approximation to the measurable part of economic welfare, and to specify what data must be adequately obtained in order to supply a satisfactory refinement of GNP. He views the task of gathering this data as feasible, and argues that his welfare indicator is, if anything, more likely to reflect real social welfare in future (on the assumption of increasing equality of income and opportunity). Even so, he admits that supplementary measures are required to index other conceptions of 'economic' welfare such as life expectancy and nutritional level, consumer wealth and assets. While work like Sametz's is able to reduce the strength of some of the criticisms of GNP, it cannot overcome all of these objections. Transformations from non-market to market activity and changes in non-market aspects of welfare may be roughly taken into account, but the distribution of wealth is ignored, and even when governmental spending on non-welfare projects is excluded from GNP (which depends upon contentious assumptions about means and ends, and the nature of welfare, e.g. Sametz's decision that defence expenditure does not contribute to welfare) the fact remains that money spent on highways, for example, contributes as much to the measure of economic welfare as does money spent on health.

A refined measure of economic welfare may yield data giving closer approximations to trends in human well-being, and enable more meaningful comparisons to be made between nations; it may prove more acceptable to critics of the use of GNP as a national yardstick. Its inevitable limitations, however, make a strong case for the use of more specific indicators of different

aspects of welfare, freed from the distortions involved in reducing them to monetary terms. The social indicators movement, as
it has been rather coyly called by some of its proponents, seems
to have been partly fuelled by a reaction to 'economic philistinism'
(Bauer, 1966).

The Social Indicators Movement

Raymond Bauer (1966), by editing a volume *Social Indicators*,
first brought this term to a wide audience. This volume contained
discussions of the uses and abuses of social indicators (SIs) which
remain unrivalled, and marked a mushrooming of interest in the
collection, interpretation and refinement of social statistics.
However, there had already been one period, in the U.S.A. at
least, of great interest in social statistics, for in the late 1920s an
annual publication concerned with social change was published
under the editorship of William F. Ogburn, and 1933 saw the
publication of *Recent Social Trends*, the Report of the President's
Research Committee on Social Trends.

These early efforts presage many of the concerns of the more
recent SI movement. While broad areas of social change such
as the family, public health and education are analysed (with
pleas for greater investment in systematic data collection),
emphasis is placed upon the inter-relationships between such
areas. In *Recent Social Trends*, Ogburn argues that in a period
of rapid change, the active planning functions of government are
vitally important, and social research should play a decisive role
in forecasting and prediction. Under the economic and political
impact of the Depression and subsequent crises the impetus of
this infant SI movement was lost, with only the U.S. Department
of Agriculture relating sponsored research and policy formulation
in the following years – and even this was destroyed by post-war
political pressures (Lyons, 1969).

The present SI movement is a response to diverse pressures.
Both scientists and policy makers feel that social change on an
unprecedented scale is taking place, that society is growing daily
more complex, and that only by improving our monitoring of
these trends can our knowledge keep pace with them. 'Modern'

techniques of management and analysis have been adopted by many institutions as a means of coping with their problems – although it may be argued that many of these problems reflect intra-institutional power struggles rather than increasing external complexity – and many of these techniques presuppose the development of information systems. The apparently successful management of national economies (more apparent in the 1960s than now?) may have encouraged application of similar philosophies of intervention on the basis of systematic knowledge to other areas of society, especially as it became increasingly obvious that economic growth alone was unable to solve social problems. As governments have assumed responsibility for a wider range of social services, concern has likewise grown that their functioning is appraised adequately so that investment is repaid. A long-term trend towards the gathering and organization of social and economic information is apparent: Flanigan and Fogelman (1970a) found that for twenty-nine countries they studied, in almost every case a clear increase in the number of serial government reports dealing with census, trade, commerce and government statistics could be observed over the period 1800–1950. There may also be a trend towards the use of SIs to disseminate information from policy makers: Biderman (1966) reports upon an accelerating tendency for U.S. State of the Union messages to employ SI material, for example. Similar themes have been cited as evidence for the growth of a technocratic ideology in Western nations (Meynaud, 1968).

These developments have coincided with a recent resurgence of interest in comparative research and studying social change among social scientists (whose attitudes have also tended to become more favourable to quantitative analysis), as the many recent publications in this field attest. Recent social turmoil and criticism of the irrelevance of much social science to real life problems has led to some scientists involving themselves in applied social research. It is also realistic to consider that advocacy of SIs in part stems from opportunism, an allegation levelled against much social science involvement in policy issues: from social science mandarins (Horowitz, 1970) seeking to legitimate their employers' policies; from displaced systems analysts (Hoos, 1972) eager to secure positions with the U.S. administration and to apply their techniques to virgin issues; or from a would-be élite of futurologists and social technicians (Lasch, 1973) bidding for power and patronage.

The SI movement contains many strands, ranging from abstract theorists to community workers, from critics of the status quo to its defenders. The use of SIs by activists and politicians may grow through a process of positive feedback as proponents of alternative policies develop and publicize social information supporting their own schemes, as champions of alternative social goals chart trends towards or away from these goals in attempts to mobilize support, and as opponents of political programmes select SIs which reflect poorly upon the programmes' impacts, and are answered by the programmes' sponsors. Transference of debate from assertions based upon subjective impressions to arguments concerning the interpretation of data does not resolve conflicting values and ideologies underlying a debate. It is possible to draw divergent conclusions from competing SIs because there are no generally accepted operational definitions of many of the broad social phenomena of interest. Poverty may be defined in various ways, for example, and trends based upon such definitions may differ – the relative proportion of wages received by the lower-paid may be increasing at the same time as the number of people falling below an estimated minimum income level also increases. The use of SIs in such debate may reinforce public scepticism about statistics, for informed judgment depends upon a clear exposition of the definition adopted for an ambiguous construct.

SIs may be used for many purposes other than plotting the progress of a nation or community through time: nations or smaller units such as regions, towns or local districts may be compared or monitored, and changes at the global level may be studied. Several international organizations are at present actively involved in the use and compilation of SI archives: for example, the United Nations Research Institute for Social Development is engaged upon a programme involving time-series data, using indicators of health, nutrition, education, housing, communications, transport etc., in which the social and economic development of nations may be analysed and compared (McGranahan, 1970). Much research involved in cross-national use of SIs has been concerned with political and economic development: the two editions of the World Handbook of

Political and Social Indicators (Russett, 1964; Taylor and Hudson, 1972) share this concern, with the first edition explicitly trying to display SIs relevant to values in the U.N. Charter of Human Rights. Regional development has been a central purpose in many accumulations of sub-national SI data, as has the study of community decision-making, social administration and localized social problems. Social forecasting may, of course, be concerned with any of these levels of analysis.

Given the diverse interests in the SI movement, it is not surprising that there is disagreement as to the definition of the term 'social indicator' itself. Sheldon and Freeman (1970) note that there is widespread agreement that a measure of some aspect of society may only be described as an SI if it may be employed regularly so as to obtain time-series data, and if it may be disaggregated to yield more specific information on persons, conditions or the contexts to which it pertains. They suggest, however, that claims that SIs are statistics of direct normative interest, and of welfare outputs rather than social resource inputs, are too restrictive: the salience of issues may change and an SI may gain or lose relevance to people's values, while measures of resources may be vital in forecasting future developments in welfare. In a subsequent discussion, Sheldon and Land (1972) distinguish between three types of SI, used for different applications. Problem-oriented SIs are direct inputs into policy decisions, descriptive SIs describe the state of society and the changes it is undergoing, and analytic SIs serve as components of explicit models of social processes. It is argued that the users of these three types of SI range respectively from administrator through social advocate to pure scientist.

An alternative perspective on SIs consists of viewing them as necessarily measures of phenomena of normative interest, and as parts of a system of indicators or model of society. This is the position of Cazes (1972) who argues that the desire to measure a phenomenon itself implies that normative considerations are associated with an SI, and that social accounting and explanation can only follow the integration of SIs into a system which reconciles apparent inconsistencies such as the divergent trends in poverty indices. When related in a causal system to other SIs which are of direct normative interest, even an SI which does not directly measure progress towards a goal may yet retain value states. Even problem-oriented and descriptive SIs are bound to be located within a mental model of the social system held by their users, within which relationships between SIs and policies may be more or less informal, intuitive and implicit.

The quality of life

The notion of quality of life (QOL) has been a central, if diffuse, element in a debate involving many critics of present social trends both real and suspected. It has been argued that the focus of policy makers upon purely economic goals has led to economic growth coupled with social stagnation. One thrust of the SI movement has been towards developing measures of the QOL of a community, measures which may appeal to the forecaster with their promise of providing a basis for normative forecasting and the evaluation of alternative futures.

QOL has become a rallying cry for social critics of many persuasions, and the ideas embodied in the concept are multifold. Despite this, its appeal to forecasters is apparent: the phrase often appears in futuristic literature, and there have even been attempts to embody quantified parameters of QOL within computer simulations. Singer (1973) includes a Q-index in his model of American economic and population dynamics; resembling the Sametz modification of GNP discussed above, it has no role in influencing other variables within the model. In his world model Forrester (1971) derives a QOL index, again of no causal significance, from measures of pollution, crowding, food and material standard of living. Apparently reaching a peak during the Second World War according to this model, QOL may also be expected to reach high levels when the world population is zero.

Attempts to quantify QOL raise many problems similar to those involved in the identification of GNP as welfare, and reflect some of the main ideological problems of the SI movement. Some opponents of the SI movement argue that nebulous concepts like QOL are not amenable to measurement, that only clearly defined aspects of society and constructs with agreed-upon operationalizations should be employed in scientific discourse. Often these arguments stem from economists, who might be seen as seeking to guard their sovereignty in societal monitoring, but there is also a body of opinion that holds that attempts to measure highly valued aspects of life, which encompass its significance for many people, will lead to a destructive, rather than life-enriching, triumph for reductionist thought, positivist language, and one-dimensional technological domination. It is certainly possible to point to many cases of social scientists naming their limited measures with a multi-faceted everyday language word, thereby reducing future discourse to the identification of this word with the simplistic fractional construct. An example is the restriction of the term 'intelligence' to signify the results of IQ tests. If QOL were to be popularly identified with Forrester's measure, for example, the term would lose many significant connotations, and our language would be enfeebled again. It may be debated whether these failures of definition imply an unbridgeable gulf between qualitative knowledge and quantitative technique, or merely lack of imagination and humility. A discussion of attempts to measure QOL will serve to throw light on this issue as well as upon some other possible abuses of SIs.

The underlying problems in most attempts to measure QOL stem from the reluctance of researchers to make any but the broadest value judgments. It is generally accepted that the QOL in a community is a composite of many of its aspects, and most QOL indices founder on the issue of aggregating these different aspects into a coherent whole. Of course, it could be argued that QOL really represents the subjective impact upon individuals of these many aspects of society, in which case QOL could be identified with happiness. Surveys of mood states (for example, Bradburn and Caplovitz, 1965) or of life satisfaction (for example, studies such as those referred to in the preceding section, Abrams, 1973; Cantril, 1965) attempt to assess this impact. Again, QOL could be identified with some behaviour suggestive of the impact of these features of society upon individuals – for example, Narrol (1969) talks of 'the sick society', employing reports of protest suicide as measures of the level of frustration within a community. He found that anthropologists were more likely to report such suicides in cultures with customs which increase the likelihood of feeling thwarted, such as wife-beating, marriage restrictions and frequent warfare.

The subjective experience of individuals, whether assessed by direct self-report techniques or by inference from other social phenomena, may reasonably be considered to comprise part of a definition of QOL. But to identify QOL solely with such measures is as restrictive and misleading as would be equating it with GNP. Among the arguments that may be advanced on this point are the viewpoints that a uniformly happy society would be stagnant and uncreative; lacking information on real conditions people could feel satisfied with an abhorrent state of affairs; relative deprivation could be reduced by restricting people's aspirations (and their potential), a policy Pool (1967, p. 26) recommends for the maintenance of order in developing countries; and that the only policy really needed to achieve the goal of mass satisfaction and content would be enforced tranquillization, say by the addition of appropriate drugs to food or water supplies. The identification of QOL with experience leads to the idea of engineering experience, a psychotherapy or adjustment of the person to his context.

Since values differ between individuals within a culture, and those typical of different cultures also differ, disagreement may naturally arise concerning the evaluation of social changes (reflected by shifts in a community's status on an SI), or concerning social differences between communities (reflected by different status on an SI). Even given a consensus of values, an SI may be ambiguously related to these values, so that different observers might locate it within different causal systems, and disagree about its implications (e.g. high rates of changing jobs may be viewed as healthy variety-seeking, or as indicative of anomie; as bringing fresh perspectives to occupations, or as imposing high costs in retraining). A similar problem relates to the possible flexibility of an SI, making the evaluation of an SI difficult even for individuals sharing the same values. Change on an indicator may reflect a real change in the social conditions which it is purported to measure, or it may indicate merely variations in flexible criteria of data collection. Flexibility may be brought about by deliberate distortion of data (e.g. an administrator seeking to present a good record) or by social changes not accounted for by the original SI designers (e.g. the stigma associated with reporting particular crimes or 'unusual' events diminishing, so that the public are more ready to acknowledge their presence to authorities). Questions of ambiguity and flexibility of SIs are open to empirical investigation, although the problems of such a task are illustrated by Biderman's analysis of the limitations of indicators of crime (Biderman, 1966, pp. 111–129). Ambiguity as to which of a series of alternative social models is appropriate to the interpretation of an SI can in principle be resolved by testing these models against new and more detailed data, while sociological and experimental techniques may be applied to checking SIs for flexibility and bias (Campbell, 1971).

A further set of problems involved in QOL assessment arises out of the multiplicity of indices of welfare, for only a highly restrictive value judgment could select one single aspect of society, and thus a single SI, as representative of QOL. In this case two issues are prominent: firstly a set of QOL indicators must be formulated, which requires setting criteria of inclusion and exclusion of SIs, and secondly the question arises of aggregation of these indices into a unique measure of QOL.

The definition of a set of social conditions relevant to QOL is itself a matter of values to the extent that if consensus exists in a population concerning the definition of attributes of QOL, then changes on the relevant SIs should be paralleled by changes in felt QOL. It is scientism to expect a value-free definition of QOL to emerge from methodologies such as survey research, just as it is to expect a scientific theory to provide a value-free basis for such definition. Both theoretical and empirical analyses may suggest factors which should be incorporated into a 'package' of QOL indicators, but criteria of inclusion and exclusion are ultimately normative. Equally, attempts to combine and weigh different SIs according to their salience to QOL must rely upon normative judgments. Each of these points has been lengthily discussed in the SI literature, and frequently ignored in QOL assessment.

Various attempts have been made to devise a system of QOL categories by survey research; for example, Dalkey (1972) describes studies in which American college students generated items they felt to be relevant to their QOL. These items were coded by researchers on a *post hoc* basis into forty-eight categories, which were then reduced to a smaller number of clusters by analysis of the original respondents' judgments of their similarity to each other. Thirteen clusters were established, closely tied to personal psychological states (e.g. novelty, peace of mind, social acceptance and comfort); this reflects the questionnaire phrasing, which could be modified to obtain aspects of QOL more closely tied to social relationships, the wider society or environment. Gallup polls in the U.S. obtain such information, in fact, by asking people to name the most important problem facing the country, their hopes and fears for themselves and for their country (e.g. Watts and Free, 1973). Abrams (1973) describes British surveys in which more detailed information was sought about which changes in various aspects of life would make respondents more or less satisfied.

The QOL categories arrived at by survey analysis are unlikely to be comprehensive. Expression of concern about a social problem may only be generated when it is believed to be remediable; Haberlein (1972) argues that concern about pollution increased as it became apparent that industry need not necessarily produce environmental damage. Threshold effects may occur: a condition, such as pollution, may have to attain a particular level or change at a particular rate to generate concern. Comparison of the conditions of other people or communities may lead to feelings of relative deprivation or gratification. The presence of large changes in the proportion of people reporting concern about particular aspects of QOL suggests that certain issues may tend to monopolize attention for periods (e.g. McEvoy, 1972, reports dramatic increases in concern with pollution in the late 1960s). The dynamics of such processes may be explored by various means: for example, Funkhouser (1973) attempts to relate concern about fifteen issues to media coverage of these issues and, less convincingly, to indicators of the 'real situation'. Definition of aspects of QOL by sounding public opinion is thus likely to mean the neglect of potentially relevant social conditions that are currently unchanging, that are regarded as natural or given, or that are more salient to other communities than the one surveyed.

Survey-derived categories should, however, be valuable additions to those derived from armchair philosophizing, social science theorizing, and the concerns of the political and academic élite. The U.S. Environmental Protection Agency (1973 Exhibit A) in reviewing the QOL literature found it possible to fit most aspects of QOL in various proposed American SI systems into six main categories: economic, political, physical, social, health and natural environment, with a further category of personal psychological aspects into which the Dalkey (1972) attributes, for example, fit. These categories neatly mirror academic disciplines, and neglect of the arts and humanities is apparent from the absence of cultural and religious categories in the above list. As a starting point for analysis, and as a reminder to those employing the QOL concept that it covers a wide range of ideas, this list should prove useful; as the product of a decade's research it is painfully unimpressive.

Most research carried out with the aim of describing QOL has used highly restrictive sets of SIs. Even if a fairly comprehensive set is established, problems remain as to the integration of its different aspects. There have been demands for the development of global QOL measures: from policy makers and programme evaluators, from academic and applied researchers. A metric is sought in which social change may be assessed by numerically trading off improvements in some conditions against deterioration in others; a system is required whereby the confusing array of statistics reflecting the relative positions of different communities may be simplified so that rapid assessment of their relative quality can be made. People may be assured that things are really getting better, despite their particular worries and complaints. The basic problem of weighting SIs calls for normative assessment of the relative importance of each. This has been obscured by three main forms of 'scientific' weighting strategy: 'idiosyncratic', 'preference' and 'statistical' weighting will serve as labels for these attempts to avoid facing the issue of value judgments.

By idiosyncratic weighting is meant the attempt by an author to assign an SI its weight on *a priori* grounds – whether of personal preference disguised as rationality, a pet social theory (which is, inevitably, given the state of social science, rudimentary and controversial enough to be termed idiosyncratic) or desperation (e.g. transforming all SIs to a common scale and weighting them equally). Francome (1972) presents a Social Index on the basis of which he argues that Britain's QOL has deteriorated over recent years, and that policy should be directed towards social amelioration rather than economic growth. This index is based upon twenty-three variables (e.g. life expectancy, suicide rates, air pollution levels and number of hours spent at work weekly), weighted according to personal criteria. Francome and Wharton (1973) present an International Social Index, with which six nations are compared in terms of twenty SIs, chosen to represent nine aspects of life. Three developed countries attained much higher scores on this index than did three underdeveloped countries. The authors suggest that the weights they assigned to different indicators reflect the choices that could be made by a rational man uninfluenced by cultural factors! Various other idiosyncratic weighting schemes have been produced (see, for example, various attempts in the E.P.A. Volume, 1973), but the resulting QOL statistics suffer from the disguising of trends in the component SIs by the process of integration, and from the absence of clear articulation of the value criteria on which the authors have based their weighting. Since ultimately QOL indices depend upon normative decisions, these need to be expressed in as precise a manner as possible so that debate may be separated between the purely moral issues, and those of scientific method SI construction and SI validation which may follow on these decisions.

Various authors have suggested that subjectivity inherent in relying upon the judgment of élite researchers could be removed, and democratization introduced, by the use of preference weighting. In this technique the relative importance placed upon each of a number of QOL areas by members of the community in question is assessed, typically by survey research. The most obvious approaches, for instance asking respondents to rate or rank order a number of social conditions in terms of their importance to his QOL, or to state whether they would wish to see more or less government activity in a particular field, have been much applied (e.g. Bettman, 1971; Dalkey, 1972; Dillman and Christensen, 1972), but are of doubtful value. While these may suggest which social changes are most likely to be favourably evaluated, they are prone to the problems of 'topicality' of concerns described earlier. Furthermore, two recent studies of life satisfaction (Andrews and Rodgers, 1972) and job satisfaction (Quinn and Mangione, 1972) have found that importance ratings add nothing to the statistical explanation of measures of overall satisfaction by measures of satisfaction with particular aspects of the situation. Techniques such as regression analysis, which can provide measures of the degree to which differences in particular aspects of the situation, or in satisfaction with these particular aspects, account for the differences in the subjective QOL of different respondents or groups in the community, probably provide a sounder approach to developing preference weightings. Research carried out using such analyses (Andrews and Withey, 1974; Hall, 1973) indicates that even within national populations such as those of the U.S.A. and U.K. the contribution of variations in different aspects of life to overall QOL differs across social groups. The use of weightings derived from the total population would bring about a 'democratization' without compromise which obscured the distinctive values of different groups, a majority rule which Maruyama (1973b) describes as domination by quantity, forced homogenization of power. A further problem with preference weightings is their inevitable historical nature, which reduces their utility for forecasting. Survey approaches may yield a crude basis for SI weighting in circumstances where value consensus is approximated and stable, and may be of value in clarifying just which clusters of values and interests are latent in a community (rather than reflecting merely those of dominant groups).

The third approach, that of statistical weighting, is also no panacea. While various statistical options are available, factor analysis, a technique for assessing the dimensionality of a number of variables by locating clusters of measures which share variance in common, has most frequently been applied to SI packages. However, the relationships between indicators thus defined do not necessarily reflect conceptual convergence or divergence of different aspects of QOL, but the presence or absence of covariation between these aspects in the communities under analysis: often, probably, a social construction rather than an inevitable natural correlation. Thus, living in poor housing and having restricted access to health care facilities may be related in our society, but they are logically distinct and alternative institutional structures in which they are unrelated or divergent may be constructed. The fact that a factor upon which they both load may emerge from an analysis of a given social context does not by any means imply, as certain authors assume, that indicators of each condition are necessarily both merely crude measures of some underlying phenomenon.

Factor analysis cannot reveal whether a correlation between two variables means that there is a direct causal link between the two, or that they are both products of a common cause. Research using factor analysis on SI data has failed to locate a single factor (dimension) that could be identified with QOL – rather a number of factors have been elicited, representing aspects of QOL that are empirically unrelated in the communities studied. Factor analytic studies of communities of various sizes have repeatedly uncovered multiple dimensions: for example, Rummel 1972) for nations, Sharkansky and Hofferbert (1969) for American states, studies reported of cities in Berry (1972), and the interesting attempts to develop measures of social needs in British local authority areas by Davies (e.g. Davies *et al*, 1972). Similarly various studies of life satisfaction and QOL using survey techniques have shown the subjective aspects of QOL also to be multi-dimensional (Allardt, 1973a,b; Andrews and Rodgers, 1972; Hall, 1973). Thus purely statistical approaches cannot hope to yield a single measure of QOL, so the proposal that SIs should be weighted according to their loadings on a QOL factor or cluster is irrelevant.

This is not to argue against the useful contribution that may be made by techniques like factor analysis to disentangling aspects of social change, and to constructing indices summarizing conveniently an otherwise cumbersome quantity of data. The work of Banks (1974) on longitudinal patterns of socio-economic development, for example, touches on many of the issues raised in this chapter and in chapter 14. Banks applies factor analysis to twelve SIs pinpointed by the U.N.R.I.S.D. project mentioned on p. 184, which has been striving to consider both social and economic aspects of development. Data for a twenty-one year period on these indicators were available for thirty-eight countries. Two dimensions were found to underlie these variables, and the larger of the two was identified as a measure of socio-economic development – economic indices loaded heavily upon it, as well as those of communications development. In terms of this measure, over the post-war period there has been some convergence between highly and intermediately industrialized nations, but the gap between the most and least industrialized countries has remained almost constant. This development measure, however, can only be marginally related to a broad definition of QOL – school enrolment levels, for example, have negligible loadings on the first factor in this analysis.

These conclusions highlight what is probably the fundamental objection to any attempt to construct a QOL index which will suffice for all communities and times. It is that human needs are multi-dimensional in essence, and may not prove to be substitutable. Simply to envisage weighting different needs so as to obtain a static trade-off function is to assume that QOL does not depend upon at least some minimal satisfaction of each need. Values, and the satisfactions attained from life, differ between individuals, times and cultures. Any QOL metric is likely to match the values of only a limited proportion of humanity.

To what extent, then, may the QOL concept prove useful for social forecasting? The conclusion arrived at above is that a single QOL measure depends upon value criteria which cannot emerge from scientific enquiry *per se*; the multiple criteria underlying a discussion of QOL should be made explicit, and openly related to particular SIs if the QOL concept is to be employed as an instrument of anything other than mystification. Since welfare is multi-dimensional, a multi-dimensional representation of QOL is called for, although broad clusters of similar values might be related together for convenience. Such a representation would enable forecasters to compare and contrast alternative futures within a common framework without imposing an *a priori* weighting scheme: once the consequences of given actions were elaborated in terms of the QOL features involved, then the alternatives could be assessed participatively by members of the community in question rather than by an élite of forecasters and planners. SIs might also be employed as provocative tools with which to stimulate public debate concerning alternative social goals and normative forecasts.

Maruyama (1973a) has argued cogently against even this approach: particular categorizations and hierarchical orderings are matters of human design rather than the real essence of things. Given this, the imposition of QOL categories and clusters of categories upon different communities might lead to a mismatch between the researcher's idea of QOL and that of a community; therefore the communities in question should generate their own categories and orderings. He does admit, however, the suggestive role of prestructured QOL lists, and it is in this spirit that the following discussion is intended. Furthermore, the cross-national surveys of Cantril (1965) reveal sufficient consensus in human hopes and fears from nation to nation to make a first attempt at such a list appear worthwhile.

Social theory has failed to generate an exclusive and comprehensive list of needs and values. The course of individual development and social evolution makes salient new categories and merges old categories of need. Nevertheless a coarsely-grained approach to social needs and QOL, free of any notions of a hierarchy or rigid sequential development, of motives and satisfactions, should provide forecasters and planners with at least some minimal QOL considerations.

Allardt (1973a,b) proposes that three broad social values, or groups of states, should be considered: he labels these 'Having', 'Loving' and 'Being'. Respectively, these refer to: levels of living and the resources an individual may command to maintain his living conditions, health and safety; his engagement in reciprocal relationships involving support, affection and meaningfulness; and his ability to influence his environment and feel purposeful, valuable and a unique individual. Categories similar to these three can prove useful for organizing more detailed aspects of QOL. It must be emphasized that the categories suggested here, and their clustering, are pragmatic and have no finality about them; they should serve to indicate the scope of the QOL concept, and alert forecasters to the various forms of human welfare to be taken into account.

What follows represents a considerable modification of Allardt's original scheme: the term 'Loving' has been replaced by 'Relating' – a term with wider coverage – and in each group QOL aspects have been divided into those more obviously dealing with security, maintenance of a standard of well-being, and the satisfaction of existing aspirations, and those more related to potential for growth and change, the exercise of control over one's development and the evolution of new aspirations.

Each of the QOL aspects delineated in Figure 12.1 remains broad, at what Gross (1966) terms the level of intermediate abstractions, since at this level values shared by a wide spectrum of cultures and communities may be subsumed. The specific operationalizations of such values in terms of QOL will vary from community to community, however, and thus a more detailed listing of SIs is bound to contain some indicators that individuals would find irrelevant to their conception of QOL. For each value aspect an almost limitless variety of SIs may be generated: for instance, when talking of health levels, physical and mental aspects of health, morbidity or mortality, etc. may be distinguished for particular purposes. Subjective indicators (e.g. of satisfaction with an aspect of QOL) may be contrasted with objective indicators of the state of affairs and indicators reflecting actual states of the population with indicators reflecting the potential choice and freedom of individuals to opt for a range of states.

The most obvious route to gathering data on SIs developed from this QOL matrix is to apply survey techniques (or even to obtain some information from regular censuses). A sample of

FIGURE 12.1.   Suggestive Classification and Definition of Scope of QOL Terms

MAINTENANCE	*Physical Health*	– fitness, life expectancy, severity of illnesses, health care services
	Nutrition and Nourishment	– consumption of foodstuffs, variety of foodstuffs
	Personal Safety	– security of self, security of property
	Housing & Shelter	– shelter from weather, space for personal activities, privacy
BEING / GROWTH	*Basic Skills*	– cognitive and intellectual abilities (e.g. literacy), schooling services
	Advanced Learning	– specialized knowledge and training
	Information Media	– dissemination of news, information about environment, other people
	Leisure Time	– quantity of time free from involuntary obligations, services to free time
	Recreation & Aesthetic Facilities	– sport and leisure activities and facilities, artistic productions
	Changing Awareness	– training and context for religious, mystical, psychodynamic experience

FIGURE 12.1 continued

HAVING	MAINTENANCE	*Disposable Resources*	– wealth, possessions that may be relinquished voluntarily
		Household Equipment	– facilities for carrying out maintenance of property
		Community Resources	– publicly-owned tools and instruments, skilled persons
		Goods Quality & Service	– range and convenience of consumer goods, repair and redress services
		Aesthetic Annoyance	– obtrusive features of environment (e.g. noise, pollution, ugliness)
	GROWTH	*Pluralism of Culture*	– variety of culture open to experience (e.g. art, gastronomy, religion)
		Occupational Mobility	– openness of occupations to entrance and departure
		Spatial Mobility	– local and long-distance transport and accommodation facilities
		Occupational Quality	– comfort, challenge, sociability, etc. of occupation
		Physical Environment	– preservation of natural environment
RELATING	MAINTENANCE	*Family Relations*	– interaction between couples, parents and children, relatives
		Social Integration	– interaction with neighbours, members of community
		Communications Facilities	– development variety of mass and private media
	GROWTH	*Civil Liberties*	– tolerance of self-expression, alternative life styles
		Neighbourhood & Workplace Control	– structure and power of influence on decisions made concerning local issues (housing, amenities, job, etc.)
		Community Decision-Making	– structure and power of influence on planning and decision-making for community, nation, etc.
		Social Mobility	– openness of various social groups (defined, for example, by culture, class, age or race) to association.

members of the community would be selected, both for interviewing and for investigation of their objective environment (e.g. pollution levels, frequency and routes of public transport, distance from home to various amenities, etc.). A recent American study of working conditions (Survey Research Center, 1970) demonstrates the utility of survey techniques in obtaining information about the perceived characteristics of various occupations, and such methods may be applied to other areas of life. However, if precise information is not necessary, it may often be possible to make use of SIs describing the characteristics of whole communities: differences between regions in terms of education levels, library facilities or crime rates suggest that average individual well-being is likely to differ correspondingly.

Such a system might be implemented as follows. Firstly, a sample from the communities for which the exercise is being carried out should be encouraged to describe their concerns and satisfactions in the various areas of life covered by the list, and thereby to suggest their own meaningful SIs of the different value aspects. Moreover, this procedure should be regularly repeated so that changes in values and in society may be responded to by a transformation of the QOL indicators to render them relevant to the changed circumstances. Indicators suggested by theory or other sources should also be presented to community members to evaluate in terms of salience and meaningfulness. Secondly, information concerning state and changes in state on all SIs considered salient should be presented for consideration by community members so that the community can work out its own weightings and trade-offs of different value areas of political processes; access should be guaranteed to information concerning SIs not considered immediately salient, and concerning the state of the communities and historical trends if comparative research has been undertaken.

How this broad scheme could best be implemented is a matter for empirical investigation. So far, little research has been carried out into the feasibility of basing either SI development or planning upon citizen participation. In town planning, for example, there have been some gestures in a participatory direction (or, perhaps, in the direction of fostering a sense of participation) involving the use of scale models of schemes; there have also been some attempts to weld survey techniques into planning by eliciting the concerns of people faced with alternative local futures. These latter studies have revealed some relevant details, such as the low level of awareness in the general public about many schemes, and the capacity of ordinary people to evaluate such schemes when properly informed of them. However, it seems likely that exploration of more adventurous techniques could be well worthwhile. Groups formed from the public, for example, might be able to provide more crucial and varied listings of QOL aspects and indicators, along the lines perhaps of brainstorming and problem-solving groups. Scenarios could be presented in various media, and the consequences of particular futures for individual welfare and life style examined in a more personally relevant fashion than exists at present. Such approaches might help counterbalance the 'artist's-impression' idealized images of the local future that currently pass for citizen-involving planning techniques.

A community-constructed QOL list along the lines suggested may be used as a framework within which alternative futures may be represented in terms of directions of changes along discrete SIs. In technology assessment the impact of a new technology may be similarly described. Scenarios should be detailed for different social groups, communities and regions, for different moderating influences such as policies and contextual changes, and the sensitivity to initial assumptions made explicit. Information may be presented at various levels of SI aggregation, following the hierarchical orderings and clusterings of SIs derived from the community, so that those interested in the fine structure of particular aspects of QOL would be able to investigate these more thoroughly, while those less concerned with these need not be bothered with cumbersome detail.

If policy making is to be a dialogue, in which laymen articulate notions of what they understand as QOL and planners respond by describing how these relevant SIs will be affected under alternative programmes, then the channels appropriate for this communication must be established, and the tasks and skills of the participants matched. Obviously it is easiest to investigate and institute participatory systems of planning when the forecasts involved are both geographically and temporally restricted. Translating such ideas into a practicable goal for global forecasting faces inevitable barriers in our present world. Even so, the list of QOL components presented here, or some similar set of SI categories, may provide a basis for a more comprehensive discussion of the ramifications of alternative futures for the individual, community, region and world.

Systems and indicators

The attempts to develop indices of QOL or of its component aspects represent a movement toward assessing the output of social systems for the people living in them. Ideally, according to Gross (1966), such research proceeds in a pyramidal fashion: the apex of this pyramid is the specification of a single grand abstraction or value (e.g. abundance, health, or equality); the middle level consists of intermediate abstractions (e.g. from abundance may be derived concepts of the production of different goods and services, and the output of wealth); and the base consists of a larger number of specific SIs relating to these intermediate abstractions. A few of the more ambitious products of the SI movement have followed this logic, but in practice research more commonly proceeds from the base of the pyramid upwards. Existing SIs are singled out as relevant to social goals and used to make sweeping assertions about the state of society, while the pyramid itself resembles an iceberg whose greater portion remains hidden.

Just how many aspects of the social process remain submerged has been made clear by those exceptional attempts to formulate comprehensive lists of values and related SIs. For example, the collections of American data and experience of Gross (1969), Sheldon and Moore (1968) and the U.S. Department of Health, Education and Welfare (1969), are concerned with issues of both methodology and comprehensiveness, and frequently admit to having no data to report on a particular aspect of social welfare. Such projects have helped to create a climate of opinion in which many academic, governmental and international organizations are collecting and appraising SIs, so it is likely that these areas of ignorance will be increasingly well charted in the future.

In the discussion above on QOL measures, little reference was made to issues of freedom, equality and justice, three values often held to be of central importance in social and political philosophy. In the SI literature these concepts are generally treated as values of the same conceptual status as abundance, health, aesthetic fulfilment, etc. However, following the leads of Allardt (1973b) and Galtung (no date), we may ask to what particular areas of life does a particular index of freedom or equality apply. It becomes appropriate to consider these concepts as metavalues rather than as simple values; there are different freedoms, equalities and justices. For example, rather than a society being typified by a given level of equality, there may be differential progress towards equality in income and wealth, in educational opportunity and health, in aesthetic fulfilment and housing conditions. Galtung and Allardt present a perspective on SI statistics that is useful in this context. Dispersion and covariation are related by these authors to equality and justice.

An SI may be viewed not only in terms of the information it yields about the average or aggregate level of well-being in a community, but also in terms of the information it can give about the dispersion of well-being in a community, and the covariation of this well-being with other community SIs. For each valued state, it is possible to index the average level of attainment, the degree to which attainments differ, and the degree to which differences in attainment are correlated with other features of the individual or community. To do this requires the collection of aggregated data, drawn by sampling among the individuals or communities being assessed, rather than global SIs based upon measures of the totality of which these are a part (Etzioni and Lehman, 1969). These SIs may then be disaggregated to yield more detailed information.

It has been suggested (Coleman, 1969) that failure to disaggregate economic indicators led American policy makers to mistaken diagnosis and policy concerning employment levels, with a false impression of the impact of labour policy being yielded due to a lack of information concerning concentrations of unemployment among certain population sub-groups. The dispersion and covariation aspects of SIs may be of vital importance in the assessment of change and the design of policy. The discussion in chapter 11 of this volume on relative deprivation and feelings of satisfaction has pointed out that the relative level of welfare, and not merely its absolute level, can determine the subjective experience of well-being, and, possibly, the public response to changes in welfare.

Much of the SI literature dealing with 'equality' really deals with covariation; given the preponderance of American research, the specific focus is usually racial injustice. While it is important to locate groups suffering multiple deprivations, to do so it is appropriate to consider equality as a metavalue, and choose appropriate indicators of dispersion accordingly. A number of statistical measures can describe the distribution of scores on an SI; a helpful comparison of selected measures of inequality is provided by Alker and Russett (1966), who recommended the Gini coefficient and the Schutz index, respectively, for cases where data is complete and incomplete. More refined measures may be in order, however, for expressing inequalities in ways which capture some of their subjective impact – it may be, for example, that a gradually sloping level of welfare from the most privileged to the most deprived has less impact than a distribution which displays a number of discontinuities. Covariation between SIs may be represented by various measures, such as regression coefficients; when specific groups or communities are being compared, a suitable measure may be the similarity index (as applied by Palmore and Whittington, 1970, 1971).

Just as it is unwise to rush into identifying the everyday notion of inequality with the dispersion of states on an SI as expressed in a particular statistical form, so identification of injustice with covariation requires much caution. It may be felt, for example, that workers in unpleasant occupations should receive more income than others. The concepts of equality and justice involve ethical assumptions which should be matched against the operations underlying the construction of SIs of the states. The statistical notions of dispersion and covariation clearly impinge upon these concepts, and are thus of utmost importance in SI research: often they may be even more important than simple aggregate statistics.

A second conception of justice focuses upon the covariation of services with needs, rather than studying the distribution of welfare outputs directly. An example of this conception in SI research is the work of Davies (1968), an analysis of conditions in different British local authority areas. He derives an index of territorial justice by correlating measures of the relative need of communities for particular social services against the actual levels of provision of these services in each community. Various measures are employed to assess both need and service levels; for example, a high need for services for the aged is inferred from the presence of a high proportion of old people without relatives to care for them. In the absence of much information on real levels of welfare, such analyses of social inputs may play an important role in the location and explanation of deviations from the existing norm of provision of QOL-enhancing services.

Freedom poses a distinct set of problems for SI construction. No statistical concepts clearly approximate it. True, Galtung (no date) suggests that measures of institutional pluralism might serve as indices, but either diversity or homogeneity may be the result of free choice or of imposition. Taken as a metavalue, freedom refers to the degree of choice available to individuals or communities to set their own goals, to decide whether to maintain or change their circumstances, to select what levels of welfare they will attain on particular SIs.

Again, subjective and objective SIs may be distinguished, and it is easy to conceive of a programme of investigation into the subjective sense of freedom. Whether the feeling that one's options are open or closed corresponds to the reality of the situation is, however, arguable. Objective assessment of available choice is bound up with assumptions about false consciousness and determinism, but a number of possible approaches, all with distinct limitations, may be mentioned. Freedom could be defined in terms of absence of coercion, and the severity of sanctions associated with different choices investigated: thus the degree of restraint imposed upon people refusing to accept norms of health, schooling, political participation, and so on could be studied. A related approach would involve assessing the amount of tolerance for particular kinds of deviation among community members and agents of social control, by survey methods for example. Again, survey research might be employed to investigate people's aspirations to attain levels of SIs other than those presently occupied. An alternative approach implies taking freedom as meaning something akin to accessibility of alternatives; a methodology might be developed for relating the resources (time, money, skill, etc.) of individuals to the demands on resources involved in attaining particular states (e.g. health, recreational facilities, higher education).

SI researchers have tended to ignore the complex problems associated with the notion of freedom, although it may be argued that the essential SIs actually are those referring to freedoms. It is an imposition of values to insist that people or communities should exist at a particular level of an SI, even if this is defined by others as indicating their welfare, for freedom involves the possibility that people might prefer to live in circumstances unpalatable to an observer. Even if a particular SI is generally identified as having a positive and negative pole, individuals may differ in the strength of their evaluations concerning it; they might then engage in different trade-offs between this and other aspects of welfare, without necessarily differing in their sense of overall well-being.

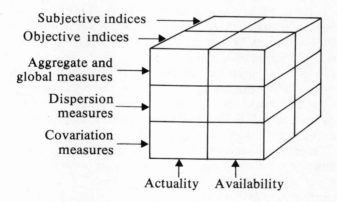

FIGURE 12.2: Taxonomy of Social Indicators

Figure 12.2 presents a taxonomy of indicators complementary to the list of indicators presented in Figure 12.1. Distinctions are drawn between aggregate, dispersion and covariation forms of SIs; between subjective and objective SIs, and between SIs which relate to the actual state of affairs and the potential availability of other states of affairs with respect to each value. SIs corresponding to different cells in this cube may be constructed for any given aspect of QOL.

This cube of different measures, along with the list of QOL areas of Figure 12.1, provides a four-dimensional matrix of SIs which might be considered as crucial features differentiating between alternative futures. Given the size of the array, and the primitive state of social theory, it is out of the question that social forecasters could make meaningful predictions about trends on any but a small fraction of these. However, if taken as a rather unwieldy set of conceptual probes into otherwise amorphous futures, these SIs can at least suggest critical divergences in QOL between alternatives. In practice researchers may often feel constrained to study merely objective dimensions of actualized states of well-being, although this demands a restrictive definition of QOL (which may also overlook important feedbacks from subjective states of well-being into social action), in which case the complexity of analysis may be much reduced.

While this SI cube has been discussed in terms of QOL indices, there is no reason why it should not be applied to make distinctions between SIs relating to other features of social systems, for example the inputs of social services to a community. As has been remarked, an SI system useful for forecasting and planning requires measures of a whole range of inputs and structures in the society in question, rather than just QOL or welfare statistics. Only by modelling the relationships between component parts of the system can the likely consequences of policies and trends be forecast. Systems viewpoints on social process, such as those presented by Easton (1965) and Salisbury (1968), which relate together characteristics of the community, the political information-processing and decision-making structure, and the forms of public policy and social services, provide a broad perspective in this context.

Indeed, Gross (1966) has applied such an approach to the analysis of SIs. While space constraints make it impossible to discuss such models at length, it is possible to summarize their advantages and weaknesses. The main criticism of systems approaches in general, their overlooking such important issues as power, inequalities and conflict, may be partly answered by the application of SIs of dispersion and covariation within such models. The secondary problem of lack of specification also carries much weight; at present satisfactory models of society cannot be constructed due to the absence of generalizable empirical knowledge about many of the relationships between system elements.

If the researcher is not concerned with establishing holistic simulations of society, however, but merely with building models of particular welfare sectors, or of explicating the relationships between different SIs relevant to such sectors, then a systems approach may be of some use. Rather than providing an invariant specification of detailed relationships, a simple mapping of SIs relating to different parts of a social system may be employed (Figure 12.3), which is applicable to a wide range of social systems.

The major advantage of such an approach is that it can aid in the explication and identification of influences upon an SI, and thereby enable contrasts to be drawn between alternative measures of the same phenomenon. It is often the case that an available SI is only tenuously related to a 'fuzzy' normative construct whose measurement is sought. An example might be the use of psychiatric hospital admissions as a measure of a community's mental health. These data are probably easier to obtain than, for example, information on the incidence of symptoms of ill health, but they reflect a variety of contaminating influences: public attitudes, hospital availability, admissions policy, etc. A systems model should suggest inter-relationships between social processes that reduce the valid range of application of an SI. Competing trends – such as Britain's declining usage of psychiatric hospital beds and increasing tranquillizer prescription levels over the past decade – should be logically related in terms of features of the system other than the level of psychiatric disturbance alone.

Systems models, by defining the context of an SI, may also clarify its normative relevance. In one context a given state of affairs may be viewed as instrumental in the attainment of a valued goal, while in another it may be viewed as dysfunctional. It must be conceded, however, that the present state of social theory makes it difficult to assess the instrumentality of many aspects of society, and the richness of a systems model will be largely dependent upon the talents of its creators rather than upon its having been constructed according to a pre-established set of rules. What is offered here, then, is not a formal theory of society nor a cookbook for producing crisp SIs (or warming up leftovers), but a broad model representing the likely impacts of social process upon SIs, which should be applicable to the

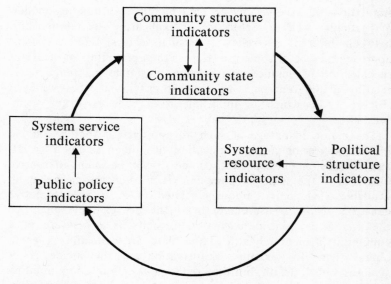

FIGURE 12.3

analysis of a wide variety of social systems and social concerns, and which provides a simple typology for SI categorization.

In this model, six types of SI are distinguished; six aspects of a social system that may be the focus of SI development are related to each other in general terms. If a specific social system were to be the object of detailed analysis, it would probably be desirable to consider additional categories of SI and SI linkages.

These six aspects of society are grouped into three blocks. One block deals with aspects of the community of concern: a community may be individually characterized and distinguished from others in terms of community structure indicators, which measure features of the social environment that are relatively slow to change, such as the age composition, cultural background and physical attributes of the community. Community state indicators measure more variable features of the community, such as, for example, levels of welfare, levels of take-up of services and satisfaction with and demands for change in these services. A second block of SIs relates to the pattern of policy and provided services within the system: indicators of public policy, such as the apportionment of expenditure to different welfare services, are distinguished from indicators of system services, the physical incorporation of these expenditures in terms of manpower, facilities, information, etc. A third block of SIs deals with the political structure and resources of the system: indicators of the properties of the policy making system, such as its representativeness of public interest, its level of institutionalization, the type and relative statuses of parties, may be distinguished from indicators of the resources of the system, such as the availability of manpower of particular types, its production capacity and wealth, etc.

Figure 12.3 displays a model relating these blocks of SIs. Interactions may occur between aspects of society tapped by SIs within each block, and the arrowed flows represent the most likely influences between blocks. The underlying conception of society is of a system in which resource allocation decisions, interacting with the prior characteristics of the community to produce changes in the state and welfare of that community, are made by a political sub-system on the basis of 'information' received from the community.

Different research traditions have involved focusing upon different parts of this model, and social monitoring has typically involved only studying trends in a given block. Often, the SIs selected to index some aspect of society are inappropriately chosen from the wrong block: thus Etzioni and Lehman (1969) point out that since the means used to attain social goals are often easier to measure than the degree to which these goals have been attained, measures of services are often substituted for measures of states – for example, health service provision and expenditure indicators employed as measures of community health levels. Often, too, explanatory research only investigates a single link between elements, although the existence of societal feedback implies the limited worth of such approaches. An exceptional study in this context is the Coleman report (Coleman et al, 1966) with its simultaneous focus upon system services (educational provisions) and community structures (ethnic, family and regional characteristics) in the determination of community states (children's educational attainments).

Measures of QOL and welfare will typically fall into the class of SIs here labelled community state indicators. It is apparent that in discussion of social policy and social justice further distinctions are sometimes drawn between community SIs. In particular, community structure SIs are often subjected to two problematic interpretations. One of these, which has already been touched upon by reference to the work of Davies (1968), is the identification of certain indicators of structure with the levels of intrinsic need for particular welfare services in a community. A related interpretation involves identifying certain of these 'background' variables with the potential of an individual or community to attain a particular social goal, within certain limits of attainment or given a particular input of services or resources. These concepts may be of value in suggesting the possibility of estimating the relative requirements of different individuals and communities for system inputs with respect to a given social goal, but the assessment of absolute needs or potential are less matters of empirical deduction than of value judgment. Even for physiological deficiencies the determination of need level requires some judgment as to tolerable degrees of human impairment, there being, for example, no sharply defined nutritional threshold below which death occurs and above which there are no ill-effects.

A systems model like the one presented here may be employed to investigate the relationships between equal opportunity and equal achievement, an issue of continuing controversy. Whereas opportunity is usually defined in terms of provision of services, this model suggests that community structure should also be viewed as a component of opportunity. The states of community welfare may result from both the degree of provision of welfare services and the take-up of these services as determined by community structure. In principle, SIs of services, structure and state (including both welfare and take-up) could be formally related together, and empirical evidence brought to bear upon the relationship between service SI dispersion and state SI dispersion. The effects of changing levels in one dimension of welfare upon take-up of other welfare services could be investigated, so that forecasters might determine the feasibility of predicting the consequences of changing policies for different forms of welfare more or less as independent closed systems.

Social indicators and social process

Social forecasting might be expected to benefit in two main ways from the accomplishments of the SI movement. Firstly SIs may be used as tools for the evaluation of policy and technological change, and secondly they may provide a basis for predictive models of society. The historical role of economic indicators may be cited to clarify both the promises and dangers of SI use. Kaldor (1971) described how British economic policy objectives of full employment, surplus balance of payments, and increasing wages, came to be expressed in terms of economic statistics. Successive governments adopted a managerial approach towards these quantitative objectives which also became accepted as goals that the public might legitimately demand, although they proved difficult to achieve simultaneously. Meade (1970) has reviewed the use of economic indicators in planning, finding several benefits: the statement of a particular goal may help reduce uncertainty about the future thus aiding rational decision-making, the co-ordination of various agencies' decisions, and the location and removal of specific constraints. Indicative planning does not, however, resolve conflicts between different interest groups, and in practice appears to have been instituted in a piecemeal, localized and unco-ordinated fashion.

It is plausible that the compilation of increasing quantities of SI data will encourage managerial attitudes toward the aspects of society indexed. Two problems may arise: firstly, a limited set of SIs will be employed as the sole guide to the soundness of policy, probably those which policy makers feel to be most objective and accessible but which will not tap many important aspects of QOL. Secondly, reification of an SI may mean that policy makers take it as more relevant than the social welfare supposedly underlying it; this would correspond to the accusation that GNP has been viewed as more real and important than the more general welfare with which governments were originally concerned.

Etzioni and Lehman (1969) argue that problems such as these call for the construction of multiple SIs for each aspect of QOL considered, for tests of the quality of data, and for the deliberate compilation of SIs for purposes of general social monitoring rather than as by-products of more limited institutional data processing. Biderman (1966) draws attention to a proposal previously made with respect to statistical series in general, that they should be subjected to quality control by a commission of technical experts. He points out its relevance in a discussion of the use of SIs for partisan political ends – the use of 'social indicators' and 'social vindicators' – in which he also stresses the misleading effects of low quality and fractional SIs, and the likelihood that proponents of alternative policies or politicians will accept statistics which confirm their particular preconceptions less critically than those which do not. Such usage of SIs may lead to public distrust in the application of statistics to QOL matters.

These issues transcend the notion of validity as usually employed in social science. For example, while the procedure of convergent validation, the use of multiple indicators of a single state, is well-known in social research (e.g. Campbell, 1969a,b) it assumes the existence of a stable underlying construct which operational indicators are each tapping with some degree of error. However, when issues of values are present such as are raised in QOL research, constructs may be unstable. Changes in social values, for example, may lead to alterations in the accepted meaning of good health or useful education. The implications of this are twofold: firstly, that compound indicators based on some fixed combination of relevant SIs, such as those obtained by factor analytic techniques, are of limited applicability (in any case they make less tangible entities for policy decisions than discrete SI parameters); and secondly, that some form of repeated monitoring of public values is called for to detect value shifts which may render some SIs irrelevant to the measurement of welfare whether or not criteria of statistical validity are fulfilled. Convergent validation can in fact contribute to the elucidation of public values: if a number of SIs cited are really measures of the same underlying phenomenon, then they should be inter-correlated, showing similar trends across time and situations. If this is not the case, then empirically distinct constructs may be confused, and, for example, factor analysis would discriminate several distinctions and the specification of value priorities. As pointed out by Biderman (1966, p. 83), 'the existence of conflicting data often provides a ready basis for examining divergent social perspectives towards a phenomenon'.

If a broad perspective on QOL is not taken, and the necessity for public participation in its definition not accepted, it is probable that one outcome of the SI movement will be to enshrine a limited set of SIs augmenting GNP as measures of social health. Important areas of human welfare will be either omitted or measured tangentially; social policies will be evaluated in terms only of these standards, which the public will be encouraged to view as ultimate criteria of the good life. The language of political debate will be 'technologically' impoverished; among possible consequences might be increasing alienation and lack of comprehension of the disjunction between 'objective social reality' and personal experience, leading to withdrawals from orthodox social and political participation. A QOL package not containing multiple measures of each area of concern, which is arbitrarily restricted to 'hard' data by prejudices against survey research and to social inputs (service measures) for reasons of convenience, and which does not capture nuances of public opinion (as expressed, say, by minority and avant-garde groups) or flexibly incorporate new dimensions of QOL that become relevant, would mainly benefit a 'social science priesthood' (Campbell, 1971). An open society needs open SIs; society has emergent rather than static concerns, and thus communities need to design and take part in their own experiments.

The use of SIs for the evaluation of social policies and pro-grammes has been held forth as one of their most valuable applications. Sheldon and Freeman (1970) have rightly com-mented that the existence of SI data *per se* cannot lead to rapid and improved understanding of the effects of policy. What is necessary for such evaluation is the application of experimental and quasi-experimental analyses, employing controlled com-parisons whereby causal influences may be assessed. The conceptual bases of such analyses are described in Campbell and Stanley (1963). Campbell (1971) has shown their application to the evaluation of policy changes in an invaluable paper. He outlines the various threats to the validity of inferences concerning the effects of policies, and appraises techniques for circumventing them. Even so, evaluation of social policies may be hindered by their impact being only evident in the long term, and as yet few of the studies of policy effects reported have attained Campbell's standard.

It has been disputed whether the development of SIs will help social theorists create more adequate models of society. Shonfield (1972) for example, argues that a satisfactory social theory is a prerequisite to setting up a comprehensive SI system; but he also describes how the early use of economic indicators enables policy makers to perceive trends and engage in crude economic analyses, the groundwork of applied economics. It seems likely that the availability of more securely founded social information will allow analysts to relate different aspects of society, test out various crude hypotheses and thus achieve some degree of explanation. This should assist both the formulation of elementary social models and the assignment of priorities in policies affecting the various causal factors influencing a given aspect of welfare. Various studies have already been published which attempt to test out social theories with data from the volumes and annuals of SI material available at present. These developments do not, of course, depend upon the existence of QOL indicators derived on the basis of community participation, so while of use to forecasters in their own right, they reveal little about the total range of QOL outputs of social changes.

Representative of current trends in the application of SIs within social models which can provide a basis for policy evaluation is the work of Anderson (1973). He analyses variations in aggregate health status across the thirty-two counties of New Mexico, relating these on the basis of cross-sectional data to variations in health services and social and demographic characteristics of the counties. The resulting causal model could, in principle, be used to assess the impact of social or policy changes, although the data base is very much open to question, and the assumption of unidirectional causal relationships between variables being no more justifiable in this context than in most other examples of social processes. However, such modelling projects represent the first steps toward the development of applicable SI systems, and the development of longitudinal SI data can only serve to encourage the sophistication of such models.

The use of SIs as instruments for policy analysis is in fact likely to meet with political obstacles to validity as much as intellectual laziness. Political demands for rapid evidence that a programme is successful may lead to unscientific reporting of data, and the establishment of satisfactory SIs may be hindered by such pressures. Conversely, the definition of social issues in clear-cut terms, as in the case of expressing a policy goal in quantitative SI terms, may make agreement on policy formation far more difficult. Maestre and Pavitt (1972) have pointed out that compromise is often made possible by the lack of clear specification of objectives. Some opposition to the development or publication of SI data may thus be based upon the possibility of its providing material for critics and creating an 'over-informed' attitude towards policy formulation, with the potential conflicts between interest groups made more manifest. Bauer (1969a) raises a related issue; that increasing the 'visibility' of social problems by preparing concrete information about them may produce frustration if the shortcomings revealed are beyond society's immediate capability of response. Harrington (1968) views social accounting as liable to provoke conflict between private interests and those concerned with public welfare, and considers that the progress in society which the SI movement proposes to monitor will only be brought about with major institutional changes. SIs may also provide forecasters with useful knowledge about current latent conflicts which may come to be recognized in the future, given the creation of new channels of communication, for example.

The issue of visibility is of relevance to dealing with social problems: many researchers into social welfare have commented upon the lack of response of authorities to social ills which are diffuse rather than concentrated in one place, private rather than in public view. Boaden (1971) in a quantitative analysis of local policy in Britain found that, while the pressure of obtrusive physical features (e.g. the amount of low-quality housing in a district) was closely related to the degree of expenditure on appropriate policies, the degree of presence of more personal problems (e.g. those associated with physical handicap) was not. Frazer (1973) links the growth of concern about social welfare during the Industrial Revolution to the concentration and multi-plication of diffuse and remote miseries, such as those associated with child labour. If the development of comprehensive SI data can make some hidden social problems more visible, then the service it will have performed should be reflected in policies directed towards these problems.

One threat perceived by some commentators is that the creation of banks of SI data may involve reduction of personal liberty, both in the issue of compulsion (as often employed in censuses, for example) and in the problems of safeguarding information concerning individuals (which is particularly relevant when longitudinal data are required, which may involve identification of the people to whom information pertains). These dangers must also be borne in mind by compilers of SI data, who must build appropriate safeguards into their data collection and storage systems.

Indicators and forecasting: conclusions

The growth of the SI movement can only be welcomed by forecasters for its promise to provide comparative data concerning trends in many areas of society about which intuitive or dubious judgments have been the only guides. Likewise, the development of useful explanatory models of social processes based upon this data would be viewed as a valuable contribution to the delineation of alternative futures.

The debate engendered by conflicting interpretations of trends, and different approaches to operationalization, may also help forecasters to clarify their own value perspectives, and become aware of the variety of value systems that can be brought to bear upon issues concerning the future. On the other hand, SIs cannot, as has sometimes been claimed, be used to formulate values or to set goals: values are the basis for our evaluation of SI data, not *vice versa*. Likewise, hopes that scientific analyses alone will automatically solve value issues, provide QOL indices, and so on, are unfounded. Making the values underlying social forecasts more explicit and open to challenge may be facilitated by reference to a set of QOL objectives.

This basis in values means that SI developments pose problems for forecasters who acknowledge the normative essence of forecasting. The issues involved in accepting participatory development of SIs underlie those of the participatory construction and choice of futures, for the generation and description of alternative futures involves use of SIs (even if not quantitatively defined, validated, or explicit). A major priority for forecasting research is the development of techniques for integrating such participation from the outset of research projects. Otherwise, it is likely that both the SI and the futures movement will serve further to entrench the values of current political and intellectual élites into planning decisions.

The suggestions made here concerning the development of QOL measures on the basis of participation, and the description of alternative futures in terms of such measures, were not intended to minimize the contribution that different kinds of forecasting groups and techniques may make. Indeed the existence of groups of forecasters prepared to criticize each other's work is an essential component of participatory planning, for the complexities of many situations make it difficult for lay people to grasp the effects of varying assumptions and models. This is particularly true when global, rather than piecemeal, planning and assessment are involved. In this vein Campbell (1971) suggests that an institute for critical re-analysis of SI data be set up, with right of free access to original data (with anonymity safeguards) for interested researchers.

The fundamental problem with SI research in a forecasting context is that such research, as largely carried out at present, may tend to increase the concentration of power in the hands of a technocratic élite. Its potentials are multifold: it can increase the visibility of social problems and locate emergent problems, thus pointing out required social and technological innovations; it can extend accepted notions of welfare, so that the responsibility of planners for the quality of life of the planned-for becomes more evident; it can provide a basis for the systematic comparison of the consequences of alternative futures for those holding alternative value perspectives and for the elaboration of both purely theoretical social science and our techniques of policy assessment and experimentation. Whether these potentials will be realized remains to be seen.

Part IV

An International Perspective for Values in Forecasting

13. Scientific and traditional technologies in developing countries 223

14. Reducing world-wide inequalities 250

Introduction to Part IV

In view of the complexity of the assumptions described in Parts I and II and the detailed critique of existing methods made in Part III, it might appear that the task of saying anything at all about alternatives for the future were almost impossible. Undoubtedly it is difficult, and what can be done should at least be illustrated, lest the reader conclude that the problems are insurmountable.

We therefore thought it advisable to add, as Part IV, two chapters which have been written in awareness of the intellectual and methodological difficulties, but nevertheless demonstrate that substantive contributions are possible.

The first of these highlights the gulf between indigenous technology and understanding of available materials at the levels of society where development is most needed and the R & D systems of many developing countries, oriented as they usually are towards the industrialized countries. The failure to link these two levels is discussed and the discussion is an implicit argument that problems, however general, need to be considered for specific regions, rather than globally, because the reasons for the failure will be different in different circumstances.

The final chapter offers quantitative support to the need for reduction of inequality between nations and explores some of the implications for the developed world if various degrees and rates of reduction are achieved.

These chapters are examples of how the aims and assumptions of Parts I and II have relevance to the real world in which decisions have to be taken; decisions which will have lasting and major effects on the world as we know it.

Chapter 13

Scientific and Traditional Technologies in Developing Countries

The purpose of this chapter is to make a brief analysis of the role that science and technology have played in the developing countries in the last decades, and of the prospects for the future. There is ample literature on the subject, and although it has greatly contributed to a better understanding of the problems involved, much of it is oriented from the point of view of the developed countries. As a result of this bias in the treatment of the subject, some of the basic characteristics of the under-developed countries are left aside as irrelevant to the main issues involved, or treated as minor features which can be easily assimilated into the general framework of the supposedly really important problems. Our main objective is to see the role of science and technology from the point of view of the under-developed countries taken as a whole, including those elements that are so commonly almost completely disregarded.

The situation that now confronts the developing countries in the field of science and technology, after several decades of effort to build up Research and Development systems appropriate for their needs, is too well-known to be worth a treatment in detail. For our purposes, it will be enough to point out the main features.

Since the beginning of the century and, above all, after the Second World War, the developing countries had tried to break the chronic stagnation of their economies through the introduction of modern methods of production. The key factor of this effort was the generation of a process of industrialization that was based on the well-known mechanism of import substitution. The general pattern adopted was more or less similar in all countries: a first stage in which only the most elementary and simple consumer goods were produced, followed by the production of increasingly sophisticated durable goods, and finally, in some countries, by the building up of an incipient heavy industry.

From the point of view of the market, this industrialization was based on the demand of the privileged minorities which constitute between 10 and 20 per cent of the total population in most developing countries, and hold most of the economic and political power. These minorities are predominantly urban, have an essentially European education, and follow the cultural habits, values and patterns of consumption of the middle classes of the advanced countries. A modern sector of the economy was thus developed in the backward countries, which in some fundamental aspects is closely integrated with the industrialized countries.

The rest of the population, mostly rural, has been hardly touched by this process of modernization, and remains more or less in the same state of poverty and backwardness that has been its lot for many generations.

It is sometimes argued that this vision is too pessimistic, and that the traditional sector of the under-developed countries is really improving, as shown by the fact that the GNP of those countries is growing at a rate of about 5 per cent a year in most cases. A closer look at the meaning of these figures, however, is enough to show that this supposed improvement is in most instances a fallacy, based on the erroneous assumption that the figures which express the GNP have the same meaning in all countries, whether developed or not. The truth is that while in developed countries the GNP reflects the economic activity of the whole society, in the developing countries it includes only that part of the production which enters the economic market, and so is included in the systems of national accounting. A great part of the population of these countries lives on a subsistence economy, which does not participate in the general economic market, and so is not included in the national statistics on which the calculation of the GNP is based. The global product is thus much larger than that reflected by the official calculated GNP and, consequently, the real rate of growth is much smaller. Considering that the rate of growth of the population of these countries is between 2 and 3 per cent, and that most of the improvement of the economy is in the modern sector, it is evident that the economy of the traditional sector is growing at a pace hardly faster than that of the population.

The evolution of the R & D systems of the developing countries shows a marked parallelism with the growth of industrialization. Before the beginning, or the acceleration, of this process, when the economy was based almost exclusively on the export of raw materials and the importation of manufactured goods from the industrialized countries, there was very little scientific activity and most of it was basic research connected with the disciplines which had some social demand, such as medicine in the most advanced of the developing countries. As industrialization started with the replacement of easily manufactured products, very little local R & D was needed. As the industrialization advanced, however, more complex goods had to be produced in areas where technology changed rapidly because of R & D carried out in developed countries. The inability of local R & D to carry out original technological research, or even to adopt intelligently technologies developed abroad, was a contributory factor in declining international competitiveness and in the stagnation of agriculture and livestock production.

It was necessary to create local R & D systems capable of efficient interaction with the productive sector. This was done by applying the same imitative criteria that were used to induce industrialization. R & D systems were created with the same structure and on the same general principles as those in existence in the advanced countries. It was assumed that once a 'modern' scientific system – in the sense of themes of research, quality of personnel, equipment, etc. – came into existence, it would become in due time naturally connected with the productive system through the classical chain of basic, applied, and development research.

As is now well-known, those expectations were not fulfilled. Despite the advice and material help of international institutions and scientific centres of the advanced countries, the R & D systems of the under-developed countries proved incapable of generating any significant amount of indigenous technology. Even in the field of adaptation, which looked more promising in recent years, they are only able to introduce minor modifications to adapt a final product or process of local raw materials, or to make a better use of the particular combination of factors of production of the country involved. As for the study and solution of the basic problems of the traditional sectors of those societies, their contribution has been negligible.

The causes of the failure of the R & D systems of the developing countries to contribute to the solution of the problems of their societies are obviously very complex, and include socioeconomic and political, as well as technological factors. For the sake of clarity, however, we will concentrate first on those elements of the problem most directly connected with the R & D systems. As a basis for our analysis, we will adopt the following criteria and definitions:

1) We will accept as a basic fact that most developing countries are dual societies, composed of a modern and a traditional sector. The modern sector comprises between 10 and 30 per cent of the population, has an average income per capita 10 to 20 times higher than the traditional sector, and has the cultural habits and patterns of consumption of the middle and upper classes of the advanced countries. The traditional sector comprises in most countries the vast majority of the population; lives mostly on a subsistence economy; and its cultural patterns are still largely based on those prevailing in the past. In the last decades mass media communications have started to change its cultural habits, without improving its material situation.

According to many social scientists, particularly those from Latin America, the relationship of the traditional sector with the modern sector is one of dependency which closely resembles the relationship between developed and developing countries. The traditional sector produces the raw materials that are exported or required as inputs by the modern sector. Most of the benefits of international trade are invested in the modern sector which, added to the great wage difference between urban and rural sectors, tends continuously to widen the economic gap between the two sectors.

2) We will consider technology broadly divided into two types: modern or scientific technology, and traditional technology based on empirical knowledge. This distinction is important, because about half of humanity and a great majority of the population

of under-developed countries uses traditional technology to solve most of the problems of the subsistence economy in which they live.

From the point of view of their structural connection with society, the two types of technology present radical differences. The scientific technology is generated by a clearly differentiated institutional framework that includes the institutions specifically devoted to scientific and technological research and the public and private organizations that produce goods and services. This complex and loose organization is what we call the R & D system of a country. The traditional technology, on the other hand, lacks any institutional arrangement, and is based on practical knowledge, which in some way is generated and dispersed in the whole community.

It is obvious that this sharp division between traditional and modern technologies is somewhat artificial. In modern societies there are technologies in use which include some elements of traditional knowledge. Conversely, in the traditional sector of society there is some penetration of modern technologies, mainly in some basic services such as health, transportation and communication. For the purpose of our analysis, however, these exceptions do not alter the overall picture.

3) For the study of the behaviour of the R & D systems, we define as the problem area of a society the set of problems that can be solved by the application of technologies, either modern or traditional.

To define what really constitutes a problem is often a very elusive question as the same social situation can be considered differently, depending on the ideological position of the observer. In relation to the first part of this analysis, in which we are mainly concerned with the behaviour of the R & D systems under present conditions, we consider only those problems which exert actual demand on the sources of technological solutions.

Demand and supply of technology

Figure 13.1 is a very simplified representation of the mechanism for generation of technologies as they work today, and its relationships with society. It refers to the whole world, but can be applied with little modification to any particular under-developed country.

The boxes at the bottom of the diagram represent the sectors into which we have divided world society: advanced countries (Ad); and modern (MS) and traditional sectors (TS) of the under-developed countries. The sizes of the boxes are approximately proportional to the size of the population included in each of these. The circles in the centre are dimensionless and depict the relationship between the problem areas of the three sectors; the amount of overlap reflects, in general terms, how much they have in common. The circles in the upper part of the diagram represent the sources of technological solutions: the R & D systems (RD) of the developed and developing countries, and empirical knowledge (EK). The sizes of the RD circles express their relative importance, although not in exact quantitative terms, as reflected by investment, personnel, etc. The broken arrows indicate the demand upon the sources of technology. The full arrows depict the 'flux' of technological solutions; their width represents the relative importance of the directions of circulation. Finally, the dash and point lines reflect the inter-connections between the sources of technology.

The diagram can be clearly divided into two parts: the left-hand side represents the relationships from the point of view of circulation of technology between the advanced countries and the modern sectors of the developing countries; the right-hand side depicts the situation of the traditional sector of the under-developed countries. We will first analyse the left-hand side of the diagram.

Most of the features shown in this part of the diagram are well-known, so we will consider only those which are more relevant to our purpose. The characteristic which determines the overall pattern of the flux of technology is the overlap of the problem areas of the two sectors under consideration. The modern sectors of the under-developed countries, having the same cultural trends and values as the developed countries, have the same patterns of consumption and, hence, exert a similar type of demand on the productive and R & D systems.

As about 98 per cent of the R & D capacity of the world is concentrated in the developed countries, it is obvious that the

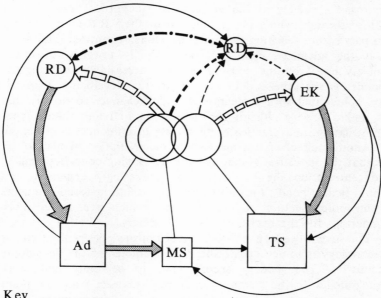

Key

RD = R and D systems
Ad = advanced countries
MS = modern sector
TS = traditional sector
EK = empirical knowledge

FIGURE 13.1

overwhelming majority of the technological solutions for the area of common problems has to come from the R & D systems of these countries. Moreover, the overlapping of technological problems is continuously enhanced by a feedback mechanism created by the way in which technology circulates in the whole system.

This mechanism is based on the fact, sometimes overlooked in the representations of the R & D systems, that the productive structure of the developing countries is not directly connected with the technological systems of the advanced countries. Of the many technical solutions explored by the R & D systems of these countries, only those that are accepted by their internal markets are finally introduced in the developing countries. In other words, the society of the industrialized countries operates as a 'filter' through which the production of their R & D system has to pass before reaching the under-developed countries. The result – as the advanced countries move rapidly towards a welfare society based on the consumption of increasingly sophisticated goods – is that the R & D systems of the developing countries are confronted with a technology which changes so rapidly that it makes it very difficult for them even to be up-to-date with information, and practically impossible to influence its direction.

Another effect of this mechanism of circulation of technology is that the industrial systems of the developing countries tend to concentrate on the production of increasingly expensive and sophisticated goods, thus diverting human and material resources from other sectors of the economy which are much more important for the backward parts of society.

The overall effect of these mechanisms of generation of technology is to accentuate the dual character of the developing countries. The modern sector tends to be more and more integrated with the advanced countries – at least from the point of view of cultural habits and patterns of consumption – thus widening the gap with the traditional sector, even if the latter has some marginal improvement in its living conditions. Besides, and this is a most important point, the *character* of the gap is changing. In the not too distant past, the gap was to a certain extent quantitative, in the sense that the more advanced parts of the population of the developing countries were still struggling to reach the satisfaction of the basic needs, as were indeed many of the inhabitants of the developed countries. There was no real basic difference from the aspirations of the more submerged part of their societies. Now, however, the values and aspirations of the post-industrial era are starting to permeate the modern sector of the under-developed countries. The basic philosophy of this 'second industrial revolution' is that the struggle for the basic needs of life is a problem of the past, and that it is necessary to look for new goals and aspirations for the future development of mankind. This crucial difference in outlook between the two parts into which developing countries are divided is what is starting to introduce a strong qualitative element in the gap that separates them, widening it in a new conceptual direction.

The above considerations also help to clarify the problems of adaptation of technology in the under-developed countries. In recent years, due to the evident failure of their attempts to create R & D systems capable of generating indigenous technologies, the attention of many developing countries has turned to the control and adaptation of imported technology. In a few countries some progress has been made in the selection of the technologies to be imported, but there has been very little success in the field of adaptation, for very understandable reasons.

The central problem can be very simply stated: adaptation to what? As we have seen, the overwhelming majority of imported technologies are devoted to satisfying the demand of the modern sector of the society. As this demand is similar to that of the advanced countries, it is difficult to see how the weak R & D systems of the developing countries could compete with the scientific and technological structures of the industrialized countries to produce different goods to satisfy the *same* needs. Even if it were possible by enormously increasing the R &D investments in the backward countries, it would be very hard to justify from the point of view of its social cost.

As for the production of these goods using more labour-intensive technologies, so as to be more in accordance with the factor endowment of the developing countries, the problem is extremely difficult to solve. In the first place, to devise such technologies to produce more or less the same goods as are now imported, requires an R & D system of a capacity comparable to those of the advanced countries. Secondly, and no less important, in the market conditions of the modern sector of the developing countries the entrepreneurs compete among themselves on the same basis as in developed countries: producing increasingly more 'up-to-date' and sophisticated goods, marketing the prestige of a particular internationally renowned brand, etc. In this situation, even if they wished otherwise (which is highly doubtful, as they have a vested interest in the conservation of the system), they can only survive by adapting the latest technologies of the advanced countries, in order rapidly to put the new products on the market.

The above considerations are enough to understand what happens in the right-hand side of the diagram. The most important feature of the traditional sector is that it comprises more than half the total population of the world, and about 80 per cent of the population of the under-developed countries. If the importance of a problem can in some way be measured by the number of people it affects, then the problems of this part of society in science and technology, as well as in any other field of human activity, are the most important that confront us.

All the characteristics of the traditional sector in relation to technology stem from the basic fact that its problem area, as we have defined it, has very little in common with that of the modern sector. The most relevant features of the traditional sector are too well-known to require a detailed description: it still greatly depends on a subsistence economy – despite the fact that it is the producer of the raw materials on which the growth of the modern sector is based – and is therefore practically outside the market integrated by the modern sector. Most important of all, it lives for the most part in a state of utter material misery. Its central problem, therefore, is to satisfy the very basic needs of everyday life.

The technologies used by the traditional sector are based mainly on practical knowledge, which is transmitted basically by verbal tradition and is the result of centuries of struggle to survive. This knowledge comprises a large amount of useful information on the physical environment and on the ways to use it to provide for the essential needs of life. Its lack of a theoretical base, however, makes the technology it generates essentially static, with very little capacity for response in the face of rapid changes.

As we have already seen, the connection of the traditional sector with the sources of modern technology is extremely weak. The technological solutions produced or adopted by the modern sector of the economy are generally not suited to the particular conditions of the traditional sector and, besides, this sector lacks the economic capacity to accede to them.

The relationships between the three sources of technology also reflect the overall situation. The R & D systems of the developing countries are strongly inter-related with the R & D systems of the advanced countries – mainly through basic research – and make their contribution, however small it might be, to the generation of the scientific knowledge which constitutes the base of modern technology. On the other hand, the body of empirical knowledge of the traditional sector has practically no connection with the R & D systems of the modern parts of society. It is not considered, in general, an object of scientific enquiry.

In conclusion, the modern and traditional sectors of the under-developed countries have two separate sources of technology, which tend to drift apart as the modern sector becomes more and more integrated with the advanced societies.

Science and technology and the gap between the modern and traditional sectors

Development by the expansion of the modern sector

How can the gap between the modern and traditional sectors in developing countries be closed, and what is the role of science and technology in this process?

The implicit assumption in the advanced countries, and in the dominant classes of the developing countries, has been that the mere expansion of the modern sector will finally transform and absorb the traditional sector. However, even a very superficial analysis of recent historical experience, and of the conditions required for that huge expansion of the modern sector, shows that this hypothesis is really untenable. The fundamental reasons can be very simply stated.

In the first place, under the circumstances we have examined very briefly above, the modern sector has had to adopt the same capital-intensive technologies that predominate in the indus-trialized countries. Even for many of these countries, with their high rate of multiplication of capital and low rate of population growth, it is not an easy task to maintain full employment. For the under-developed countries, with low rates of capital accumu-lation, a high rate of demographic growth and 70 or 80 per cent of the population still in the pre-industrial traditional sector, the problem is virtually hopeless. It is interesting to remember that during the Industrial Revolution a considerable part of the population of the Western European countries had to migrate to other continents – particularly America – due to the incapacity of their productive systems to provide enough employment. However, the technologies used at the time were more labour-intensive than those prevailing today, and the rate of population growth was significantly lower than that of the present developing countries.

In the second place, the problem of the availability of resources merits a special consideration. According to the most reliable forecasts, around the beginning of the next century the population of the earth will be approximately 7 billion, with more than 5.5 billion belonging to the under-developed countries. By the most optimistic assessments, the world population might stabilize at about 10 billion during the first half of the 21st century.

If this huge population is going to have the same type and volume of consumption that the average industrialized country has today – not to mention the level of consumption they would probably require thirty years from now – the pressures on the natural resources of the earth would be tremendous. It is not so much a problem of the ultimate physical limit of those resources – which we believe is too far away to be of any relevance to the foreseeable future – but of the generation of the enormous capital required to develop even conventional resources in the next thirty or forty years. Besides, even taking into account that some of the basic natural resources are located mostly in under-developed countries, the developed world – due to its superior economic and technological capacity – will still have a clear advantage in the competition for the traditional sources of raw materials for many years to come.

Another point also related to the material constraints is that environmental considerations will make it increasingly difficult to reach the rate of growth in the exploitation of non-renewable natural resources that would be required to raise the level of living of the whole world to the standards that are still now foreseen by the advanced countries. It is still impossible to predict the exact form these environmental restrictions will take, but they will surely impose some limitations on the unrestricted exploitation of natural raw materials.

A new road to development

We have been referring to the material constraints on development, but the basic question is whether it would be desirable, even if possible, to repeat the road followed in the past by the now developed countries. We believe it is not, as it would lead to the same situation of social and international inequality, wasteful use of resources, destruction of the natural environment and growing social alienation, that confronts Western culture today.

The problem is, then, how to define a new path to development that, being viable from the material point of view, represents a rational answer to the needs and aspirations of the deprived majority of mankind. As has been pointed out in Part III, it is very difficult to identify aspirations in a community. However, the problem changes its character if we consider two different levels: a level of basic general values, and a level of specific needs and social goals which changes with time and with different human groups.

If we accept that the fundamental objective of development has to be the creation of a society in which each human being has the opportunity fully to develop its potentialities, the first level comprises those values and elements of social organization which are the preconditions to make that basic goal at least possible. The first one, which is treated in the last chapter of this book, is the reduction of inequalities. In such basic needs as nutrition, housing, health and education, the final goal should be an essentially egalitarian humanity.

Besides the basic needs, which are the most pressing at the moment because without an adequate satisfaction of them no human being can be free in any meaningful sense, there are many other forms of inequality that have to be taken into account. Some of them, such as those based on racial, sexual, or political discrimination, are obviously unjust and should also be reduced and eventually eliminated. There are others, however, stemming from the genetic endowment of individuals or from the cultural values and traditions of different human groups, that are not the result of social oppression, and contribute to the rich diversity of mankind. Using an ecological analogy, these inequalities constitute the genetic reservoir of future cultural options.

However, it is frequently very difficult to differentiate between what we can call 'legitimate' inequalities, and those which are the result of social oppression, sometimes subtle enough to make them appear as real free options. There is no easy way to escape this dilemma; any external judgment as to what constitutes a legitimate inequality is necessarily highly subjective, in that legitimacy depends on a very complex inter-relationship between social, cultural and psychological elements, which are very difficult to evaluate. The only solution to this problem is to generate, through the effective participation of the populace in social decisions, a mechanism which makes it impossible, or at least very difficult, to impose arbitrary inequalities on individuals or social groups.

At the level of specific social needs and aspirations – which is above the level of basic needs and represents the level of cultural options at which a society expresses its essential originality – the necessity of full participation is still greater. Since by their very nature these options cannot be anticipated, the only way to ensure that they represent a legitimate social expression is by the active and conscious participation of the members of the community at all levels of decision, as discussed in Part III. The lack of this condition is certainly the most important element of the present alienation of a great part of mankind; in a certain way, such options are alien to their own cultural forms, as they have little participation in their origin and evolution.

The problem of how to ensure wide social participation is one of the most difficult of our time, and is treated elsewhere in this book. Here, we refer only to some of its implication in the field of technology, particularly for the developing countries, because, as we have already shown, they are the passive recipients of technological forms originated in quite different social and cultural environments.

Technology, defined in a wide anthropological sense, is possibly the most important component of culture. It determines the relationship of a community with its natural environment, and is the most concrete expression of its values. We believe, therefore, that one of the main objectives of any process of liberation by the developing countries should be to revive technology as one of the central elements of their own cultural creativity.

Traditional cultures and social change

The concept that the development of the backward countries can be solved by simply expanding the modern sector has produced grave disruptive effects on the social fabric of the traditional sector, without significantly improving its material standard of life. The massive immigration of peasants to the cities, which are unable to provide employment for them, is probably the most widely known of those disruptive phenomena.

The real problem, however, is not whether the material condition of living of the developing countries can be improved, but whether they have cultural values worth preserving. We believe that they have, and that their preservation is essential to maintain the rich cultural diversity of mankind. At a moment when, for the first time in history, humanity is confronting fundamental problems on a planetary scale, the contributions of different cultural visions of the world could prove essential in finding new roads to development more compatible with the physical and human environment than the ones being currently postulated in the Western world.

There is also a direct instrumental value in the preservation of some of the basic elements of traditional cultures. A different conception of development necessarily means, as we have already stated, a different system of social and cultural values. The only ones we have to begin with – besides the general ones of eliminating illegitimate inequalities and ensuring social participation – are the basic traditional values of the societies to be transformed. The task to be undertaken – which is very difficult indeed, but the only one that offers any hope of success – is the transformation of the traditional societies by the gradual and non-disruptive introduction of modern scientific knowledge, so as to reach a stage at which the essential material needs of every human being are really satisfied, in a new cultural context where the basic goals of equality and participation are harmoniously blended with the old traditional values.

It is obvious that such a process of transformation requires deep institutional and social changes which can only be achieved by political means. However, as history has repeatedly proved, the changes in the relations of power inside a society are not enough in themselves automatically to adapt the superstructural elements to the new situation. This is particularly important in the case of R & D systems, because a social change of the magnitude we are envisaging requires a tremendous amount of scientific and technological knowledge. The R & D systems of modern societies, whether of the advanced or of the developing countries, have traditions and criteria to form and orient research which were developed as a part of the mechanism of progress of the advanced Western societies. This is the main reason, leaving aside the political constraints, why the R & D system has proved so inefficient when confronted with the radically new situation posed by the traditional sector of the under-developed countries.

In what follows here, we will try to point out which are the main obstacles now hindering the effective use of science and technology by the backward countries, from the point of view of the R & D systems themselves, and in very general terms, what should be done to remove them or, more accurately, which are the problems that require research.

In the analysis we will leave aside the main political issues in the sense that we assume the existence of a political will to produce the necessary changes. It is pertinent here to remember that the will to change is to be considered in relative rather than in absolute terms. Despite the variety of political systems, most developing countries are becoming increasingly conscious that the traditional approach to development has consistently failed, and that something new has to be done. Although in most cases this attitude has very well-defined limits, it gives the opportunity to initiate new experiences, and it is a well-known fact that small, well-directed changes are the best catalysts of radical transformations.

The assumptions of the R & D systems

The first point we have to consider is to what extent the present R & D systems determine the orientation and content of the research connected with social problems from the point of view of the specific technologies required to solve them. As is known, some developed countries have very well-defined institutional structures for establishing the direction and content of the scientific effort in relation to their main objectives of development. In other countries such formal arrangement is almost completely lacking, and the R & D system works more or less independently of the formal structure of national planning. In both cases, however, the efficiency of the R & D systems, in terms of their contribution to the general objectives of their countries, is more or less the same. Of course, as we have already made clear, this statement does not represent a value judgment on the intrinsic desirability of the direction of development: it only expresses the fact that the R & D systems of the developed countries respond relatively efficiently to the implicit demands of their societies.

The explanation of this fact is very simple, and we are going to examine it briefly only because it is often almost entirely forgotten in the analysis of the problems of the developing countries.

The determination of the adequacy of a technology to a given society is a problem with many variables, only a few of them being strictly technological. Most of these belong to the fields of economics, sociology and social psychology, and form what might be called a set of assumptions, which constitute the frame of reference of the R & D system. Some of those relating to the advanced countries can be stated as follows: the scarce factor of production is labour, so the more capital-intensive technology is the better; it is necessary to stimulate consumption by producing as many varieties as possible of goods to satisfy the same needs; the dynamics of the economy depend to a great measure upon a rapid circulation of goods, so a relatively fast rate of obsolescence is desirable; a considerable part of the population has its basic needs more than fulfilled, so its consumption can only be stimulated by the production of more and more sophisticated goods, irrespective of their real social value; it is a highly competitive economy in which innovations are essential to survival, and they have to be stimulated even when they waste resources, in the sense that they result in the production of more complex and expensive goods which add nothing, or very little, to the rational satisfaction of the needs at which they are directed; natural resources or their substitutes, with a very few exceptions, are available in unlimited amounts.

These are only a few examples of the set of assumptions which directs the effort of the R & D systems of the developed countries of the capitalist world. They are the expression of the most basic characteristics of those societies, and are seldom explicitly stated since they have become assimilated by every member of the R & D systems. This is the reason why any scientist or technologist of the developed world, whatever his personal social position or political ideology, when faced with a technological problem rejects automatically, almost unconsciously, any solution which does not conform to the accepted paradigms. This is the first filter that sorts out any possible technological solution which could be of application to the specific problems of the developing countries. The trivial but important point here is that without that set of assumptions or any other equivalent, no technological problem can be stated in meaningful terms. In other words, a technological problem can be an object of scientific research only when the social and economic parameters and variables are unambiguously defined.

In the developing countries the R & D systems have evolved with the modern sector of the economy, and in close connection with the R & D systems of the advanced countries. Their paradigmatic determinants are very similar to those of the developed societies, and this similarity is continuously enhanced by the process we have already described.

In the traditional sector, on the other hand, the problem area is almost entirely different from that of the modern sector, and consequently the paradigms of the R & D system cannot be applied to its solution. It is an essentially non-explored problem area and there is no set of assumptions which could form the basic framework to direct the efforts of the R & D systems. In other words, the basic specific problems of the traditional sector cannot be stated in terms such as to make them objects of direct scientific research. The consequence which is widely known, is that the traditional sector does not in practice exert demand on the R & D systems of the under-developed countries.

This statement does not contradict the fact that the R & D systems do perform some research on the problems of the traditional sector which results in the introduction of a few modern technologies. The important point, however, is that this research is directed on the implicit assumption that the criteria applied to the modern sector are also valid for the traditional sector. This necessarily results in a piecemeal approach which induces the introduction of some 'modern' technologies, without taking into account the overall social effects. The mechanization of agriculture, which increases unemployment and drives millions of peasants to the misery of the city slums without much improving crop yields, and the build-up in extremely poor countries of expensive Western-style universities, which can absorb only a privileged minority of the population to receive a training entirely disconnected from the real needs of the country, are but two examples of a widespread phenomenon.

What the R & D systems of the developing countries lack to direct their research is a set of assumptions embodying a whole new concept of development. This would give the under-developed countries, not merely the modern sector, a frame of reference for defining adequately the type and character of the technologies required.

The role of the R & D systems in a new approach to development

The adoption of the new concept of development that we have defined in very general terms, is obviously a basic political problem, and much of its specific content will vary according to the particular conditions of the country involved. Moreover, a social project of that magnitude is not born at once, but is constructed through a long and hard process of trial and error, starting from a few basic goals. The minimum necessary precondition is the existence of the political will to improve the situation of the submerged part of the society, as fast as materially possible.

Given the political decision, one of the most important elements of success is the existence of an efficient R & D system, capable of exploring and solving the material and cultural problems of under-development. As we have already shown, the present R & D systems of the developing countries are not adequate for the new task. Thus a prime objective of the process of change should be to adapt them to the new situation.

A necessary prerequisite for even a very brief analysis of how the R & D systems should be modified is to have at least a general idea of the basic characteristics of the new approach to development from the point of view of technological requirements. The central ones, in our opinion, have to be the following:

(a) The main objective of development, at least in its first and fundamental phase, has to be the satisfaction of those basic needs such as food, shelter, health and education which are essential for any human being to be wholly incorporated into its culture.

(b) The development of every country or region will have to be based, as much as possible, on its own resources – natural as well as human.

(c) New technologies should not be socially disruptive, so as to allow a smooth continuous transition from traditional societies to better forms of social organization, preserving the best cultural elements of the old order. One essential prerequisite to this purpose is to provide socially useful employment to the active population.

(d) The rational management of the physical environment should be one of the guidelines of economic and social development. In other words, it is essential to build a society intrinsically compatible with its environment.

We believe that these four principles are an adequate starting point to reorientate the scientific and technological activities of developing countries. We want to emphasize also that the restructuring of the R & D systems is a long-term objective, and that the definition of its external context always involves a certain degree of risk. Besides, the role of an R & D system in society is not a totally passive one, and as they now actively contribute to the maintenance of social inequality in developing countries, so with different objectives they could also be a driving force in the direction of change.

In accepting this reasoning, it is clear that the under-developed countries have to start from a situation which has some similarities to that facing Western European countries at the beginning of the Industrial Revolution. At that time, those countries were starting a new social project, less explicitly defined but no less concrete than the one now confronting the developing countries. For our purposes, the important point is that they had to start by using technologies produced by the resourcefulness and craftsmanship of common people whose abilities were almost entirely based on traditional empirical knowledge. The obvious reasons were, in the first place, that the body of scientific knowledge of the time had little application to the concrete needs of the incipient process of industrialization and, in the second place, and most important, because history shows that technology commonly stems from previous technology, that the traditional one was the only one available at the time. In a more advanced stage of the process some entirely new technologies appear, based on scientific discoveries, but the fact still remains that most technology evolves from previous technologies, although with an increasingly larger scientific component.

The situation of the under-developed countries is similar, in the sense that they have to start a process of which there is little previous experience, and have to rely to a great extent on the empirical knowledge of the physical and social environment accumulated in the traditional societies. On the other hand, there is also an essential difference from the circumstances of the Industrial Revolution: the existence of a rich and diversified body of scientific knowledge which, rationally used, can enormously contribute to the technological foundations of a new approach to development.

The central problem, then, is to unite the capacity of the modern R & D systems with the experience and knowledge of the environment of the traditional societies, in order to face the technological problems of development. The main objectives of such complementary mechanisms would be the following:

(a) To define broadly – taking into account the premises previously stated, and the particular conditions of each country or region – the set of parameters which is to be used as a frame of reference for the technological solutions. This amounts to a very general description of the conditions which have to be met by the required technologies.

(b) To study the technologies being currently used – above all in the traditional sector – their empirical foundation, and how they can be used by the R & D system to find technological solutions to satisfy the basic social needs.

(c) On the basis of the previous analysis, to define for each field of activity the type and characteristics of the technologies to be used, in terms of the functions they have to fulfil. The final results of this stage are well-defined programmes of research rather than blueprints of finished operational technologies.

(d) To control the assessment of the adequacy of the resulting technologies.

It is obvious that these four stages do not constitute a strict time sequence since they will take place simultaneously. The main task of building up a comprehensive valid paradigm will constitute a dialectical process. A few initial parameters will be the framework to start to define technologies, but the experience gained in their building and application will revert on the paradigm to modify, enlarge or complete it. This is the process now operating in the advanced countries, which allows them 'spontaneously' to generate technologies adequate to their needs and aspirations, but which has yet to be induced in the developing countries.

An important point to keep in mind is that we are referring to a stage of transition, although it may well be a rather long one. Once the traditional technologies and their base of empirical knowledge have been more or less wholly incorporated, and the new paradigm assimilated, the R & D system will operate as a 'normal' one, although with an organization probably quite different from the one now prevailing in the advanced countries.

For a number of reasons already discussed, the R & D systems of the developing countries, with their present organization and methodology of work, are unable to perform the functions just defined; they lack the necessary link with the problems and the body of empirical knowledge of the traditional sector of their societies. An intermediate stage is necessary in the circuit of demand and supply of technology, where, by connecting the R & D system with the body of traditional knowledge, the problems of the traditional sector can be stated in concrete scientific terms and so exert demand on the R & D system.

What we have defined as lacking in the R & D systems is a function, and not necessarily an institutional or organizational form. However, given the complexities of the problem and the historical evidence, it seems indispensable to introduce some modifications in the organization and methodology of the R & D systems so that they can adequately perform the new function. At this stage we cannot determine precisely the institutional form of the required modifications, but we can give some idea of the type of methodology to be utilized.

In the first place, the formulation of the problem areas of the developing countries in such a way as to make them concrete subjects of scientific and technical enquiry, would require an interdisciplinary research of a type somewhat different from that being currently performed. In most cases, multidisciplinary research is understood as the collaboration of specialists of different scientific fields on a particular project. The planning of river basins, some ecological projects, and urban planning are but a few examples. In all these cases, the characteristics of the project have been predetermined, and the specialists are temporarily incorporated into the group to treat the special problems of their specific fields, although with a certain amount of interaction among them. In other words, the research is confined mostly to the stage of development.

The new form of interdisciplinary research, which should include the human and social, as well as the physical sciences, should start at the stage of *basic* research in which problems and objectives of research are defined. This implies a type of interaction which obviously requires new forms of organization in the R & D structure.

To give just one example of the type of problem involved in this stage, in order to illustrate the implications of the task to be performed, we can take the case of the tropical jungle. The recent announcement of the Brazilian Government of its intention to colonize the Amazonian Basin has been received with deep concern by the environmentalists of the advanced countries who consider that region to be the most important of the remaining 'green lungs' of the earth. The interesting point is that to utilize the jungle for economic development seems to mean to the Brazilians, as well as to the rest of the world, to destroy it. Apparently the European tradition of crop farming and stock raising in terms of closed and cleared areas, which leads to destruction of the forest, is accepted as the only practical way to utilize the land economically. However, is it really the only rational approach? Why not consider the jungle a virgin natural renewable resource with enormous potential possibilities of economic exploitation without completely destroying it?

This approach to the problem is much more in accordance with the basic paradigm we have stated above – utilization of local resources, rational management of the environment, etc. – than with the traditional one. To explore its possibilities, the only knowledge we have to start with is that accumulated through many generations by the people living in close contact with the jungle, or with similar environments. Complemented and enlarged by the scientific study of the biological, economic, environmental and social implications of the occupation of the jungle, it can give rise to a completely new concept of rational utilization.

The case of the jungle is just one example to which innumerable others can be added. Most under-developed countries are located in the tropical areas, in natural environments that have been scarcely studied by the R & D systems of the Western countries, and where local knowledge would be an essential contribution in finding new roads to development.

A central problem is what type of mechanisms we have to devise to facilitate the incorporation of local knowledge and experience into the operative capacity of the R & D systems. It is a most difficult question because in most cases it is not a problem of simply adopting the traditional specific technologies being used, but one of extracting the original ideas they might contain, and of studying them by applying the resources of modern science. The most important local contributions would probably be, more than in specific technologies, in new approaches to the solution of old problems which may stimulate scientific research in hitherto unexplored directions. Besides the methodological difficulties, this approach requires an unprejudiced and open-minded attitude, which is not one of the remarkable characteristics of the R & D systems in regard to traditional knowledge.

Some tentative approaches in this direction have been made in the last few years, and the Chinese experience is undoubtedly the most important one. Although we do not have enough information of the results, it seems that it fell short of achieving the objective of fully utilizing the creative capacity of the traditional sector, probably because of the lack of effective links with the R & D system. However, it constitutes a valuable experience, and deserves a careful analysis to detect its shortcomings and potential possibilities. Some programmes are also being tried in India, but it is still too early to extract conclusions.

An interesting possibility would be to combine the 'conventional' methods with some of the elaborate tools currently being used in technological forecasting. A promising instrument could be the morphological analysis which allows the systematic and exhaustive examination of all the possible technological solutions to a given problem. It has the great advantage that it helps to break the pre-established schemes, since one of its basic principles is that no possible solution can be left aside *a priori*, however unorthodox it may appear.

We have only given a brief description of the problems involved in the adaptation of the R & D systems of the developing countries to a new concept of development; its main purpose is to outline a field of work in which much research is required.

Long-term perspectives

What could be the consequences on the overall problem areas of the developing countries of a change in the objectives of their R & D systems, such as the one we have just outlined? It is a very difficult question to answer in detail, but some general results can be anticipated.

In the first place, a rapidly growing demand on the R & D systems will be generated by the same type of mechanisms that operated in the developed countries during the more advanced stages of the Industrial Revolution. That mechanism was based on the demand for technological solutions by the productive system, as the increasing complexity of the goods and services produced required a greater amount of specialized knowledge. In other words, the connecting chain with the R & D systems was built mainly in an upward direction.

An important difference between that process and the one likely to develop in the developing countries is that in the latter there will be a strong demand for basic research from the beginning, as they will have to confront problems which have never been thoroughly studied by the R & D systems of the advanced countries. This will activate a downward directed interconnection between the different sub-systems of the scientific structure that will tend to multiply the effect of the upward movement.

The growing demand of the traditional sector will divert an increasingly important part of the productive capacity of the modern sector, particularly to supply the capital goods required for the new technologies. Production of the highly sophisticated goods necessary to emulate the pattern of consumption of the rich countries will have to be drastically reduced as the economy is gradually transformed to satisfy the basic requirements of a much enlarged but poorer market. As a consequence, the developing countries will tend to be more homogeneous, and more differentiated from the advanced countries.

The concentration of the effort of the local R & D systems on the specific problems of development will also allow a more rational and coherent attitude towards foreign generated technologies. The science-based technologies will have to be imported, at least for the transitional period, with minor modifications needed to adapt them to different endowment of factors and raw materials. Until a more advanced stage is reached, the main task of the R & D systems in the field of science-based technologies would be to make enough research up-to-date so as to be able to introduce the most adequate technologies to the particular needs of a new society. In the less research-intensive technologies which will still have to be imported, the problem of selection and adaptation would be, at least from a conceptual point of view, much easier, as the social goals and basic values of the developing countries would be significantly different from those now prevailing in the advanced countries.

The general effect of this evolution in the mechanisms of demand and supply of technologies is depicted in Figure 13.2, built on the same assumptions as Figure 13.1, and representing the transitional phase. STP represents the intermediate stage where, by connecting the R & D systems with the body of empirical knowledge, the problems of the under-developed countries can be stated in concrete scientific terms.

This examination of the failure of R & D to aid development as much as was originally expected shows that it arose from misconceptions concerning the results of introducing highly evolved technologies into developing countries and from an incomplete understanding of the factors contributing to the distribution of wealth, and therefore of welfare, in developed countries. We have suggested that the problem of integrating indigenous empirical knowledge into the development process requires the definition of new aims, and have indicated possible ways of fulfilling these and of avoiding some of the pitfalls encountered to date. The approach is that the intermediate stage leading up to full integration of the indigenous sector with the R & D system is a learning phase, needing to be flexible and to maintain a variety of options for as long as possible. In this respect it resembles the approach of the other contributors to this book in attempting to assess available technologies by postulating their likely future effects and provides, in some ways, a practical application of this approach.

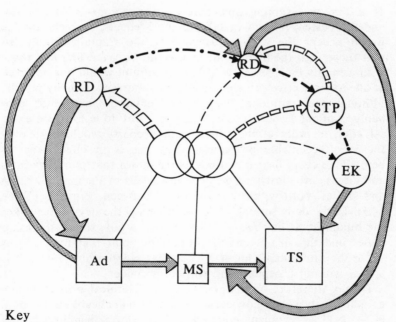

Key

RD = R and D systems
Ad   = advanced countries
MS = modern sector
TS   = traditional sector
EK = empirical knowledge
STP = intermediate stage

FIGURE 13.2

Chapter 14
Reducing World-Wide Inequalities

If a ship was sinking anywhere on the oceans of the world, and the passengers had to take to the lifeboats, scarcely anyone would accept the ethical principle if the Captain announced that those with the highest income would be saved first and those with a family income below $1000 per annum would not be saved at all. Any selective principle would be abhorrent to many people, although the traditional 'women and children' first would probably command more general support. But to rank people for salvation in order of their income or property would be one of the least acceptable procedures. Yet this is in effect what is being done every day; it can be clearly shown that mortality rates and disease are closely associated with levels of income, nutrition and shelter, both within countries and between countries (Table 14.1). In the daily scramble for the lifeboats the devil often takes the hindmost. It has become fashionable to talk about 'spaceship earth' and this brings out the important point that humanity is all in the same boat. But as Vickers has pointed out (1968), it is a boat without a captain and without a rudder.

It may therefore be maintained that an ethical principle such as that which we are advocating is simply inapplicable until there is a world government which could take responsibility for all citizens of the world, and for the diminution of inequalities. Although we would like to see some form of world government, we do not accept this view, and believe on the contrary that one of the most important responsibilities of forecasters is to take account of global issues which are outside the prerogative of national governments but nevertheless affect everyone in the world. The consciousness of important issues of national concern

Table 14.1.   Some economic and social data about groups of countries with different annual incomes per head (1955–60)

	I	II	III	IV	V	VI
			Gr	*oup*		
Annual income in $ per head	1000 & above	576– 1000	351– 575	201– 350	100– 200	100
Total population in millions	275	340	165	320	270	1390
% of the national income from agriculture	11	11	15	30	33	41
Expectation of life at birth	71	68	65	57	50	45
Inhabitants per doctor	885	1044	1724	3132	5185	13450
Infant deaths in first year per 1000 live births	24	34	68	75	100	150
% of illiterates	2	6	19	30	49	71
Consumption of energy per head (1000 kilogrammes of coal equivalent)	4	2.8	1.9	0.7	0.4	0.2
School attendance (%)	90	83	75	60	43	37
Caloric consumption per head (in 1000 units)	3.2	2.8	2.8	2.5	2.2	2
Carbohydrate content of food (%)	44	52	60	72	68	82

Source: Jan Tinbergen, *Development Planning* (Weidenfeld & Nicolson, 1967) and Wilfred Beckerman, *International Comparisons of Real Income* (Development Centre of the OECD, Paris, 1968).
Reproduced from D. Seers and L. Joy *Developments in a Divided World* (Pelican, 1971).

preceded the formation of nation states and the same must be true of global issues (Ward, 1971).

There are, of course, already international organizations which do take a supra-national view, especially the agencies of the United Nations. These may be regarded as an embryonic form of world government, in that they do attempt to assume some responsibility for world security, world health, world nutrition, world environment, world trade and finance, and many other social problems, and to take a global view of all these issues. It is notable that the very *attempt* to think in this way, despite the severe constraints on the actual operations of the U.N., leads directly to the type of approach which we are advocating. To think and act responsibly in global terms necessarily involves deep concern for the issue of world-wide inequalities. Each of the U.N. agencies has been attempting to introduce measures which would particularly benefit the poorest countries and the poorest part of the population in all member countries. They have also been trying (without very much success) to persuade the wealthier countries to commit resources on a large scale to support these efforts. Moreover, the representatives of almost all countries nominally accept the moral obligation of reducing inequalities. This may be regarded as the purest hypocrisy; but if we accept La Rochefoucauld's dictum that hypocrisy is the tribute paid to virtue by vice, then we must regard the ethical principle as well established.

However, even if the moral principle is conceded, the very lack of success of the U.N. may be taken by the cynical and the sceptical as evidence for the view that, despite the fact that all member countries are committed to the reduction of world poverty, malnutrition and disease, and make high-sounding speeches about 'one world' and aid for the poor, in practice they continue policies which widen the gulf between member countries, and do not honour the obligations which they have undertaken, especially when these appear to conflict in any way with short-term national self-interest, or the interests of powerful and privileged groups within these nations. Moreover the U.N. itself is frequently hamstrung by internal disputes, lack of resources and managerial incompetence.

These arguments must be taken very seriously indeed since they are some of the explicit or implicit assumptions of those who believe either that the issue of world-wide inequalities is unimportant, or that nothing much ever can or will be done about it. We shall argue that whether or not the U.N. plays a leading part in resolving these problems (and we hope that it will), and whether or not the existing national governments are guided by the normal considerations we have outlined (and we believe that they are not), the issue is one which cannot be evaded even by those who are motivated primarily or exclusively by considerations of expediency and self-interest.

From the experience of this work, we have become intensely aware of the strength of feeling in the developing countries on the issue of rich-poor country relationships, and the issue of foreign tutelage and interference. We have also become aware of the central importance of the choice and control of technology to the whole issue of social and economic development in the Third World. Obviously technical change is crucial for overcoming poverty, malnutrition and disease, but the choice of technology and the way in which it is introduced will also have a very great effect on social inequalities.

We therefore turn now from discussion of the moral issue to consideration of feasibility and probability. The argument will be set out in the following way: first the elementary but essential point will be made that to forecast the long-term future of any nation state (and especially Britain) in isolation from the global system would be a dubious procedure. The growing interdependence of the world system is a fact, whatever we may think about the issue of global inequalities. Secondly, a slightly longer section will summarize the essential available evidence about the extent of existing inequalities. This is necessary background to the consideration of the feasibility of reducing these inequalities. Thirdly, a brief section considers the present *trend*, i.e. whether inequality is increasing or diminishing now. Finally, in the concluding section we return to the central issue: is it realistic to believe that world-wide pressures for the reduction of inequalities will be a major feature of world politics for the next generation or two? And if so, is it realistic to believe that they could be effective and to devise ways in which this social process might be facilitated, through international, political, economic and technical co-operation, rather than frustrated by international conflict, or terminated by a third world war?

Global interdependence

First then, let us take the issue of global interdependence. It is probably unnecessary now to labour the point that to produce long-term forecasts about the future of Britain except in a global context makes little sense. The OPEC crisis is a sufficiently powerful reminder of this. For a country so dependent on international trade it is obvious that trends in world supply of food, materials and energy are of vital importance. Although we have strongly criticized the MIT computer simulation world models (Cole *et al*, 1973), we do not dissent from their view that population, resource and environmental problems must be studied in a global context. This is no less true of the movement of ideas and of social and political change. We do not have to believe in McLuhan's concept of a 'global village' to accept his point that the world communications network is now so effective that interdependence is very much an everyday reality. Finally, nuclear, chemical and biological weapons have reinforced the lessons of two world wars on the impossibility of self-sufficient isolation from the world system of international relations and international conflict. Consequently we believe it is not only ethically sound but also the starkest realism to take account of global issues, even though they are not yet the responsibility of any world government or authority.

Measures of inequality

Following this introductory discussion we now turn to a summary of the available evidence on world-wide inequalities.

The most obvious and important measure is the difference in output and income between people and between nations. It is important because so many of the other undesirable differences appear to stem from this single basic cause. Estimates of wealth and income have been made in many countries and these are the statistics which are most often used to make international comparisons. However, it is the social inequalities frequently resulting from maldistribution of wealth and income which provide the major reasons for concern and we are well aware that economic measures can be very unsatisfactory indicators of quality of life (see, for instance, McLean and Hopkins, 1974).

The most commonly used measures are also open to considerable doubt as to their accuracy. However, provided they are used with caution, they serve to indicate the orders of magnitude of world inequalities, and it is only in this way that we intend to use them here. The figure most frequently used to compare the differences in wealth between countries is GNP per capita. There are many criticisms of this measure (see chapter 12, 'The assault on GNP' and the preceding chapter in this section). GNP measures only some of the goods and services which are produced in a country and in itself says nothing about how the goods and services are distributed. It also measures some of the 'bads' as well as the 'goods'. In many countries both GNP and the level of population are very imperfectly known so that there is doubt about the accuracy of the index. In making comparisons between countries there are two other factors to be considered. Firstly, in order to make the comparisons, local currencies are usually converted to U.S. dollars at official exchange rates, and these do not accurately reflect the differences in actual cost of living in different countries. Also, in the poor countries, many people are not part of the market economy and it is very difficult to estimate their contribution to GNP. For both these reasons the use of GNP per capita figures probably overstates the actual gap in income between the rich and the poor countries. Some economists have attempted to compensate for this by making elaborate corrections to the data (Escott Reid, 1973, p. 246–7; Ranis, 1972, pp. 8–11; and Beckerman, 1966). The adjusted figures would usually imply a per capita income as much as 50 per cent higher for the poorest countries.

Table 14.2.   Income distribution between countries

Countries	Per Capita 1970 $	GNP Total 1970 $ Billion	Average annual growth rate 1960–70	Population Total 1970 Million	Percentage of world population	Average annual growth 1960–70
Rich	2,790	2,567	4.4	920	25	1.1
Middle	870	268	4.5	309	8	2.0
Poor	300	155	3.2	516	14	2.8
Very poor	120	232	1.8	1,933	52	2.2
Total	880	3,222	4.1	3,678	100	2.0

Source: Escott Reid (1973)

Table 14.2 summarizes the available data on GNP per capita and is compiled from the World Bank Atlas by Escott Reid (p. 235). The world has been divided into four groups of countries and the data aggregated for the four groups. The 'rich' countries include the Soviet Union, and account for one quarter of the total world population. From this table it can be seen that approximately half the world population lives in the very poor countries, and two-thirds in the poor and very poor combined. The per capita income of the rich countries is approximately twenty times greater than that of the very poor countries. Thus, the Lorenz curve for world income distribution is far more skew than that for any single country. The study of the more detailed tables of GNP per capita in different countries (Reid, pp. 227–234) reveals that most of the people in the very poor countries live in Asia and Africa south of the Sahara. In fact nine-tenths of the people in the very poor countries live in only six countries: China, India, Pakistan, Bangladesh, Indonesia and Nigeria. Another estimate which dramatizes the inequality in the world is that the poorest 10 per cent of the people account for 2 per cent of world consumption, and the richest 10 per cent account for 35 per cent of world consumption (Jolly, 1974). Just as there are important differences between countries, so too there are major differences between regions of the same country and between individuals within regions. The differences in wealth between the poor North-East of Brazil and the rich districts of Sao Paulo are obvious to any traveller to Brazil. Similarly, there are major variations between the states and regions of almost all countries though probably few so extreme as in Brazil. Brazil and India have almost the same proportion of population with annual incomes below $50 (U.S. 1964) although the average per capita income of Brazil is more than twice as high. The regional variations in income distribution and poverty for India are summarized by Dharma Kumar (1974). Most people are now familiar with the general picture of acute rural poverty leading to migration to the vast urban shanty slums of Asia and Latin America.

Most standard measures of inequality within countries ignore the regional variations and concentrate on the measurement of the proportion of total income earned by different groups within the country. Extreme caution must be exercised in interpreting these statistics. Most of them are based on sample surveys whose accuracy is open to question. Ahluwalia (1973) points out some of the pitfalls, but has compiled available statistics for the Chenery (1974) book on world poverty. His estimates show that the countries with the most extreme inequality are poor, while most of the industrialized countries have a somewhat less unequal distribution of income.

One of the useful indicators of distribution is the percentage of total income received by the bottom 40 per cent of the population in each country. This varies from a high of about

25 per cent for some socialist countries in Eastern Europe, to a minimum of about 6 per cent for a number of countries such as Brazil, Peru, Gabon, Iraq and South Africa. The U.K., Canada and the U.S.A. show about the same percentage (20) as Israel and Taiwan. It is unfortunate that income distribution data for China are not available, for they would almost certainly show that, although the per capita GNP is low, thus putting China among the very poor countries, the distribution would be much more equal than that in any of the other large countries, rich or poor. Whilst this conclusion is supported by information for particular enterprises or communes, and by overall impressions, to the best of our knowledge there are no nation-wide data on this point.

The main importance of these statistics for our purposes is to demonstrate that simply to increase *average* per capita incomes in poor countries will not resolve the problem of extreme inequality, unless redistribution measures are taken within countries as well, and unless the traditional rural sector is transformed. This point is taken up in chapter 13. Whilst they give a crude indication of degrees of inequality, care must be taken not to read too much into these estimates. The data are derived in different ways for different countries. Secondly, income in kind is very important in many countries including the socialist countries. Finally, the figures are based on income rather than capital. Ownership of capital is obviously an extremely important element in all considerations of the issue of inequality. Whilst it is known that the distribution of capital is far more unequal than income distribution in almost all capitalist and Third World countries, no international comparative statistics are available.

The income measures considered so far are probably the best single measures of inequality. However, they do not provide a direct measure of the physical and social characteristics which together help determine the quality of life. Some development planners (Habakuk ul Huq, 1973) have argued forcefully that it is these social indicators and other economic structural indicators which provide a truer measure of development. He urges that each country should define minimum levels of such characteristics as nutrition, education, health and housing and should aim to reach these levels within a specified time. Space does not permit us to develop the argument but we certainly agree that this move towards the identification and measurement of other economic and social indicators of development and inequality is a useful and desirable trend. Kuznets (1966) has analysed a large number of these characteristics and a few of them are summarized in Table 14.1. Both Kuznets and Ahluwalia have also analysed the correlation between several of these economic relationships. This is an area where much more research is needed before firm conclusions can be drawn, but for our purposes it is sufficient to make the general point that a substantial improvement in living standards and quality of life is possible only as a result of a widespread process of socio-economic change and a substantial improvement of productivity in agriculture and in industry. Such a process of economic transformation would certainly be reflected in a growth of measured GNP per capita. But although an improvement in the quality of life in the poorest countries is almost inconceivable without a growth of GNP, it is by no means the same thing, and it is important not to confuse the two issues. The promotion of economic efficiency and growth is not an *end* but only a means to other goals.

GNP figures give only a rough idea of the numbers of people who live in absolute poverty, i.e. who live in what can only be called sub-human conditions. Several analysts have tried to come to grips with defining where this poverty line lies in different countries, but the problem of making international comparisons is great. The minimum requirements for food, shelter and clothing differ from region to region, although there is international agreement on some things, such as the minimum number of calories required to prevent malnutrition. As a very first approximation, Ahluwalia (1974) has collected data for sixteen different countries and shown the percentage of population in 1969 receiving less than $75 per annum (measured in $U.S. for 1964). The problems of estimating income levels in subsistence non-market economies are very great, but it is probably a fair inference that many of the people below some such per capita income level are living in sub-human conditions of deprivation. As much as a quarter or a third of the whole world population is living in such conditions and their numbers are probably increasing, because of the combination of high population growth rates, low rates of real improvement in productivity in some poor countries and extreme inequalities in distribution of national income within these countries. They are concentrated overwhelmingly in the very poor countries, but there are appreciable numbers even in the rich countries.

Are the gaps widening?

We turn now to consider the evidence on whether the degree of inequality is increasing or diminishing. Kuznets (1972) and Olin (1972) have analysed the trends in per capita GNP statistics over the past hundred years. There is general agreement between these and other analysts that the gap between the rich and the poor countries has widened during this period and that the reason is the increase in wealth of the rich, rather than a decrease in wealth of the poor. There is less agreement about when the gap began to grow, or why it grew.

The measurements which have been made since the Second World War show that the gap in GNP per capita between rich and poor countries has continued to widen, at least until 1970. This has largely been due to the fact that the population increase has been greater in the poor countries than in the rich (Table 14.3), but the latest figures (1971–1974) suggest that the rates of growth of per capita GNP may now be slightly faster in the poor countries than in the rich. But even if the per capita GNP growth rate was to be 2 per cent greater in the poor countries than in the rich, then given existing levels of per capita GNP the gap would take over a century to close. And if chapter 13 is right in arguing that existing GNP growth measures exaggerate the real improvement in the poor countries, it would take even longer.

Table 14.3.   Changes in income in rich and poor countries: 1950–67

	Average percentage annual increases	
	1950–60	*1960–67*
Total income		
Rich	4.0	4.8
Poor	4.6	5.0
Income per capita		
Rich	2.8	3.6
Poor	2.3	2.5

There has been a good deal of uncertainty about whether inequality has been increasing within the poor countries over the past decade. It has been suggested that the evidence from India points not only to greater inequality of income, but also to greater absolute numbers of people living below the poverty line. Dharma Kumar (1974) has reviewed 71 papers related to income distribution in India and concludes that although there is conflicting evidence, on balance it appears that the income distribution has marginally improved and that there are fewer, not more, people living below the poverty line.

The data for Brazil are less equivocal. Census data taken in 1959 and 1970 show without doubt that income distribution became more unequal during those years.

Information from the other poor countries is sparse and unreliable. Information from the richer countries is more plentiful but even here the interpretation of the facts is disputed. At best it can be said that outside the socialist countries the reduction of inequalities has made little progress since 1945. However, Kuznets (1972) has pointed out that, even though the GNP gap has continued to widen, the gaps between some of the other economic and social indicators have narrowed. Most notable has been the convergence of such indices as death rate and literacy. This is important in considering quality of life indicators and the extent to which they may diverge from GNP indicators.

Conclusions

In summary, the following points emerge as being particularly significant:

1) There are income inequalities between countries which are greater than those existing within the most unequal countries.

2) Although most published measures of inequalities are related to per capita income, there is growing demand from planners for measures more directly related to the physical and social well-being of people.

3) Many people, perhaps as much as 30 per cent of the world population, live in sub-human conditions, below an absolute poverty line.

4) According to most indices the gap in incomes between the rich and poor nations has widened over the past 100 years. A few other indices however show a convergence within the past few decades.

5) Even if growth rates per capita now become faster in the poor countries than in the rich, the absolute income gap may continue to grow for some years.

The prospects are therefore daunting. Not only is the evidence of extreme inequality overwhelmingly strong, but the evidence is also pretty strong that at least between countries the degree of inequality has been increasing. Is it then realistic or even desirable to try and reverse the tide? Or would any attempts in this direction simply be Canute-like gestures?

We do not under-estimate the problem, but despite its massive nature, we do believe that it is both feasible and highly desirable to reverse these long-term trends and to move in the opposite direction. In a short chapter such as this it is not possible to work through all the many complex political, social, economic and technical aspects. We are attempting to do this in our research programme over the next few years, particularly in relation to the technological alternatives, and we shall be publishing the results of this work. Here it is possible only to indicate very briefly why we believe the objective is feasible, and finally to return to the issue of desirability, and our own bias in relation to these problems.

First, looking at the issue in the crude terms of average per capita GNP, with all the reservations which we have made about these statistics, the picture is not quite so black as it appears. Quite a number of both socialist and capitalist developing countries and some which appear to be hybrids have succeeded recently in achieving and sustaining rather high rates of growth – as much as 10 per cent per annum. Whilst it is true that a difference of 2 per cent between poor country per capita growth rates and rich country growth rates would imply about 150 years to close the international gap, a difference of 4 per cent would imply that the gap could be closed in 75 years.

Such a difference between rich and poor growth rates is by no means inconceivable, particularly if allowance is made for a gradual slowing down of growth rates per capita in the rich countries, for example from an average of 3–4 per cent in the

1960s to 2–3 per cent in the 1980s and 1990s and 1–2 per cent in the 21st century. There are already indications from attitude surveys and from many other sources that a slow-down of rich country growth rates is quite a plausible scenario. We do not ourselves believe that a complete cessation of growth in richer countries would benefit the poor countries because of international economic interdependencies and the risk of a worldwide slump, as well as because of acute social problems remaining within the rich countries. But a substantially faster average rate of growth in most poor countries is by no means inconceivable, and is indeed in line with what many economists, such as Keynes (1936), confidently expected would happen in the second half of this century.

That their expectations have not hitherto been fulfilled is due to a complex combination of circumstances, but among these circumstances are certainly some which can and are being changed. First of all, social and political upheavals involving the replacement of feudal and colonial regimes in many developing countries have been necessary to permit the type of economic development which Keynes and others envisaged. These changes are far from complete, but it can hardly be denied that things are very different now in Asia, Africa and Latin America compared with the 1920s or even the 1950s.

Secondly, the international economic and political order since the Second World War has not been particularly favourable to the poor countries, despite the efforts of some U.N. agencies and the expectations of some economists. Many of the potential benefits of 'aid' and higher rates of investment in the poor countries were dissipated through adverse movements in terms of trade, interest payments and other invisible flows. It is too early to assess the long-term effects of the OPEC crisis, but at least it is one indication that major shifts in the terms of trade and other world economic arrangements in favour of at least some of the poorer countries are a more realistic prospect than they appeared in the 1960s.

Thirdly, the political support necessary for such changes in both rich and poor countries is now more apparent than in the immediate post-war period. One indication of this is the growing militancy of the poor countries themselves. Another is the attitude of such people as McNamara in the rich countries. He attributes most of the local wars since 1945 to international inequalities, and sees the reduction of these inequalities as an essential way of preventing world wars and other severe international conflicts. A third indication is the change in attitude of development economists and others specializing in these problems who increasingly see the reduction of inequalities within and between countries as the central issue of world development, rather than economic growth *per se.*

We believe that these indications are more than just straws in the wind and that they add up to a realistic possibility of reversing some of the trends towards greater inequality in the next two generations. This is even more true if we drop the over-simplified and crude type of measures involved in GNP comparisons and concentrate on the quality of life issues, which are far more important, and the issues of choice of technology which underlie the quality of life.

It may be contended that those who believe in a scenario of increasing inequalities are the ones who are most lacking in realism, since they are overlooking or under-estimating the most powerful world-wide pressures of social, political and international institutional change, and numerous indications of attitude changes especially amongst young people.

Consequently, although we would acknowledge our own biases, we believe that they may be in some respects a healthy antidote to the more nationally biased forecasts, and particularly those which tend to disregard or minimize the aspirations of the Third World countries and the impact which these are likely to have on global development.

We are aware that in this necessarily sketchy outline we have been obliged to omit consideration of some extremely important issues, such as the relationship between economic inequalities and racial, sexual, and political inequalities. This is not because we under-estimate the importance of these other types of inequality, but because this chapter is intended only as the first sketch of our approach, which will be amplified in our future work.

Bibliography

Abrams, Mark (1971) 'Mass views of the future' *Futures* **3**, 103–15.

Abrams, Mark (1973) 'Subjective Social Indicators' in M. Hissel (ed) *Social Trends No. 4* London: HMSO, pp 35–50.

Adelman, M. A. (1972) *The World Petroleum Market* Baltimore: Johns Hopkins for Resources for the Future.

Ahluwalia, M. S. (1973) 'Taxes, subsidies and employment' *Quarterly Journal of Economics* August, 393–409.

Alker, Hayward M. and Russet, Bruce M. (1966) 'Indices for Comparing Inequality' in R. L. Merrit and S. Rokkan (eds) *Comparing Nations* New Haven: Yale University Press, pp. 349–72.

Allardt, Erik (1973a) 'A welfare model for selecting indicators of national development' *Policy Sciences* **4**, 63–74.

Allardt, Erik (1973b) *About Dimensions of Welfare* Helsinki, Finland: University of Helsinki, Research Group for Comparative Sociology Research Reports, No. 1.

Almond, Gabriel and Verba, Sidney (1963) *The Civic Culture* Princeton: Princeton University Press.

Amara, R. C. and Salancik, G. R. (1972) 'Forecasting: From conjectural art to science' *Technological Forecasting and Social Change* **3**, 415–26.

Ament, R. H. (1970) 'Comparison of Delphi forecasting studies in 1964 and 1969' *Futures* **2**, 35–44.

Anderson, James G. (1973) 'Causal models and social indicators: Towards the development of social systems models' *American Sociological Review* **38**, 285–301.

Andrews, Frank M. and Rodgers, W. (1972) *Some Analyses of Measures of Satisfaction, Dissatisfaction and Importance* Ann Arbor, Michigan: Institute for Social Research, Survey Research Centre, project 462150, document 8.

Andrews, Frank M. and Withey, Stephen B. (1974) 'Developing measures of perceived life quality: Results from several national surveys' *Social Indicators Research* **1** (in press).

Armytage, W. H. (1965) *The Rise of the Technocrats* London: Routledge and Kegan Paul and Toronto: University of Toronto Press.

Ash, J. C. and Smyth, D. J. (1973) *Forecasting the U.K. Economy* London: Saxon House.

Ashby, Sir E. (1973) 'Prospect for pollution' *Journal of Royal Society of Arts, Man and Community* June, 443–54.

Baier, K. E. M. (1969) 'What is Value?' in K. E. M. Baier and N. Rescher *Values and the Future* New York: Free Press, pp. 33–68.

Ball, R. J. (1968) 'Econometric models' in *Mathematical Model Building in Economics and Industry* London: Griffin.

Banks, Arthur S. and Textor, Robert B. (1962) *A Cross-Polity Survey* Cambridge, Mass.: MIT Press.

Banks, Arthur S. (1971) *Cross-Polity Time-Series Data* Cambridge, Mass. and London: MIT Press.

Banks, Arthur S. (1974) 'Industrialization and development: A longitudinal analysis' *Economic Development and Cultural Change* 22, 320–37.

Barnowe, J. Thad, Mangione, Thomas W. and Quinn, Robert P. (1972) 'Quality of employment indicators, occupation classifications, and demographic characteristics as predictors of job satisfaction' *Proceedings American Psychological Association's 80th Annual Convention*, 437–8.

Bauer, Raymond A. (1966) *Social Indicators* Cambridge, Mass.: MIT Press.

Bauer, Raymond A. (1969a) 'Societal Feedback' in Gross (1969), pp. 63–77.

Bauer, Raymond A. (1969b) *Second Order Consequences* Cambridge, Mass.: MIT Press.

Beckerman, W. (1966) *International Comparisons of Real Incomes* Paris: OECD, Development Centre Studies.

Bell, D. (1967) 'Toward the Year 2000' *Daedalus* Summer, 646.

Bender, D. A. (1969) 'Delphic study examines developments in medicine' *Futures* 1, 2, June.

Berry, Brian L. J. (ed) (1972) *City Classification Handbook: Methods and Applications* New York: Wiley-Interscience.

Bertalanffy, L. von (1956) 'General system theory' in *General Systems Yearbook* 1.

Bettman, James R. (1971) 'Measuring individuals' priorities for national goals: A methodology and empirical example' *Policy Sciences* 2, 373–90.

Biderman, Alfred D. (1966) 'Social Indicators and Goals' in Bauer, pp. 68–153.

Bjerrum, C. A. (1969) *Forecasts 1968–2000 of Computer Developments and Applications* Copenhagen: Parsons and Williams; also reported in *Futures* June 1969.

Blandy, R. *et al* (1973) 'The Bachue employment model' *International Labour Review* June.

Boaden, Noel (1971) *Urban Policy–Making: Influences on County Boroughs in England and Wales* Cambridge, U.K.: Cambridge University Press.

Bogart, Leo (1972) *Silent Politics* New York: Wiley-Interscience.

Bonilla, Frank (1970) *The Failure of Elites* Cambridge, Mass.: MIT Press.

Bowen, R. (1947) *German Theories of the Corporative State* New York: McGraw-Hill.

Bowers, R. and Frey, J. (1972) 'Solid state microwave devices' *Scientific American* February.

Bradburn, Norman and Caplovitz, David (1965) *Reports on Happiness* Chicago: Aldine.

Brannon, Robert *et al* (1973) 'A field experiment joined to a general population survey' *American Sociological Review* 38, 625–36.

Brewer, G. D. (1973) *The Politician, the Bureaucrat, and the Consultant – A Critique of Urban Problem Solving* New York: Basic Books.

Brewer, G. D. and Hall, O. P. Jr. (1973) *Policy Analysis by Computer Simulation – The Need for Appraisal* Santa Monica: RAND Corporation.

Brigard, R. de and Helmer, O. (1969) *Some Potential Societal Developments 1970–2000* Connecticut: Institute for the Future, Report R–7,

September.

Briones, Guillermo and Waisanen, F. B. (1966) 'Educational Aspirations, Modernization and Urban Integration', paper read at American Sociological Association annual meeting at Miami.

Brooks, D. G. and Andrews, P. W. (1974) 'Mineral resources, economic growth and world population' *Science* **185**, 4145, 5th July, 13–19.

Buckley, W. (1967) *Sociology and Modern Systems Theory* Englewood Cliffs, N.J.: Prentice-Hall, p. 41.

Bunge, M. (1967) *The Search for System* New York: Springer-Verlag, p. 536.

Bunge, M. (1973) 'The role of forecast in planning' *Theory and Decision* **3**, 207–21.

Bureau of Mines (1970) *Minerals Facts and Problems 1970* Washington, D.C.: U.S. Government Printing Office.

Business Week (1974) 'Review: The year the forecasters went wrong', May.

Campbell, Angus and Converse, Philip E. (1972) *The Human Meaning of Social Change* New York: Russell Sage Foundation.

Campbell, Donald T. (1963) 'Social Attitudes and Other Acquired Behavioural Dispositions' in S. Koch (ed) *Psychology: A Study of a Science* vol. 6, New York: McGraw-Hill.

Campbell, Donald T. (1969a) 'Definitional versus multiple operationism' *Et Al* **2**, 14–17.

Campbell, Donald T. (1969b) 'Reforms as experiments' *American Psychologist* **24**, 409–29.

Campbell, Donald T. (1971) 'Methods for the Experimenting Society' paper read to American Psychological Association, Washington, September.

Campbell, Donald T. and Stanley, Julian C. (1963) 'Experimental and Quasi-Experimental Designs for Research on Teaching' in N. L. Gage (ed) *Handbook of Research on Teaching* Chicago: Rand McNally. Reprinted in 1966 as *Experimental and Quasi-Experimental Designs of Research*.

Cantril, Hadley (1965) *The Pattern of Human Concerns* New Brunswick, N.J.: Rutgers University Press.

Cantril, Albert H. and Roll, Charles W. Jr. (1971) *Hopes and Fears of the American People* New York: Universe Books.

Carpenter, R. A. (1972) 'Technology Assessment and Congress' in Kasper (ed).

Carr, E. H. (1946) *The Soviet Impact on the Western World* London: Macmillan, ch. 2.

Carr, E. H. (1951) *The New Society* London: Macmillan, p. 2.

Carr, E. H. (1961) *What is History?* London: Macmillan and New York: Knopf (Vintage Books).

Cazes, Bernard (1972) 'The Development of Social Indicators: A Survey' in A. Shonfield and S. Shaw *Social Indicators and Social Policy* London: Heinemann, pp. 9–22.

Cazes, Bernard *et al* (1972) *France Face au Choc du Futur* Paris: Armand Colin.

Cetron, M. and Bartocha, B. (1973) *Technology Assessment in a Dynamic Environment* London: Gordon and Breach.

Chein, I. (1972) *The Science of Behaviour and the Image of Man* London: Tavistock Publications and New York: Basic Books.

Chenery, H. *et al.* (1974) *Redistribution with Growth* Oxford: Oxford

University Press.
Clark, J. *et al.* (1974) *Science and Technology Choices for the EEC in the Light of EEC External Dependencies* Brighton: SPRU.
Clark, J. *et al* (1975) *Global Simulation Models* London and New York: John Wiley.
Clarke, A. C. (1964) *Profiles of the Future* London: Gollancz.
Clarke, I. F. (1970) *Voices Prophesying War* London: Panther Books.
Clarke, I. F. (1971a) 'Anxious anticipations' *Futures* March.
Clarke, I. F. (1971b) 'The utility of utopia' *Futures* December.
Club of Rome (1974) *3rd Report on New Directions in Science and Technology.*
Coates, Joseph F. (1972) 'The future of crime in the United States from now to the year 2000' *Policy Sciences* 3, 27–45.
Coates, V. T. (1971) *Manned Space Stations* Staff Discussion Paper 212 of the Program of Policy Studies in Science and Technology, George Washington University.
Coburn, T. M. *et al* (1960) *The London–Birmingham Motorway* Road Research Laboratory Technical Report 46, London: HMSO.
Coen, P. G., Gomme, E. D. and Kendall, M. G. (1969) 'Lagged relationships in economic forecasting' *Journal of Royal Statistical Society,* series A, **132**, 1.
Cole, H. S. D. (1974) 'World models – their progress and applicability' *Futures* May.
Cole, H. S. D. and Curnow, R. C. (1973) 'An Evaluation of the World Models' in Cole *et al.*
Cole, H. S. D., Freeman, C., Jahoda, M. and Pavitt, K. L. R. (eds) (1973) *Thinking about the Future* London: Chatto and Windus/Sussex University Press. Issued in the U.S. as *Models of Doom* New York: Universe Books.
Coleman, James S. *et al* (1966) *Equality of Educational Opportunity* Washington, D.C.: U.S. Office of Education.
Coleman, James S. (1969) 'The Methods of Sociology' in R. Bierstedt (ed) *A Design for Sociology: Scope, Objectives and Methods* Philadelphia: American Academy of Political and Social Science, monograph 9, pp. 86–114.
Congressional Research Service of the U.S. Library of Congress (1972) *Science Policy – A Working Glossary* Washington, D.C.: U.S. Government Printing Office.
Converse, Philip E. (1963) 'Attitudes and Non-attitudes: Continuation of a Dialogue', paper read at 17th International Congress of Psychology at Washington; reprinted in E. R. Tufte (ed) (1970) *The Quantitative Analysis of Social Problems* Reading, Mass.: Addison-Wesley.
Cooper, M. H. (1974) 'Rationing health' *New Society* 18th April, 131–2.

Daedalus (Summer 1967) 'Toward the Year 2000' Boston: American Academy of Arts and Sciences.
Dalkey, Norman C. (1972) *Studies in the Quality of Life: Delphi and Decision-Making* Lexington, Mass.: D. C. Heath and Co.
Dalkey, Norman C. and Helmer, O. (1963) 'An experimental application of the Delphi method to the use of experts' *Management Science* **IX**.
Davies, Bleddyn (1968) *Social Needs and Resources in Local Services* London: Michael Joseph.
Davies, Bleddyn, Barton, Andrew and McMillan, Ian (1972) *Variations in*

Children's Services among British Urban Authorities London: G. Bell.
Davis, R. C. (1973) *Organising and Conducting Technological Forecasting in a Consumer Goods Firm* Englewood Cliffs, N.J.: Prentice-Hall.
Demerath, N. J. (1968) 'Trends and Anti-trends in Religious Changes' in Sheldon and Moore (eds).
Dharma Kumar (1974) 'Changes in income distribution and poverty in India: A review of the literature' *World Development* 2, 1, January, 31–42.
Dillman, Don A. and Christensen, James A. (1972) 'The Public Value for Pollution Control' in William A. Burch Jr., Neil H. Cheek Jr. and Lee Taylor *Social Behavior, Natural Resources and the Environment* New York: Harper and Row, pp. 237–56.
Dorfmann, R. (ed) (1965) *Measuring Benefits of Government Investment* Washington, D.C.: Brookings Institution.
Dupuit, J. (1834) *On the Measurement of Utility of Public Works* published in English in International Economic Papers (1952) and in Munby (1968).

Easton, David (1965) *A Systems Analysis of Political Life* New York: John Wiley.
Edwards, D. V. (1969) *International Political Analysis* New York: Holt, Rinehart and Winston.
Ehrlich, P. and Holdren, J. P. (1972) *Human Population and the Global Environment* Stockholm: U.N.
Ellul, J. (1964) *The Technical Society* New York: Knopf and London: Cape.
Environmental Protection Agency (1973) *The Quality of Life Concept* Washington: E.P.A. Office of Research and Monitoring, Environmental Studies Division.
Etzioni, Amitai and Lehman, Edward W. (1969) 'Some Dangers in Valid Social Measurement' in Gross pp. 45–62.
Etzioni, Amitai and Remp, R. (1972) 'Technological "short cuts" to social change' *Science* 7th January, 31–37.

Fairweather, George W. (1967) *Methods for Experimental Social Innovation* New York: John Wiley.
Feldman, Arnold S. and Hurn, Christopher (1966) 'The experience of modernization' *Sociometry* 29, 378–95.
Fishbein, Marvin (1967) 'Attitudes and the Prediction of Behaviour' in M. Fishbein (ed) *Readings in Attitude Theory and Measurement* New York: John Wiley.
Flanigan, William and Fogelman, Edwin (1970a) 'Patterns of political violence in comparative historical perspective' *Comparative Politics* 3, 1–20.
Flanigan, William and Fogelman, Edwin (1970b) 'Patterns of Political Development and Democratization: A Quantitative Analysis', paper first presented to American Political Science Association in Chicago, September 1967; published in John V. Gillespie and Betty A. Nesvold (1970) *Macro-Quantitative Analysis* Beverly Hills: Sage Publications.
Flechtheim, O. (1966) *History and Futurology* Meisenheim-am-Glan: Anton Hain, pp. 63 and 103.
Form, William K. (1971) 'The accommodation of rural and urban workers to industrial discipline and urban living' *Rural Sociology* 36, 488–508.
Forrester, Jay (1968) *Industrial Dynamics* Cambridge, Mass.: MIT Press.

Forrester, Jay (1969) *Urban Dynamics* Cambridge, Mass.: MIT Press.

Forrester, Jay (1971) *World Dynamics* Cambridge, Mass.: Wright-Allen Press.

Forrester, Jay (1972) 'Counter Intuitive Behaviour of Social Systems' in J. Bieshon *Systems Behaviour* Bletchley: Open University Press.

Foster, C. D. (1963) *The Transport Problem* Glasgow: Blackie.

Foster, C. D. and Beesley, M. E. (1963) 'Estimating the social benefit of constructing an underground railway in London' *Journal of the Royal Statistical Society* **126**; reprinted (fully or partially) in Munby (1968) and Layard (1973).

Franck, James (1945) in A. K. Smith *A Peril and a Hope* Chicago: University of Chicago Press.

Francome, Colin (1972) *The Poverty of Growth* London: Voluntary Committee for Overseas Aid and Development and Academics Against Poverty.

Francome, Colin and Wharton, Bob (1973) 'An international social index' *New Internationalist* **7**, September, 19–21.

Frazer, Derek (1973) *The Evolution of the British Welfare State* London: Macmillan.

Freedman, Deborah S. (1972) 'Consumption Aspirations as Economic Incentives in a Developing Country – Taiwan' in Strumpel, Morgan and Zahn (eds).

Freeman, C. (1970) 'Technology assessment and its social context' *Studium Generale* **24**, 1048.

Freud, S. (1920) *The Psychogenesis of a Case of Homosexuality in a Woman*. Standard edition, vol. 18, 1958, London: Hogarth Press and New York: W. W. Norton.

Freud, S. (1930) *Civilisation and its Discontents*. Standard edition, vol. 21, 1960, London: Hogarth Press and New York: W. W. Norton.

Friday, James (1971) *Windows on the Future – Science Fiction and Forecasting* SPRU, mimeo.

Fuchs, Claudio J. and Landsberger, Henry A. (1973) ' "Revolution of Rising Expectations" or "Traditional Life Ways"? A study of income aspirations in a developing country' *Economic Development and Cultural Change* **21**, 212–26.

Funkhouser, G. Ray (1973) 'The issues of the sixties: An exploratory study in the dynamics of public opinion' *Public Opinion Quarterly* **37**, 62–75.

Galtung, Johan (no date) 'From Value Dimensions for Social Analysis to Social Indicators' mimeo, Oslo: International Peace Research Institute.

Gardner, M. and Ashby W. R. (1970) 'Connectance of large dynamic (cybernetic) systems: Critical values for stability' *Nature* **228**, 21st November.

Gellner, E. (1964) in J. Gould and W. L. Kobb (eds) *A Dictionary of the Social Sciences* London: Tavistock Publications, p. 435.

Gerardin, L. (1973) 'Study of alternative futures: a scenario writing method' in T. J. Bright *A Guide to Practical Technological Forecasting* Englewood Cliffs, N.J.: Prentice-Hall.

Gibson, Q. B. (1960) *The Logic of Social Enquiry* London: Routledge, and New York: Humanities Press, p. 196.

Glenn, Norval D. (1967) 'Massification versus differentiation: Some trend data from national surveys' *Social Forces* **46**, 172–80.

Glenn, Norval D. (1974) 'Recent trends in intercategory trends in attitudes'

Social Forces **52**, 395–401.

Goel, M. Lal. (1970) 'The relevance of education for political participation in a developing society' *Comparative Political Studies* **3**, 333–46.

Goldthorpe, J. H., Lockwood, D., Bechofer, F. and Platt, W. J. (1969) *The Affluent Worker* Cambridge, U.K.: Cambridge University Press.

Goldthorpe, J. H. (1971) 'Theories of industrial society' *Archives Européennes de Sociologie* **12**, 263–88.

Gordon, T. J. and Hayward, H. (1968) 'Initial experiments with the cross-impact method of forecasting' *Futures* **1**, 2, December, 100–16.

Grabb, E. M. and Pyke, D. L. (1973) 'An evaluation of the forecasting of information processing technology and applications' *Technological Forecasting and Social Change* **4**, 2, 143–50.

Greeley, Andrew M. and Sheatsley, Paul B. (1971) 'Attitudes toward racial integration' *Scientific American* **225**, 13–19.

Greene, J. E. (1972) 'Participation, integration and legitimacy as indicators of developmental change in the politics of Guyana' *Social and Economic Studies* **21**, 243–83.

Gross, Bertram M. (1966) *The State of the Nation* London: Tavistock Publications. First printed in Bauer (1966) pp. 154–271.

Gross, Bertram M. (ed) (1969) *Social Intelligence for America's Future* Boston: Allyn and Bacon. First published as May and September issues of *Annals of American Academy of Political and Social Science* (1967).

Gurin, Gerald, Veroff, Joseph and Field, Sheila (1960) *Americans View their Mental Health* New York: Basic Books.

Gvishiani, D. M. (1974) 'Scientific and Technological Revolution and Scientific and Technological Policy' paper delivered at 8th World Congress of Sociology, Toronto, Canada.

Habakuk ul Huq (1973) 'Crisis in development planning' *World Development* **1**, 7, July, 29–32.

Haberlein, Thomas A. (1972) 'The land ethic realized: Some social psychological explanations for changing environmental attitudes' *Journal of Social Issues* **28**, 79–87.

Hall, J. (1928) *Alma Mater, or the Future of Oxford and Cambridge* London: Kegan Paul, p. 32.

Hall, John (1973) 'Measuring the Quality of Life using Sample Surveys' in G. J. Stöber and D. Schumacher (eds) *Technology Assessment and Quality of Life* Amsterdam: Elsevier.

Hamming, R. W. (1973) *Numerical Methods for Scientists and Engineers* New York: McGraw-Hill (second edition).

Harrington, Michael (1968) 'A Subversive Version of the Great Society' in Herman D. Stein (ed) *Social Theory and Social Invention* Cleveland: Press of Case Western Reserve University, pp. 47–69. First published in Harper's Magazine (December 1966).

Harris, Louis (1974) *The Anguish of Change* New York: W. W. Norton.

Harrison, A. J. and Quarmby, D. A. (1973) 'The Value of Time' in Layard.

Heilbroner, R. L. (1967) 'Do machines make history?' *Technology and Culture* **8**, 342–45.

Heilbroner, R. L. (1974) 'The human prospect' *New York Review of Books* January 24.

Herrera, A. (1974) *Latin American World Model: Progress Report* mimeo, Rio Negro, Argentina: Fundacion Bariloche.

Hirschman A. O. (1973) 'The changing tolerance for income inequality in the course of economic development' *World Development* **1**, 12, December, 29–36.

Hoghton, Charles de, Page, William and Streatfield, Guy (1971) . . . *And Now the Future* London: P.E.P., Broadsheet **37**, No. 529.

Hoos, Ida R. (1972) *Systems Analysis and Public Policy: A Critique* Berkeley: University of California Press.

Horowitz, Irving Louis (1970) 'Social science mandarins: Policy making as a political formula' *Policy Sciences* **1**, 339–60.

Huber, Bettina J. (1971) 'Studies of the Future: A Selected and Annotated Bibliography' in Wendell Bell and James A. Mau *The Sociology of the Future* New York: Russell Sage Foundation, pp. 339–454.

Hyman, Herbert (1955) *Survey Design and Analysis* Glencoe, Ill.: Free Press.

Hyman, Herbert (1972) *Secondary Analysis of Sample Surveys* New York: John Wiley.

Hymans, Saul H. (1970) *Consumer Durable Spending* Brookings Papers on Economic Activity. Washington, D.C.: Brookings Institution.

Inglehart, Ronald (1971) 'The silent revolution in Europe: Intergenerational change in post-industrial societies' *American Political Science Review* **65**, 991–1017.

Inkeles, Alex (1960) 'Industrial man: The relation of status to experience, perception and value' *American Journal of Sociology* **66**, 1–31.

Inkeles, Alex (1969a) 'Making men modern: The causes and consequences of individual change in six developing countries' *American Journal of Sociology* **75**, 208–25.

Inkeles, Alex (1969b) 'Participant citizenship in six developing countries' *American Political Science Review* **63**, 1120–41.

Inkeles, Alex and Rossi, Paul (1956) 'National comparisons of occupational prestige' *American Journal of Sociology* **61**, 329–39.

Inkeles, Alex and Smith, David H. (1970) 'The fate of personal adjustment in the process of modernization' *International Journal of Comparative Sociology* **11**, 81–114.

Jansson, B. O. (1973) *Ecosystem Approach to the Baltic Problem* University of Stockholm.

Jantsch, E. (1967) *Technological Forecasting in Perspective* Paris: OECD.

Japanese Prime Minister's Office (no date) 'Public Opinion Poll on Daily Life', part of report on *Problems of Modern Society in Japan* submitted to U.N.

Jolly, R. (1974) 'International Dimensions', ch. 8 in H. Chenery *et al.* (eds).

Josling, J. E. (1973) *An International Grain Reserve* London: British–North American Research Committee.

Jouvenel, B. de (1967) *The Art of Conjecture* London: Weidenfeld and Nicolson.

Kahl, Joseph A. (1968) *The Measurement of Modernism* Austin, Texas: University of Texas Press.

Kahn, H. and Wiener, A. (1967) *Toward the Year 2000 – A Framework for Speculation* New York: Macmillan.

Kajanoja, J. (1973) *The Problem of Aggregation in Location Models* Stockholm: Conference on Dynamic Allocation in Space.

Kaldor, Nicholas (1971) 'Conflicts in National Economic Objectives' in N. Kaldor (ed) *Conflicts in Policy Objectives* Oxford: Basil Blackwell, pp.

1–19.

Kaplan, A. R. and Becker, R. R. (1972) 'Technology Assessment and the Federal Drug Administration' in Kasper.

Kasper, R. G. (ed) (1972) *Technology Assessment* New York: Praeger.

Katona, George (1960) *The Powerful Consumer* New York: McGraw-Hill.

Katona, George, Strumpel, B. and Zahn, E. (1971) *Aspirations and Affluence* New York: McGraw-Hill.

Kaya, Y. (1972) *On the Future Japan and the World – A Model Approach* Japan Techno-Economics Society.

Kaya, Y. (1973) *Towards a Global Vision of Human Problems* Japan Techno-Economics Society.

Keynes, J. M. (1936) *The General Theory of Employment, Interest and Money* New York: Harcourt, Brace.

Kiefer, D. M. (1972) 'Technology Assessment: A Layman's Overview' in Cetron and Bartocha.

Klarman, H. E. (1965) 'Syphilis Control Problems' in Dorfmann.

Kleiner, Robert J. and Parker, Seymour (1969) 'Social Mobility, Anomie and Mental Disorder' in Stanley C. Plog and Robert B. Edgerton (eds) *Changing Perspectives on Mental Illness* New York: Holt, Rinehart and Winston.

Kuznets, S. (1972) *Modern Economic Growth, Rate Structure and Spread* New Haven: Yale University Press, pp. 374–84.

Lasch, Christopher (1973) 'Take me to your leader' *New York Review of Books* **20**, October 18, 63–66.

Layard, R. (ed) (1973) *Cost–Benefit Analysis* Harmondsworth: Penguin Modern Economics Readings.

Lee, D. B. Jr. (1973) 'Requiem for large scale models' *A.I.P. Journal* May.

LeMasters, E. E. (1971) 'The passing of the dominant husband-father' *Impact of Science on Society* **21**, 21–30.

Lindblom, C. (1959) 'The science of "muddling through" ' *Public Administration Review* **19**.

Linneman, H. (1973) *Problems of Population Doubling* Free University of Amsterdam, mimeo.

Little, M. D. and Mirrlees, J. A. (1969) *Manual of Industrial Project Analysis in Developing Countries. Vol. 2: Social Cost–Benefit Analysis* Paris: OECD.

Lloyds Bank (1972) *The British Economy in Figures* London, p. 4.

Lyons, Gene M. (1969) *The Uneasy Partnership* New York: Russell Sage Foundation.

MacKenzie, N. and J. (1973) *The Time Traveller – A Biography of H. G. Wells* London: Weidenfeld and Nicolson.

Maestre, C. and Pavitt, Keith (1972) *Analytic Methods in Government Science Policy* Paris: OECD.

Malinowski, B. (1960) *A Scientific Theory of Culture* London: Oxford University Press.

Mannheim, K. (1951) *Freedom, Power and Democratic Planning* London: Routledge and Kegan Paul.

Marsh, Alan (in print) 'The "silent revolution", value priorities and the quality of life in Britain' *American Political Science Review*.

Maruyama, Margoroh (1973a) 'Cultural, social and psychological considerations in the planning of public works' *Technological Forecasting and*

Social Change 5, 135–43.

Maruyama, Margoroh (1973b) 'The non-economic ghetto' *Man-Environment Systems* 3, 225–32.

Maslow, Abraham H. (1954) *Motivation and Personality* New York: Harper.

Mathiason, John R. and Powell, John O. (1972) 'Participation and efficacy: Aspects of peasant involvement in political mobilization' *Comparative Politics* 4, 303–70.

Maynard–Smith, J. (1974) *Models in Ecology* Cambridge, U.K.: Cambridge University Press.

Mazlish, Bruce (ed) (1965) *The Railroad and Space Program: An Exploration in Historical Analogy* Cambridge, Mass.: MIT Press.

McClelland, David C. (1961) *The Achieving Society* Princeton, N.J.: Van Nostrand.

McEvoy III, James (1972) 'The American Concern with Environment' in William A. Burch Jr., Neil H. Cheek Jr. and Lee Taylor *Social Behavior, Natural Resources and the Environment* New York: Harper and Row, pp. 214–36.

McGranahan, Donald (1970) 'The interrelations between social and economic development' *Social Science Information* 9, 61–77.

McLean, M. and Hopkins, M. (1974) 'Problems of world food and agriculture' *Futures* August.

Meade, J. E. (1970) *The Theory of Indicative Planning* Manchester: Manchester University Press.

Meadows, Donella H., Meadows, Dennis L., Randers, Jørgen and Behrens, William W. III (1972) *The Limits to Growth* New York: Potomac Books.

Medford, D. (1973) *Environmental Hazard or Technology Assessment?* Amsterdam: Elsevier.

Merton, R. K. (1957) *Social Theory and Social Structure* Glencoe, Ill.: Free Press, ch. 1.

Mesarovic, M. and Pestel, E. (1974) *Mankind at the Turning Point* New York: Dutton/Readers Digest Press.

Meynaud, Jean (1968) *Technocracy* London: Faber and Faber and New York: Free Press.

Miles, Ian (1974) 'Social forecasting: From impressions to investigation' *Futures* 6, 240–252.

Ministry of Transport (1963) *Proposals for a Fixed Channel Link* London: HMSO; extracts in Munby (1968).

Mishan, E. J. (1970) 'What is wrong with Roskill?' *Journal of Transport Economics and Policy* 4, 3; reprinted in Layard (1973).

Mishan, E. J. (1971) *Cost–Benefit Analysis* London: Unwin University Books and New York: Praeger.

Mitchell, Robert Edward (1971) 'Some social implications of high density housing' *American Sociological Review* 36, 18–29.

MITRE for the Office of Science and Technology (1971–2) *Automobile Emissions Control; Computer Communications Networks; Industrial Enzymes; Sea Farming; Water Pollution – Domestic Wastes* MITRE Corporation.

Moore, W. E. (1966) 'The utility of utopias' *American Sociological Review* 31, 6, 765–72.

Moser, C. A. and Kalton, G. (1971) *Survey Methods in Social Investigation* London: Heinemann and New York: Basic Books, 1972 (2nd ed.).

Moses, L. N. and Williamson, H. F. (1963) 'Value of time, choice of mode and the subsidy issue' *Journal of Political Economy* **71**, 247–64.
Mueller, Eva (1967) *Technological Advance in an Expanding Economy: Its Impact on a Cross-section of the Labour Force* Ann Arbor, Michigan: Survey Research Center.
Munby, D. (ed) (1968) *Transport* Harmondsworth: Penguin Modern Economics Readings.
Musgrave, C. (1973) *Life in Brighton* London: Faber.
Muskin, S. (1971) quoted in Mishan.

Namenwirth, J. Zvi (1973) 'Wheels of time and the interdependence of value change in America' *Journal of Interdisciplinary History* **3**, 649–83.
Narrol, Raoul (1969) 'Cultural Determinants and the Concept of the Sick Society' in Stanley C. Plog and Robert B. Edgerton *Changing Perspectives on Mental Illness* New York: Holt, Rinehart and Winston, pp. 128–55.
National Academy of Engineering (1969) *A Study of Technology Assessment* prepared for the Committee on Science and Astronautics, U.S. House of Representatives, July; Washington, D.C.: U.S. Government Printing Office.
National Academy of Sciences (1969) *Technology: Processes of Assessment and Choice* Washington, D.C.: U.S. Government Printing Office.
National Resources Committee (1937) *Technological Trends and National Policy* Washington, D. C.: U.S. Government Printing Office.
Naylor, T. and Finger, J. M. (eds) (1971) *Computer Simulation Experiments with Models of Economic Systems* New York: John Wiley.
Nef, J. U. (1950) *War and Human Progress* New York: W. W. Norton, p. 129.
Nissel, Muriel (ed) (1970) *Social Trends, No. 1, 1970* London: HMSO.

Office of Population Censuses and Surveys (annually since 1971) *Population Projections* London: HMSO.
Ogburn, William F. (ed) (1929–33) *Social Changes in 1928–1932* Chicago: University of Chicago Press.

Page, W. (1973) 'Population Forecasting', ch. 11 in Cole *et al.*
Palmore, Erman and Whittington, Frank (1970) 'Differential trends toward equality between whites and non-whites' *Social Forces* **49**, 108–17.
Palmore, Erman and Whittington, Frank (1971) 'Trends in the relative status of the aged' *Social Forces* **50**, 84–91.
Parker, E. F. (1969) 'Some experiments with the application of the Delphi technique' *Chemistry and Industry*, 1317.
Patel, Surendra (1964) 'The economic distance between nations' *Economic Journal* March, 122–9.
Pettigrew, Thomas F. (1967) 'Social Evaluation Theory: Convergences and Applications' in D. Levine (ed) *Nebraska Symposium on Motivation, 1967* Lincoln, Neb.: University of Nebraska Press.
Pettigrew, Thomas F. (1969) 'Radically separate or together?' *Journal of Social Issues* **25**, 43–69.
Pool, Ithiel de Sola (1967) 'The Public and the Polity' in I. Pool (ed) *Political Science: Toward Empirical Theory* New York: McGraw-Hill.
Popper, K. R. (1945) *The Open Society and its Enemies* London: Routledge and Princeton, N.J.: Princeton University Press; 1966 (5th rev. ed.).
President's Research Committee on Social Trends (1933) *Recent Social*

Trends New York: McGraw-Hill.
Prest, A. R. and Turvey, R. (1967) 'Cost–Benefit Analysis: A Survey' in *Survey of Economic Theory, Vol. III* American Economic Society and Royal Economic Society.
Prigogine, I., Nicolis, G. and Babloyantz, A. (1972) 'Thermodynamics of evolution' *Physics Today* **25**, No. 11, 23–28, No. 12.

Quinn, Robert P. and Mangione, Thomas W. (1972) 'Evaluating weighted measures of job satisfaction: A Cinderella story' *Proceedings* American Psychological Association's 80th Annual Convention, 435–6.

Rae, J. B. (1967) 'The Rationalisation of Production' in M. Kransberg and C. W. Pursell (eds) *Technology in Western Civilisation, Vol. II* London: Oxford University Press, p. 47.
RAND Corporation (1964) 'Report on a long-range forecasting study' in O. Helmer, B. Brown and T. Gordon *Social Technology* New York: Basic Books.
Ranis, Ed. G. (1972) *The Gap between Rich and Poor Countries* London: Macmillan.
Ray, G. F. and Crum, R. E. (1963) 'Transport – Notes and Comments' *National Institute of Economics Review* **24**, May.
Read, H. (1967) *Art and Society* London: Faber and New York: Schocken Books (4th edition), p. 7.
Reid, Escott (1973) *Strengthening the World Bank* Chicago, Ill.: Adlai E. Stevenson Institute.
Research Services Ltd (1970) *Future Perspectives* London: report prepared for the S.S.R.C., J6869/IM/JP.
Richardson, Bradley M. (1973) 'Urbanisation and political participation: The case of Japan' *American Political Science Review* **62**, 433–52.
Robinson, John P. (1969) 'Measures of Life Satisfaction and Happiness' in J. J. Robinson and P. M. Shaver *Measures of Social Psychological Attitudes* Ann Arbor, Michigan: Survey Research Center.
Rogers, Everett M. (1969) *Modernization among Peasants: The Impact of Communication* New York: Holt, Rinehart and Winston.
Rogers, Everett M. (1971) *Communication of Innovations* New York: Free Press.
Rokeach, Milton and Parker, Seymour (1970) 'Values as social indicators of poverty and race relations in America' *Annals of the Academy of Political and Social Science* **388**.
Roskill, Mr Justice (Chairman) (1970) *Committee on the Third London Airport: Report* London: HMSO.
Rummel, Rudolph J. (1972) *The Dimensions of Nations* Beverly Hills: Sage Publications.
Runciman, W. G. (1966) *Relative Deprivation and Social Justice* London: Routledge and Kegan Paul.
Russett, Bruce M. (1964) *World Handbook of Political and Social Indicators* I, New Haven: Yale University Press.
Rutovitz, D. (1966) 'Pattern Recognition' *Journal of Royal Statistical Society,* series A, **129**, 4.

Salancik, G. R. (1973) 'Assimilation of aggregated inputs into Delphi forecasts' *Technological Forecasting and Social Change* **5**, 243–7.
Salisbury, Robert (1968) 'Analysis of Public Policy: The Search for

Theory and Roles' in A. Ranney (ed) *Political Science and Public Policy* Chicago: Markham, pp. 151–75.

Sametz, A. W. (1968) 'Production of Goods and Services' in Sheldon and Moore, pp. 77–96.

Schmoelders, Guenter and Biervert, Bernd (1972) 'Level of Aspiration and Consumption Standard: Some General Findings' in Strumpel, Morgan and Zahn.

Schnaiberg, Allen (1970) 'Measuring modernism: Theoretical and empirical explorations' *American Journal of Sociology* 36, 399–425.

Schon, D. A. (1971) *Beyond the Stable State* London: Temple Smith, pp. 142–4.

Schultze, L. (1968) *The Politics and Economics of Public Spending* Washington, D.C.: Brookings Institute.

Schwartz, Mildred A. (1967) *Trends in White Attitudes towards Negroes* Chicago: National Opinion Research Center.

Seers, S. W. (1973) 'The use of simulation in the field of urban and regional planning' *Simulation Today* 13.

Shapiro, Harold T. (1972) 'The Index of Consumer Sentiment and Economic Forecasting: A Reappraisal' in Strumpel, Morgan and Zahn.

Sharkansky, Ira and Hofferbert, Richard I. (1969) 'Dimensions of state politics, economics and public policy' *American Political Science Review* 63, 867–79.

Sharp, J. (1974) *Extensions to the Theory of Dynamic Modelling* University of Bradford, Ph.D. thesis.

Sheldon, E. B. and Freeman, H. E. (1970) 'Notes on social indicators: Promise and potential' *Policy Sciences* 1, 97–111.

Sheldon, E. B. and Land, K. C. (1972) 'Social reporting for the 1970s' *Policy Sciences* 3, 137–51.

Sheldon, E. B. and Moore, W. E. (eds) (1968) *Indicators of Social Change* New York: Russell Sage Foundation.

Sherril, Kenneth S. (1969) 'The attitudes of modernity' *Comparative Politics* 1, 184–220.

Shonfield, Andrew (1972) 'Research and Public Policy. Lessons from Economics' in A. B. Cherns, R. Sinclair and W. I. Jenkins *Social Science and Government: Policies and Problems* London: Tavistock Publications and New York: Barnes & Noble.

Shubkin, V. N. (1966) 'Youth starts out in life' *Soviet Sociology* 4, 3–15.

Silva Michelena, Jose A. (1967) 'Venutopia I: An experimental model of a national polity' in Frank Bonilla and J. A. Silva Michelena *A Strategy for Research on Social Policy* Cambridge, Mass.: M.I.T. Press.

Simonson, G. R. (1960) 'The demand for aircraft and the aircraft industry 1907–1950' *Journal of Economic History* XX, 3, September, 372.

Sinclair, T. C. (1971) 'The incorporation of health and welfare risks into technological forecasting' *Research Policy* 1.

Sinclair, T. C. (1973) 'Technology and Risks of Fatalities' in Cetron and Bartocha.

Singer, S. Fred (1973) 'Is there an Optimum Level of Population?' in Andrew Weintraub *et al* (eds) *The Economic Growth Controversy* London: Macmillan. First published New York: International Arts and Services Press.

Sklair, Leslie (1973) *Organized Knowledge,* London: Hart Davis–MacGibbon.

Smith, David H. and Inkeles, Alex (1966) 'The O–M scale: A comparative socio-psychological measure of individual modernity' *Sociometry* **29**, 353–77.

Spangler, M. B. (1973) 'Technological Alternatives for Enhanced Urban Use of Water and Related Land Resources' in Cetron and Bartocha.

Spiro, M. E. (1958) *Children of the Kibbutz* Cambridge, Mass.: Harvard University Press.

SPRU (1974) *Application of Dynamic Analysis and Forecasting to World Problems* Brighton: SPRU.

Starr, Chauncey (1973) 'Benefit–Cost in Socio-Technical Systems' in Cetron and Bartocha.

Steiner, P. O. (1959) 'Choosing among alternative public investments in the water resources field' *American Economic Review* **49**, December.

Stouffer, S. A., Suchman, E. A., De Vinney, I. C., Star, S. A. and Williams R. H., Jr. (1949) *The American Soldier* Princeton: Princeton University Press.

Streeten, P. (ed) (1970) *Unfashionable Economics – Essays in Honour of Lord Balogh* London: Weidenfeld and Nicolson.

Strumpel, Burkhard, Morgan, James N. and Zahn, Ernest (1972) *Human Behaviour in Economic Affairs* Amsterdam: Elsevier.

Surrey, J. (1973) in Cole *et al.*

Survey Research Center (1970) *Survey of Working Conditions* Washington, D.C.: U.S. Department of Labor.

Szalai, Alexander (1972) *The Use of Time* The Hague and Paris: Mouton.

Tanter, R. (1973) 'The policy relevance of models in world politics' *Conflict Resolution* **XVI**, 4.

Taylor, Charles L. and Hudson, Michael C. (1972) *World Handbook of Political and Social Indicators* II, New Haven: Yale University Press.

Turner, P. (1965) 'Introduction' to Thomas More, *Utopia* Harmondsworth: Penguin, pp. 16–21.

U.S. Department of Health, Education and Welfare (1969) *Toward a Social Report* Washington, D.C.: U.S. Government Printing Office.

Vajda, S. (1956) *Theory of Games and Linear Programming* London: Methuen.

Verba, Sidney (1971) 'Cross–National Survey Research: The Problem of Credibility' in Ivan Vallier (ed) *Comparative Methods in Sociology* Berkeley: University of California Press, pp. 309–56.

Verba, Sidney, Ahmed, B. and Bhatt, A. (1971) *Caste, Race and Politics* Beverley Hills: Sage Publications.

Verba, Sidney, Nie, Norman H. and Kim, Jae–On (1971) 'The Modes of Democratic Participation: A Cross-National Comparison' *Sage Professional Papers in Comparative Politics* **2**, Beverly Hills: Sage Publications.

Verba, Sidney *et al* (1973) 'The modes of participation: Continuities in research' *Comparative Political Studies* **6**, 235–50.

Vickers, G. (1968) *Science and the Regulation of Society* New York: Columbia University Institute for the Study of Science in World Affairs.

Ward, Barbara *et al* (1971) *The Widening Gap* New York: Columbia University Press.

Ward, Barbara and Dubos, Rene (1972) *Only One Earth* New York: W. W. Norton and Co.

Watts, William and Free, Lloyd A. (1973) *State of the Nation* Washington, D.C.: Potomac Associates.

Weaver, T. (1969) 'An exploration into the relationships between conceptual level and forecasting future events' PhD thesis, Syracuse University.

Webb, E. J., Campbell, D. T., Schwartz, R. D. and Sechrest, L. (1966) *Unobtrusive Measures: Non-reactive Research in the Social Sciences* Chicago: Rand, McNally.

Weiss, E. (1972) 'Processes of Technology Assessment: The National Transportation Safety Board' in Kasper.

Wells, John (1974) 'Distribution of earnings, growth and the structure of demand in Brazil during the 1960s' *World Development* 2, 1, January, 9–24.

Werskey, P. G. (ed) (1973) *Science at the Crossroads* London: Frank Cass.

Wilcox, Leslie D. *et al* (1972) *Social Indicators and Societal Monitoring: An Annotated Bibliography* Amsterdam: Elsevier.

Willems, Edwin P. (1973) 'Behavioural Ecology and Experimental Analysis: Courtship is not Enough' in John R. Nesselroade and Hayne W. Reese (eds) *Life–Span Developmental Psychology* New York: Academic Press.

Winthrop, H. (1968) 'The sociologist and the study of the future' *American Sociologist* 3, 136–45.

Winthrop, H. (1971) 'Utopia Construction and Forecasting' in W. Bell and J. A. Mau (eds) *The Sociology of the Future* New York: Russell Sage Foundation.

Young, M. (ed) (1968) *Forecasting and the Social Sciences* London: Heinemann.

Name Index

Abrams, M. 142–3, 154, 156, 187, 191
Adelman, M. A. 73
Ahluwalia, M. S. 256, 258
Ahmed, B. 162
Allardt, E. 194, 196, 202
Alker, H. M. 203
Almond, G. 160, 161
Amara, R. 74
Ament, R. 79, 80
American Academy of Arts & Sciences 130
Anderson, I. 214
Andrews, F. M. 160, 192
Andrews, P. W. 77
Armytage, W. H. 113
Ash, J. C. 97
Ashby, Lord 29, 34
Ashby, W. R. 107
Augustine 32

Bacon, F. 6
Baier, K. E. M. 14
Ball, R. J. 97
Banks, A. S. 194
Barnowe, J. T. 160
Barton, A. 194
Battelle Institute 109
Bauer, R. A. 130, 182, 215
Beard, C. 4
Becker, R. R. 122
Beckerman, W. 251, 255
Beesley, M. E. 118
Bell, D. 5, 32, 56
Bell, M. 66
Bender, D. A. 80, 82
Berry, B. L. J. 194
Bertalanffy, L. von 26, 77
Bettman, J. R. 192

Bhatt, A. 162
Biderman, A. D. 183, 189, 212
Biervert, B. 157
Bjerrum, C. A. 80
Blandy, R. 110
Boaden, N. 215
Bonilla, F. 160
Bowen, R. 11
Bowers, R. 118
Bradburn, N. 157, 187
Brannon, R. 152
Brewer, G. D. 100
Brigard, R. de 80
Briones, G. 159
Brooks, D. G. 77
Brown, B. 71, 79, 81
Buckle, H. T. 10
Buckley, W. 41
Bunge, M. 12, 43–4
Bureau of Mines 75, 76
Business Week 98
Butler, S. 6

Campbell, A. 175, 176
Campbell, D. T. 151, 166, 189, 212, 213, 217
Cantril, A. H. 154, 155, 156, 158, 187
Čapek, K. 6
Caplovitz, D. 157, 187
Carpenter, R. A. 129
Carr, E. H. 3, 4, 11
Cazes, B. 13, 185
Chein, I. 24
Chesney, Lt.-Col. G. T. 63, 64, 70, 86
Christensen, J. A. 192
Clark, J. 93, 105
Clarke, A. C. 65

Clarke, I. F.   7, 10, 63
Coates, J. F.   172
Coates, V. T.   118
Coburn, T. M.   118
Coen, P. G.   68
Cole, H. S. D.   19, 29, 93, 104, 105
Coleman, J. S.   202, 209
Congressional Research Service
    121
Converse, P. E.   175, 176
Crum, R. E.   130
Curnow, R. C.   93

Daddario, E.   121
Dalkey, N. C.   78, 189, 192
Davies, B.   194, 203, 210
Demerath, N. J.   152
Dillman, D. A.   192
Dubos, R.   251
Dupuit, J.   117

Easton, D.   206
Edwards, D. V.   65, 67, 69
Eliot, T. S.   3
Ellul, J.   170
Environmental Protection Agency
    190, 192
Etzioni, A.   122, 202, 211

Fairweather, G. W.   116
Falk, C.   124
Feldman, A. S.   169
Federal Drug Administration   122
Finger, J. M.   93
Fishbein, M.   151
Flanigan, W.   170, 183
Flechtheim, O.   3
Fogelman, E.   170, 183
Food & Agriculture Organisation
    110
Form, W. K.   171
Forrester, J. W.   28, 32, 93, 100,
    102, 109, 111, 186, 253
Foster, C. D.   118, 130
Fourier, F. M. C.   15
Franck, J.   118
Francome, C.   190, 192
Frazer, D.   215
Free, L. A.   155, 190
Freedman, D. S.   157
Freeman, C.   15, 124
Freeman, H. E.   185, 213
French Water Control Agency   120

Freud, S.   24, 39
Frey, J.   118
Friday, J.   7
Fuchs, C. J.   156
Fuller, B.   170
Funkhouser, G. R.   191

Galtung, J.   202
Gardner, M.   107
Gerardin, L.   88
Gibson, Q. B.   3
Glenn, N. D.   171
Goel, M. L.   162
Goldthorpe, J. H.   56, 159, 167
Gomme, E. D.   68
Gordon, T. J.   71, 79, 80, 81, 83
Grabb, E. M.   79
Graves, R.   5
Greeley, A. M.   148
Greene, J. E.   159
Gross, B. M.   176, 196, 201, 206
Gurin, G.   154
Gvishiani, D. M.   11

Habakuk ul Huq   257
Haberlein, T. A.   190
Haldane, J. B. S.   5
Hall, J.   5
Hall, John   154, 160, 193, 194
Hall, Joseph   6
Hall, O. P.   100
Hamming, R. W.   93
Harris, L.   25
Harrison, A. J.   130
Hayward, H.   83
Heilbroner, R.   24, 40
Helmer, O.   71, 78, 79, 80, 81, 82,
    83
Herrera, A.   106
Hofferbert, R. I.   194
Hoghton, C. de   9, 64, 65, 145
Hoos, I. B.   113, 183
Hopkins, M.   254
Horowitz, I. L.   183
Howard, E.   10
Hoyle, F.   28
Huber, B. J.   142
Hudson, M. C.   185
Hurn, C.   176
Huxley, A.   5, 6
Huxley, T. H.   4
Hyman, H.   142, 164

Inglehart, R. 146–7, 159
Inkeles, A. 148, 149, 150, 152, 154, 159, 161, 163, 168, 169, 171
Institute of Development Studies 256
International Labour Organisation 110

Jansson, B. O. 110
Jantsch, E. 9, 64, 65, 69, 70
Japanese Prime Minister's Office 159
Jenkins, R. 33
Jolly, R. 256
Josling, J. E. 108
Jouvenel, B. de 3, 18
Juvenal 83

Kahl, J. A. 159, 168
Kahn, H. 36, 37, 56, 75, 77–8, 86–8
Kajanoja, J. 100
Kaldor, N. 98, 211
Kalton, G. 142
Kaplan, A. R. 122
Katona, G. 156, 163
Kaya, Y. 106
Kendall, M. G. 68
Kennedy, R. 91
Keynes, J. M. 262
Kiefer, D. M. 124
Kim, J.-O. 161, 162
Kleiner, R. J. 156
Kumar, D. 256, 260
Kuznets, S. 258, 259

Land, K. C. 185
Landsberger, H. A. 156
Lasch, C. 184
Lee, D. B. 99, 100
Lehman, E. W. 202, 211
LeMasters, E. E. 171
Lindblom, C. 114
Linneman, H. 109
Little, M. D. 127
Lorenz, P. 70
Lyons, G. M. 182

MacKenzie, N. & J. 4
Maestre, C. 64, 99, 100, 215
Malthus, T. 4, 117
Mangione, T. W. 192
Mannheim, K. 11

Marsh, A. 150
Maruyama, M. 193, 195
Marx, K. 15, 39
Maslow, A. H. 146
Mathiason, J. R. 162
Maynard-Smith, J. 107
Mazlish, B. 70, 130
McClelland, D. C. 145
McEvoy, J. 190
McGranahan, D. 184
McLean, J. M. 254
McLuhan, M. 170, 254
McMillan, I. 194
McNamara, R. 262
Meade, J. E. 211
Meadows, D. H. 28, 32, 34, 37, 66, 70, 73, 87, 93, 104, 105, 106, 109, 111, 164, 253
Medford, D. 118, 120
Mesarovic, M. 105
Meynaud, J. 183
Miles, I. 170
Mill, J. S. 68
Mirrlees, J. A. 127
Mishan, E. J. 121
Mitchell, R. E. 171
M.I.T.R.E. 118, 125, 127, 132
Moore, T. 6, 7
Moore, W. E. 176
Morgan, J. N. 164
Moser, C. A. 142
Moses, L. N. 130
Muckfield 81
Mueller, E. 171
Mumford, L. 170
Musgrave, C. 119

Nader, R. 93
Namenwirth, J. Z. 145
Narrol, R. 187
National Academy of Engineering (USA) 118, 121
National Academy of Sciences (USA) 139
National Transportation Safety Board 122
Naylor, T. 93
Nie, N. H. 161, 162
Nissel, M. 174, 175, 176

Office of Population Censuses & Surveys (U.K.) 65, 75

Ogburn, W. F.   9, 175, 176, 182
Olin   259
Orwell, G.   6

Page, W.   9, 23, 64, 65, 145
Palmore, E.   203
Parker, E. F.   80
Parker, S.   156, 159
Parsons, T.   56
Pavitt, K.   64, 99, 100, 215
Pestel, E.   105
Pettigrew, T. F.   148, 155, 156
Plato   7, 38
Pool, I. de S.   188
Popper, K.   3, 15
Powell, J. O.   162
Prest, A. R.   120
Prigogine, I.   108
Pyke, D. L.   79

Quarmby, D. A.   130
Quinn, R. P.   192

Rae, J. B.
RAND Corpn.   71, 79, 81
Ranis, E. G.   255
Ray, G. F.   130
Read, H.   18
Reid, E.   255, 256
Remp, R.   122
Research Services   143
Richardson, B. M.   162
Robinson, J. P.   154, 156
Rochefoucauld, La   252
Rodgers, W.   159
Rogers, E. M.   163, 167, 192, 194
Rokeach, M.   159
Roll, C. W.   155
Roskill, Lord   118, 123, 124, 129,
   131, 137
Rummel, R. J.   194
Runciman, W. J.   154, 155
Russell, B.   15
Russett, B. M.   185, 203
Rutovitz, D.   68

Salancik, G. R.   74, 82
Salisbury, R.   206
Sametz, A. W.   180, 181, 186
Schmoelders, G.   157
Schnaiberg, A.   167
Schon, D. A.   12
Schwartz, M. A.   145, 148, 150, 152

Seers, S. W.   100
Shapiro, H. T.   164
Sharkansky, I.   194
Sheatsley, P. B.   148
Sheldon, E. B.   176, 185, 201, 213
Sherril, K. S.   168
Shubkin, V. N.   159
Shonfield, A.   214
Silva Michelena, J. A.   164, 165
Sinclair, T. C.   26, 120
Singer, S. F.   186
Smith, D. H.   168, 171
Smyth, D. J.   97
Sorokin, P.   56
Spangler, M. B.   118
Spengler, O.   4, 56
Spiro, M. E.   171
Stanley, J. C.   166, 213
Starr, C.   117
Stouffer, S. A.   155
Streatfield, G.   9, 64, 65, 145
Strumpel, B.   156, 164
Survey Research Center   199
Swift, D.   6
Szalai, A.   163

Taylor, C. J.   127
Taylor, C. L.   185
Textor, R. B.   194
Tinbergen, J.   251
Toynbee, A.   56
Turner, P.   6
Turvey, R.   120

U.K. Ministry of Technology   131
U.K. Ministry of Transport   118,
   123, 125, 127
U.K. Office of Population Censuses
   & Surveys   65, 75
U.S. Bureau of Mines   75, 76
U.S. Committee on Social Trends   9
U.S. Dept of Health, Education &
   Welfare   201
U.S. Environmental Protection
   Agency   190, 192
U.S. Federal Drug Administration
   122
U.S. National Resources Committee
   9
U.S. National Transportation Safety
   Board   122

Vajda, S.   67

Verba, S.   160, 161, 162
Verne, J.   7
Vickers, G.   250

Waisanen, F. B.   159
Ward, B.   251
Watts, W.   155, 190
Weaver, T.   81
Wells, H. G.   4, 6, 7, 18
Welty   81
Wharton, R.   192
Whittington, F.   203
Wiener, A.   36, 37, 56, 75, 77–8,

86–8
Willems, E. P.   171
Williamson, H. F.   130
Winthrop, H.   7, 14
Withey, S. B.   160, 193
World Bank   256

Yeager, P.   117
Young, M.   23

Zahn, E.   156, 164
Zamyatin, A.   6
Zwicky, F.   85

Subject Index

Alternative futures, need for   23–5
Analogy   68, 70, 130; see also Extrapolation
Association   70, 75; see also Extrapolation
Astrology   67
Attitudes: and behaviour   151–3, 161; forecasting   142–3, 146–153

Bariloche model   106
Brighton   119

Causality   68, 194
Chance   67
Cliometrics   5–6, 174
Concorde   124, 127
Consumer surplus   135–6
Content analysis   145
Continuity   10, 68, 70, 106–7; see also Extrapolation
Corfam   127
Correlation   68

Cost-benefit analysis   116–140, definitions   117–122, evaluation   116, 132–3, and forecasting   126, 128–133, procedure   122–140
Counter-intuitive behaviour   103–4
Cross-impact matrices   70, 71, 83–5

Data, adequacy of   58–9, 72, 76–7, 99, 174
Delphi   71, 78–83, 85
Delphic Oracle   69
Determinism   5, 7, 15, 24, 53–4, 180
Dialectic   69
Discounting   125, 138–9

Economic change, psychological consequences   167–70
Economic needs and quality of life   156–7, 178
Economic indicators: international comparisons   254–63 (tables 251,

255), meaning 178–9, 224–5
Envelope curves 69, 71
Environment and goals 147
Equality 15–17; *see also* Inequalities, Normative Approach, Goals
Extrapolation 73–4, 75–8, 142, 145–153, 153–4

Forecasts and forecasting: approaches 36–8; central issues 23–50, 51–60; dangers of isolationism 27–8, 60, 142; definitions 6, 12, 23–4, 33, 53, 65, 250; history of 4–5, 6–8, 9–11, 25, 63–4, 69; history, use of 3–6, 57, 130, 143–4; influence of values 4, 5, 14–15, 27–8, 95, 128–130, 133–4, 137, 141; and planning 10–13, 15, 24, 27, 31, 46, 52, 59–60, 80, 90–1, 98–101, 102, 108; role and uses 23–5, 64, 72, 89–91, 96–97; misuses 52–3, 76; short- v. long-term 26, 55, 75, 92, 109, 126, 139
Forecasting techniques: assessment criteria 71–5, 89, 96, 100, 102, 140; common elements 66–7, 69–71; open v. closed systems 31, 43, 73–4, 76; taxonomies 65–6, 67–9
France 13, 120
Franck Report 118

Gaming 68
Goals 15–17, 25, 27, 28–30, 33, 38–40, 147, 166, 195, 257–8; *see also* Normative approach
Gross National Product: international comparisons 254–63 (tables 251, 255), meaning 178–9, 224–5

Hindsight testing 23, 46–7, 133
History: of forecasting 4–5, 6–8, 9–11, 25; of social indicators 182–3; use in forecasting 3–6, 57, 130, 143–4
Historicism 15, 56–7
Holism 57–8, 103

Imagination 7, 15, 70, 130–1, 132
Income distribution: *see* Inequalities, Quality of life
Inequalities (international) 250–65; feasibility of change 252–3, 261–

2; increasing gap? 259–60; international comparisons 254–63 (tables 251, 255); moral issues 250–3, 261
Inequalities (national) 235–6, 254–6, 260–3; and quality-of-life research 155, 235–6
Inequalities: *see also* Goals, Normative Approach
Innovation, diffusion of 163
Input-output methods 46, 99
Interdisciplinary research 35–7, 142
Intuition 67–8, 69–70; *see* Delphi

Job satisfaction 193

Logic 41–51, 71; *see* Intuition
Lorenz curve 256
Luddites 118

Measuring units 26, 45–6, 135, 136, 254–6
Metals, future demand 73–74
Models and modelling: definitions 41–45, 70, 101; economic models 97–99; global models 104–115; size 99–100, 109; testing 94, 105, 113; urban 99–100, 103, 113; uses & merits 101–4, 109–113, 147, 153
Models of Doom 19, 104
'Modernity' 167–9
Morphology 85–6

Normative approach 15–17, 27–8, 121, 166, 185, 195, 257–8; *see also* Goals

Objectivity v. publicity needs 34, 64, 66–7
Opportunity costs 136
OPEC 73, 88, 253

Peer judgment 74, 81, 134
Physical limits 10, 28–9, 37, 234
Planning 10–13, 15, 24, 27, 31, 46, 52, 59–60, 80, 90–1, 98–101, 102, 108
Plausibility 74, 87
Political beliefs & structural regularities 160–4; *see also* Values
Pollution 29–30
Projection 68
Prophecy 67, 69

Public debate   132–3, 150, 236
Public mystification   102, 140
Publication, implications of   34, 63, 66–7

Quantification   58, 119, 134–137
Quality of life   26–7, 38–40, 154–7, 257–8; definition & scope   186–7 (table 197–8); and economic needs 156–7, 178; measures   188–195, 199–201, 202; uses   195–6; see also Social indicators

R and D in developing countries: future possibilities   233–40; origins 225–6; traditional v. modern   227–9, 232–5
Recent Social Trends   182
Reductionism   6, 35, 57
Reproducibility of results   74–5, 79, 129

S-curves   76, 145
Scenarios   63, 64, 70, 86–9
Science fiction   7–8
Shadow prices   127–8
Simplification   57–8, 187
Simulation   68; see Models
Social change   165–6, 170–2
Social indicators: definition & scope 174–8, 185–6 (tables 176–7); international comparisons   254, 257–61, 262–3 (tables 251, 255); the S.I. movement   182–4; uses   98, 183, 184, 185–6
Social v. natural science   35–6
Socio-technical systems   37–8
Species/individual problem   49
Stability   12, 107–8
Statistical methods (general)   95–6, 193–4

Stock Exchange   67, 68
Strategy for Survival   105–6
Survey research: problems of   136–7, 143; and social models 163–5; uses   131, 142, 145, 166, 189–90, 193, 197–9

Technological changes   165; see also R and D
Technology assessment   116–140; definition   117–122; see Cost-benefit analysis
Technological 'fix'   122
Theory, adequacy of   56–7, 99, 101–3, 104–5, 129, 130
The Art of Conjecture   18
The Battle of Dorking   63, 64, 72, 86
The First Alternative World Model 106
The Limits to Growth   28, 32, 34, 37, 66, 70, 73, 87, 93, 104, 105, 106, 109, 111, 164, 253
The Year 2000   36, 37, 56, 75, 77–8, 86–8
Thinking About the Future
Third London Airport   118, 129
Thresholds   190
Time horizons   125

United Nations & agencies   184, 194, 251–2
U.S. President's Research Committee on Social Trends   9, 182
U.S.S.R.   11
Utopia   6–8, 15

Values   4, 5, 14–15, 27–8, 95, 128–30, 133–4, 137, 141
Victoria Line (London)   118, 119

DATE DUE